IMPLIED-IN-FACT CONDITION

Implied-in-fact conditions arise by physical or moral inference from what the parties have expressed (i.e., reasonable expectations of the parties). *Jacob & Youngs, Inc. v. Kent*, 230 N.Y. 239, 129 N.E. 689 (1921).

IMPLIED-AT-LAW (CONSTRUCTIVE) CONDITION

"Constructive" conditions function to fix the order of performance when the express terms of the bargain are silent in this region.

DUTY OF PERFORMANCE

Once a condition has been met, a duty of performance arises.

SATISFACTION OF DUTY

Performance is the most desirable way to "discharge" a duty that arises from a contract. Once a party performs a duty required by a contract, that duty is "discharged."

DISCHARGE OF DUTY

Duty to perform may be discharged by one of the following methods:

1. Impossibility: As measured by the objective standard, the impossibility must arise after the contract was entered into. The destruction of the subject matter of the contract gives rise to an impossibility, as does the subsequent passing of a law that renders the contract matter illegal. And if the services required in the contract were unique to one person (such as an artist or performer), then the death of the person will give rise to impossibility and discharge the duty inherent in the contract.
2. Impracticability: Occurs when subsequent factors have rendered the cost of performing a contract grossly in excess of what was foreseen. The key is whether the unreasonable increase in price was foreseeable. If it was foreseeable, the impracticability may NOT be used to discharge the duty.
3. Frustration of purpose: Occurs when a subsequent development not foreseeable at the time of entering the contract completely destroys the purpose of the contract (as understood by both parties).
4. Rescission: Duties to a contract may be rescinded by mutual agreement of both parties.
5. Novation:
   a. Novation substitutes a new party for an original party to the contract.
   b. All parties must assent to the substitution.
   c. Once the substitution occurs, then the original party is released from the contract.
6. Accord and Satisfaction: An accord and satisfaction releases debtor from a disputed debt through a new agreement. A valid accord and satisfaction must have consideration and the amount paid to satisfy the debt must be less than the debtor was originally entitled to.
   a. If the debt is undisputed, there is no accord and satisfaction.
   b. There is no consideration involved in releasing someone from a debt that is agreed upon—the debtor may seek additional payment.
   c. If the debt is disputed, then there is a valid accord and satisfaction.

EXCUSE OF CONDITIONS

However, there are intervening factors t prematurely "discharge" a duty, thus rel party of fulfilling the earlier promise.

1. Anticipatory Repudiation (applies onl, bilateral contracts). *Hochster v. De La Tour*, 2 Ellis. & Bl. 678 (1853).
   a. The anticipatory repudiation must be unequivocal, definite, and communicated before the time of performance (must be more than a mere expression of doubt).
   b. Upon the anticipatory repudiation, the non-repudiating party may:
      i. Suspend own performance and sue other party immediately, OR
      ii. Affirm the contract and await the due date for performance.
2. Waiver: A party may voluntarily relinquish a known contract right, such as a condition or a contract, thus excusing the underlying condition or promise. *Clark v. West*, 193 N.Y. 349, 86 N.E. 1 (1908).
3. Estoppel: If a party who has the protection of a condition precedent or concurrent creates an impression that she will NOT insist upon its satisfaction, and the other party reasonably relies on such, the advantaged party will be estopped from insisting upon satisfaction.
4. Prevention or Failure to Cooperate: If a party wrongfully prevents a condition from occurring, whether by prevention or failure to cooperate, she will no longer be given the benefit of it.
5. Substantial Performance:
   a. Only applies to where implied-at-law (constructive) conditions are involved.
   b. Where a party has almost completely performed her duties, but has breached in a minor way, forfeiture of a return performance may be avoided by this rule.

   [Remember, substantial performance does not apply in the sale of goods (Article 2) context; the "perfect tender" rule applies.]
6. Conditions may also be excused by impossibility, impracticability, or frustration.

CROSSING OFFERS

If there are two crossing offers that are identical and are mailed at the same time to the other party in such a way that they cross in the mail, a contract is not formed.

PAROL EVIDENCE RULE

INTERPRETATION OF TERMS

1. Ignorant party wins against knowing party. Restatement § 201.
2. When both parties knew of the differing intent, there is no contract
3. In order of preference:
   a. Express terms.
   b. Course of performance (negotiations).
   c. Course of dealing (previous contracts).
   d. Usage of trade.

and final expression of the p

   a. "Merger clause": A clause included in the contract intended to buttress the presumption that the written contract is a complete and final expression of the parties. *ARB Inc. v. E-Systems, Inc.*, 663 F.2d 189 (D.C. Cir. 1980).
   b. Such a contract outlined above is said to be "integrated."
2. Exceptions to the Parol Evidence Rule (evidence of the following may be admitted despite the Parol Evidence Rule):
   a. Subsequent modifications to the contract.
   b. Collateral agreement.
   c. Formation defects.
   d. Ambiguous terms.
   e. Existence of a condition precedent.
   f. Partial integration.

SUBSEQUENT ASSIGNMENTS

Subsequent assignments automatically revoke the former assignment; an assignment in writing is, however, irrevocable. If the assignments are "equal," then usually one applies the "American Rule": first in line is first in right.

BREACH OF CONTRACT

MATERIAL v. MINOR BREACH

1. Material breach: One may suspend performance AND sue for damages. *K & G Contr. Co. v. Harris*, 223 Md. 305, 164 A.2d 451 (1960).
2. Minor breach: One may only sue for damages (which may be nominal). It is important to remember that this does NOT suspend the duty to perform. *Walker & Co. v. Harrison*, 347 Mich. 630, 81 N.W.2d 352 (1957).
3. The test for materiality for a breach weighs several factors:
   a. The benefit received by the injured (non-breaching) party.
   b. Adequacy of compensation for the injured party.
   c. The extent to which the non-injured (breaching) party has partly performed.
   d. Hardship to the non-injured party.
   e. Negligence or willful behavior of the breaching party.
   f. The likelihood that the breaching party will perform the remainder of contract.

LATE PERFORMANCE

1. Usually a minor breach.
2. May become a material breach only where:
   a. Contract requires timely performance (usually UCC).
   b. Contract contains language such as "time is of the essence."

THIRD-PARTY RIGHTS

THIRD-PARTY BENEFICIARIES

The third party must have been present at the formation of the contract. If third party was added later, look into assignment or delegation.

THIRD-PARTY BENEFICIARIES

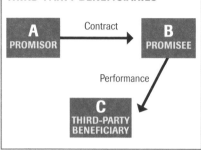

ENFORCEMENT

- A creditor beneficiary may sue the promisor OR the promisee (not both). *Lawrence v. Fox*, 20 N.Y. 268 (1859).
- A donee beneficiary may sue the promisor but may NOT sue the promisee unless there was detrimental reliance.

INTENDED BENEFICIARIES

Only intended beneficiaries have contractual rights. Incidental beneficiaries do not. Intended beneficiaries are usually:
1. Identified in the contract; OR
2. There is some indication by the original parties to intend a benefit.

VESTING

A third-party beneficiary may only enforce a contract if her rights have vested.
1. Three ways a third party vests her rights:
   a. Detrimental reliance.
   b. Filing of a lawsuit (can only assert rights at time of suit).
   c. Third party accepts in a manner expressly invited by the original contracting parties
2. If not vested, original parties may freely modify.
3. Third-party beneficiary has no greater rights than original contracting parties.

ASSIGNMENT OF RIGHTS

IN GENERAL

1. Assignor must adequately describe rights to be assigned and manifest an intention to presently vest those rights in the assignee.
2. Certain tasks may NOT be assigned:
   a. Rights in a future contract are generally not assignable.
   b. Assignment of rights is banned if it will substantially change the obligor's duty.
   Common Law: Requirements contracts are not assignable, substantially changes the obligor's duty.
   UCC: Assignment is permissible if reasonable.

---

3. Consideration is not needed; a gratuitous assignment is effective. *Speelman v. Pascal*, 10 N.Y.2d 313, 178 N.E.2d 723 (1961).
4. Subsequent assignments revoke the former assignment. However, an assignment becomes irrevocable if there is one of the following:
   a. Consideration.
   b. Writing.
5. A valid assignment creates privity of contract between the obligor and the assignee while extinguishing privity between the obligor and the assignor.

ENFORCEMENT

Assignee may sue the obligor. Obligor cannot raise any defenses that the assignor may have against the assignee.

ASSIGNMENT

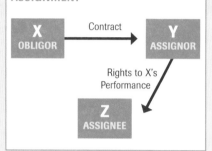

DELEGATION OF DUTIES

IN GENERAL

1. Most duties may be delegated with the following exceptions:
   a. Duties involving personal judgment and skill.
   b. Changes the obligee's expectancy (such as requirements and output contracts).
   c. There is a contractual prohibition on delegation.
2. Generally, a delegator remains liable on the contract, even if delegate has expressly assumed the duty.
3. When obligee consents (expressly) to a transfer of duties, then this is an offer of novation, and the original delegator is relieved of any liability.

Note: This is different from a novation.

DELEGATION

DAMAGES

MEASURE OF DAMAGES

1. Contracts for the Sale of Land

   Contract price
   - Fair market value

   Damages

   Specific performance may be requested, since land is unique. *Parker v. Twentieth Century-Fox Film Corp.*, 89 Cal. Rptr. 737, 474 P.2d 689 (1970).
2. Employment Contracts
   a. Employer breach:

      Full contract price
      - Wages earned elsewhere after breach

      Damages
   b. Employee breach:

      Cost of replacement
      (to find another employee)
      - Wages due to the employee

      Damages
3. Construction Contracts: *Jacob & Youngs v. Kent*, 230 N.Y. 239, 129 N.E. 889 (1921).
   a. Builder breach:
      i. Non-performance: owner recovers cost of completion.
      ii. Deficient performance: diminution in market value is the measure of damages. (Cost of completion would unjustly enrich the owner.)
   b. Owner breach:

      Cost
      + Expected profit

      Damages

OTHER DAMAGES

1. Consequential Damages: Damages must have been foreseeable at the time of entering the contract. *Hadley v. Baxendale*, 9 Exch. 341, 156 Eng. Rep 145 (1854).
2. Punitive Damages: Usually reserved for tort and are unusual in a commercial contract case, but have been applied in cases by insureds against their insurance companies for failure to settle or defend in good faith (*Comunale v. Traders & General Ins. Co.*, 50 Cal.2d 654, 328 P.2d 198 (1958)), and in other limited contexts. *Nicholson v. United Pacific Ins. Co.*, 219 Mont. 32, 710 P.2d 1342 (1985).
3. Specific Performance: Available for land and unique goods, but not for services.

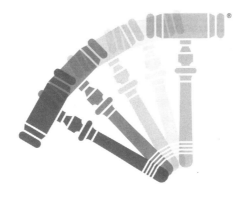

Casenote® *Legal Briefs*

CONTRACTS

Keyed to Courses Using

Knapp, Crystal, and Prince's
Problems in Contract Law
Seventh Edition

Wolters Kluwer
Law & Business

Copyright © 2012 CCH Incorporated. All Rights Reserved.

Published by Wolters Kluwer Law & Business in New York.

Wolters Kluwer Law & Business serves customers worldwide with CCH, Aspen Publishers, and Kluwer Law International products. (www.wolterskluwerlb.com)

No part of this publication may be reproduced or transmitted in any form or by any means, electronic or mechanical, including photocopy, recording, or utilized by any information storage and retrieval system, without written permission from the publisher. For information about permissions or to request permission online, visit us at wolterskluwerlb.com or a written request may be faxed to our permissions department at 212-771-0803.

To contact Customer Service, e-mail customer.service@wolterskluwer.com, call 1-800-234-1660, fax 1-800-901-9075, or mail correspondence to:

Wolters Kluwer Law & Business
Attn: Order Department
P.O. Box 990
Frederick, MD 21705

Printed in the United States of America.

1 2 3 4 5 6 7 8 9 0

ISBN 978-1-4548-0804-6

About Wolters Kluwer Law & Business

Wolters Kluwer Law & Business is a leading global provider of intelligent information and digital solutions for legal and business professionals in key specialty areas, and respected educational resources for professors and law students. Wolters Kluwer Law & Business connects legal and business professionals as well as those in the education market with timely, specialized authoritative content and information-enabled solutions to support success through productivity, accuracy and mobility.

Serving customers worldwide, Wolters Kluwer Law & Business products include those under the Aspen Publishers, CCH, Kluwer Law International, Loislaw, Best Case, ftwilliam.com and MediRegs family of products.

CCH products have been a trusted resource since 1913, and are highly regarded resources for legal, securities, antitrust and trade regulation, government contracting, banking, pension, payroll, employment and labor, and healthcare reimbursement and compliance professionals.

Aspen Publishers products provide essential information to attorneys, business professionals and law students. Written by preeminent authorities, the product line offers analytical and practical information in a range of specialty practice areas from securities law and intellectual property to mergers and acquisitions and pension/benefits. Aspen's trusted legal education resources provide professors and students with high-quality, up-to-date and effective resources for successful instruction and study in all areas of the law.

Kluwer Law International products provide the global business community with reliable international legal information in English. Legal practitioners, corporate counsel and business executives around the world rely on Kluwer Law journals, looseleafs, books, and electronic products for comprehensive information in many areas of international legal practice.

Loislaw is a comprehensive online legal research product providing legal content to law firm practitioners of various specializations. Loislaw provides attorneys with the ability to quickly and efficiently find the necessary legal information they need, when and where they need it, by facilitating access to primary law as well as state-specific law, records, forms and treatises.

Best Case Solutions is the leading bankruptcy software product to the bankruptcy industry. It provides software and workflow tools to flawlessly streamline petition preparation and the electronic filing process, while timely incorporating ever-changing court requirements.

ftwilliam.com offers employee benefits professionals the highest quality plan documents (retirement, welfare and non-qualified) and government forms (5500/PBGC, 1099 and IRS) software at highly competitive prices.

MediRegs products provide integrated health care compliance content and software solutions for professionals in healthcare, higher education and life sciences, including professionals in accounting, law and consulting.

Wolters Kluwer Law & Business, a division of Wolters Kluwer, is headquartered in New York. Wolters Kluwer is a market-leading global information services company focused on professionals.

Format for the Casenote® Legal Brief

Nature of Case: This section identifies the form of action (e.g., breach of contract, negligence, battery), the type of proceeding (e.g., demurrer, appeal from trial court's jury instructions), or the relief sought (e.g., damages, injunction, criminal sanctions).

Fact Summary: This is included to refresh your memory and can be used as a quick reminder of the facts.

Rule of Law: Summarizes the general principle of law that the case illustrates. It may be used for instant recall of the court's holding and for classroom discussion or home review.

Facts: This section contains all relevant facts of the case, including the contentions of the parties and the lower court holdings. It is written in a logical order to give the student a clear understanding of the case. The plaintiff and defendant are identified by their proper names throughout and are always labeled with a (P) or (D).

Palsgraf v. Long Island R.R. Co.

Injured bystander (P) v. Railroad company (D)

N.Y. Ct. App., 248 N.Y. 339, 162 N.E. 99 (1928).

NATURE OF CASE: Appeal from judgment affirming verdict for plaintiff seeking damages for personal injury.

FACT SUMMARY: Helen Palsgraf (P) was injured on R.R.'s (D) train platform when R.R.'s (D) guard helped a passenger aboard a moving train, causing his package to fall on the tracks. The package contained fireworks which exploded, creating a shock that tipped a scale onto Palsgraf (P).

🏛 RULE OF LAW
The risk reasonably to be perceived defines the duty to be obeyed.

FACTS: Helen Palsgraf (P) purchased a ticket to Rockaway Beach from R.R. (D) and was waiting on the train platform. As she waited, two men ran to catch a train that was pulling out from the platform. The first man jumped aboard, but the second man, who appeared as if he might fall, was helped aboard by the guard on the train who had kept the door open so they could jump aboard. A guard on the platform also helped by pushing him onto the train. The man was carrying a package wrapped in newspaper. In the process, the man dropped his package, which fell on the tracks. The package contained fireworks and exploded. The shock of the explosion was apparently of great enough strength to tip over some scales at the other end of the platform, which fell on Palsgraf (P) and injured her. A jury awarded her damages, and R.R. (D) appealed.

ISSUE: Does the risk reasonably to be perceived define the duty to be obeyed?

HOLDING AND DECISION: (Cardozo, C.J.) Yes. The risk reasonably to be perceived defines the duty to be obeyed. If there is no foreseeable hazard to the injured party as the result of a seemingly innocent act, the act does not become a tort because it happened to be a wrong as to another. If the wrong was not willful, the plaintiff must show that the act as to her had such great and apparent possibilities of danger as to entitle her to protection. Negligence in the abstract is not enough upon which to base liability. Negligence is a relative concept, evolving out of the common law doctrine of trespass on the case. To establish liability, the defendant must owe a legal duty of reasonable care to the injured party. A cause of action in tort will lie where harm,

though unintended, could have been averted or avoided by observance of such a duty. The scope of the duty is limited by the range of danger that a reasonable person could foresee. In this case, there was nothing to suggest from the appearance of the parcel or otherwise that the parcel contained fireworks. The guard could not reasonably have had any warning of a threat to Palsgraf (P), and R.R. (D) therefore cannot be held liable. Judgment is reversed in favor of R.R. (D).

DISSENT: (Andrews, J.) The concept that there is no negligence unless R.R. (D) owes a legal duty to take care as to Palsgraf (P) herself is too narrow. Everyone owes to the world at large the duty of refraining from those acts that may unreasonably threaten the safety of others. If the guard's action was negligent as to those nearby, it was also negligent as to those outside what might be termed the "danger zone." For Palsgraf (P) to recover, R.R.'s (D) negligence must have been the proximate cause of her injury, a question of fact for the jury.

▶ ANALYSIS
The majority defined the limit of the defendant's liability in terms of the danger that a reasonable person in defendant's situation would have perceived. The dissent argued that the limitation should not be placed on liability, but rather on damages. Judge Andrews suggested that only injuries that would not have happened but for R.R.'s (D) negligence should be compensable. Both the majority and dissent recognized the policy-driven need to limit liability for negligent acts, seeking, in the words of Judge Andrews, to define a framework "that will be practical and in keeping with the general understanding of mankind." The Restatement (Second) of Torts has accepted Judge Cardozo's view.

▬

Quicknotes
FORESEEABILITY A reasonable expectation that change is the probable result of certain acts or omissions.

NEGLIGENCE Conduct falling below the standard of care that a reasonable person would demonstrate under similar conditions.

PROXIMATE CAUSE The natural sequence of events without which an injury would not have been sustained.

▬

Party ID: Quick identification of the relationship between the parties.

Concurrence/Dissent: All concurrences and dissents are briefed whenever they are included by the casebook editor.

Analysis: This last paragraph gives you a broad understanding of where the case "fits in" with other cases in the section of the book and with the entire course. It is a hornbook-style discussion indicating whether the case is a majority or minority opinion and comparing the principal case with other cases in the casebook. It may also provide analysis from restatements, uniform codes, and law review articles. The analysis will prove to be invaluable to classroom discussion.

Issue: The issue is a concise question that brings out the essence of the opinion as it relates to the section of the casebook in which the case appears. Both substantive and procedural issues are included if relevant to the decision.

Holding and Decision: This section offers a clear and in-depth discussion of the rule of the case and the court's rationale. It is written in easy-to-understand language and answers the issue presented by applying the law to the facts of the case. When relevant, it includes a thorough discussion of the exceptions to the case as listed by the court, any major cites to the other cases on point, and the names of the judges who wrote the decisions.

Quicknotes: Conveniently defines legal terms found in the case and summarizes the nature of any statutes, codes, or rules referred to in the text.

Wolters Kluwer Law & Business is proud to offer *Casenote® Legal Briefs*—continuing thirty years of publishing America's best-selling legal briefs.

Casenote® Legal Briefs are designed to help you save time when briefing assigned cases. Organized under convenient headings, they show you how to abstract the basic facts and holdings from the text of the actual opinions handed down by the courts. Used as part of a rigorous study regimen, they can help you spend more time analyzing and critiquing points of law than on copying bits and pieces of judicial opinions into your notebook or outline.

Casenote® Legal Briefs should never be used as a substitute for assigned casebook readings. They work best when read as a follow-up to reviewing the underlying opinions themselves. Students who try to avoid reading and digesting the judicial opinions in their casebooks or online sources will end up shortchanging themselves in the long run. The ability to absorb, critique, and restate the dynamic and complex elements of case law decisions is crucial to your success in law school and beyond. It cannot be developed vicariously.

Casenote® Legal Briefs represents but one of the many offerings in Legal Education's Study Aid Timeline, which includes:

- *Casenote® Legal Briefs*
- *Emanuel® Law Outlines*
- Emanuel® *Law in a Flash* Flash Cards
- Emanuel® *CrunchTime®* Series
- *Siegel's Essay and Multiple-Choice Questions and Answers Series*

Each of these series is designed to provide you with easy-to-understand explanations of complex points of law. Each volume offers guidance on the principles of legal analysis and, consulted regularly, will hone your ability to spot relevant issues. We have titles that will help you prepare for class, prepare for your exams, and enhance your general comprehension of the law along the way.

To find out more about Wolters Kluwer Law & Business' study aid publications, visit us online at *www.wolterskluwerlb.com* or email us at *legaledu@wolterskluwer.com*. We'll be happy to assist you.

A. Decide on a Format and Stick to It

Structure is essential to a good brief. It enables you to arrange systematically the related parts that are scattered throughout most cases, thus making manageable and understandable what might otherwise seem to be an endless and unfathomable sea of information. There are, of course, an unlimited number of formats that can be utilized. However, it is best to find one that suits your needs and stick to it. Consistency breeds both efficiency and the security that when called upon you will know where to look in your brief for the information you are asked to give.

Any format, as long as it presents the essential elements of a case in an organized fashion, can be used. Experience, however, has led *Casenote® Legal Briefs* to develop and utilize the following format because of its logical flow and universal applicability.

NATURE OF CASE: This is a brief statement of the legal character and procedural status of the case (e.g., "Appeal of a burglary conviction").

There are many different alternatives open to a litigant dissatisfied with a court ruling. The key to determining which one has been used is to discover *who is asking this court for what*.

This first entry in the brief should be kept as *short as possible*. Use the court's terminology if you understand it. But since jurisdictions vary as to the titles of pleadings, the best entry is the one that addresses who wants what in this proceeding, not the one that sounds most like the court's language.

RULE OF LAW: A statement of the general principle of law that the case illustrates (e.g., "An acceptance that varies any term of the offer is considered a rejection and counteroffer").

Determining the rule of law of a case is a procedure similar to determining the issue of the case. Avoid being fooled by red herrings; there may be a few rules of law mentioned in the case excerpt, but usually only one is *the* rule with which the casebook editor is concerned. The techniques used to locate the issue, described below, may also be utilized to find the rule of law. Generally, your best guide is simply the chapter heading. It is a clue to the point the casebook editor seeks to make and should be kept in mind when reading every case in the respective section.

FACTS: A synopsis of only the essential facts of the case, i.e., those bearing upon or leading up to the issue.

The facts entry should be a short statement of the events and transactions that led one party to initiate legal proceedings against another in the first place. While some cases conveniently state the salient facts at the beginning of the decision, in other instances they will have to be culled from hiding places throughout the text, even from concurring and dissenting opinions. Some of the "facts" will often be in dispute and should be so noted. Conflicting evidence may be briefly pointed up. "Hard" facts must be included. Both must be *relevant* in order to be listed in the facts entry. It is impossible to tell what is relevant until the entire case is read, as the ultimate determination of the rights and liabilities of the parties may turn on something buried deep in the opinion.

Generally, the facts entry should not be longer than three to five *short* sentences.

It is often helpful to identify the role played by a party in a given context. For example, in a construction contract case the identification of a party as the "contractor" or "builder" alleviates the need to tell that that party was the one who was supposed to have built the house.

It is always helpful, and a good general practice, to identify the "plaintiff" and the "defendant." This may seem elementary and uncomplicated, but, especially in view of the creative editing practiced by some casebook editors, it is sometimes a difficult or even impossible task. Bear in mind that the *party presently* seeking something from this court may not be the plaintiff, and that sometimes only the cross-claim of a defendant is treated in the excerpt. Confusing or misaligning the parties can ruin your analysis and understanding of the case.

ISSUE: A statement of the general legal question answered by or illustrated in the case. For clarity, the issue is best put in the form of a question capable of a "yes" or "no" answer. In reality, the issue is simply the Rule of Law put in the form of a question (e.g., "May an offer be accepted by performance?").

The major problem presented in discerning what is *the* issue in the case is that an opinion usually purports to raise and answer several questions. However, except for rare cases, only one such question is really the issue in the case. Collateral issues not necessary to the resolution of the matter in controversy are handled by the court by language known as *"obiter dictum"* or merely *"dictum."* While dicta may be included later in the brief, they have no place under the issue heading.

To find the issue, ask *who wants what* and then go on to ask *why did that party succeed or fail in getting it*. Once this is determined, the "why" should be turned into a question.

The complexity of the issues in the cases will vary, but in all cases a single-sentence question should sum up the issue. *In a few cases,* there will be two, or even more rarely, three issues of equal importance to the resolution of the case. Each should be expressed in a single-sentence question.

Since many issues are resolved by a court in coming to a final disposition of a case, the casebook editor will reproduce the portion of the opinion containing the issue or issues most relevant to the area of law under scrutiny. A noted law professor gave this advice: "Close the book; look at the title on the cover." Chances are, if it is Property, you need not concern yourself with whether, for example, the federal government's treatment of the plaintiff's land really raises a federal question sufficient to support jurisdiction on this ground in federal court.

The same rule applies to chapter headings designating sub-areas within the subjects. They tip you off as to what the text is designed to teach. The cases are arranged in a casebook to show a progression or development of the law, so that the preceding cases may also help.

It is also most important to remember to *read the notes and questions* at the end of a case to determine what the editors wanted you to have gleaned from it.

HOLDING AND DECISION: This section should succinctly explain the rationale of the court in arriving at its decision. In capsulizing the "reasoning" of the court, it should always include an application of the general rule or rules of law to the specific facts of the case. Hidden justifications come to light in this entry: the reasons for the state of the law, the public policies, the biases and prejudices, those considerations that influence the justices' thinking and, ultimately, the outcome of the case. At the end, there should be a short indication of the disposition or procedural resolution of the case (e.g., "Decision of the trial court for Mr. Smith (P) reversed").

The foregoing format is designed to help you "digest" the reams of case material with which you will be faced in your law school career. Once mastered by practice, it will place at your fingertips the information the authors of your casebooks have sought to impart to you in case-by-case illustration and analysis.

B. Be as Economical as Possible in Briefing Cases

Once armed with a format that encourages succinctness, it is as important to be economical with regard to the time spent on the actual reading of the case as it is to be economical in the writing of the brief itself. This does not mean "skimming" a case. Rather, it means reading the case with an "eye" trained to recognize into which "section" of your brief a particular passage or line fits and having a system for quickly and precisely marking the case so that the passages fitting any one particular part of

the brief can be easily identified and brought together in a concise and accurate manner when the brief is actually written.

It is of no use to simply repeat everything in the opinion of the court; record only enough information to trigger your recollection of what the court said. Nevertheless, an accurate statement of the "law of the case," i.e., the legal principle applied to the facts, is absolutely essential to class preparation and to learning the law under the case method.

To that end, it is important to develop a "shorthand" that you can use to make marginal notations. These notations will tell you at a glance in which section of the brief you will be placing that particular passage or portion of the opinion.

Some students prefer to underline all the salient portions of the opinion (with a pencil or colored underliner marker), making marginal notations as they go along. Others prefer the color-coded method of underlining, utilizing different colors of markers to underline the salient portions of the case, each separate color being used to represent a different section of the brief. For example, blue underlining could be used for passages relating to the rule of law, yellow for those relating to the issue, and green for those relating to the holding and decision, etc. While it has its advocates, the color-coded method can be confusing and time-consuming (all that time spent on changing colored markers). Furthermore, it can interfere with the continuity and concentration many students deem essential to the reading of a case for maximum comprehension. In the end, however, it is a matter of personal preference and style. Just remember, whatever method you use, underlining must be used sparingly or its value is lost.

If you take the marginal notation route, an efficient and easy method is to go along underlining the key portions of the case and placing in the margin alongside them the following "markers" to indicate where a particular passage or line "belongs" in the brief you will write:

N   (NATURE OF CASE)
RL   (RULE OF LAW)
I   (ISSUE)
HL   (HOLDING AND DECISION, relates to the RULE OF LAW behind the decision)
HR   (HOLDING AND DECISION, gives the RATIONALE or reasoning behind the decision)
HA   (HOLDING AND DECISION, APPLIES the general principle(s) of law to the facts of the case to arrive at the decision)

Remember that a particular passage may well contain information necessary to more than one part of your brief, in which case you simply note that in the margin. If you are using the color-coded underlining method instead of marginal notation, simply make asterisks or checks in the margin next to the passage in question in the colors that indicate the additional sections of the brief where it might be utilized.

The economy of utilizing "shorthand" in marking cases for briefing can be maintained in the actual brief writing process itself by utilizing "law student shorthand" within the brief. There are many commonly used words and phrases for which abbreviations can be substituted in your briefs (and in your class notes also). You can develop abbreviations that are personal to you and which will save you a lot of time. A reference list of briefing abbreviations can be found on page xii of this book.

C. Use Both the Briefing Process and the Brief as a Learning Tool

Now that you have a format and the tools for briefing cases efficiently, the most important thing is to make the time spent in briefing profitable to you and to make the most advantageous use of the briefs you create. Of course, the briefs are invaluable for classroom reference when you are called upon to explain or analyze a particular case. However, they are also useful in reviewing for exams. A quick glance at the fact summary should bring the case to mind, and a rereading of the rule of law should enable you to go over the underlying legal concept in your mind, how it was applied in that particular case, and how it might apply in other factual settings.

As to the value to be derived from engaging in the briefing process itself, there is an immediate benefit that arises from being forced to sift through the essential facts and reasoning from the court's opinion and to succinctly express them in your own words in your brief. The process ensures that you understand the case and the point that it illustrates, and that means you will be ready to absorb further analysis and information brought forth in class. It also ensures you will have something to say when called upon in class. The briefing process helps develop a mental agility for getting to the *gist* of a case and for identifying, expounding on, and applying the legal concepts and issues found there. The briefing process is the mental process on which you must rely in taking law school examinations; it is also the mental process upon which a lawyer relies in serving his clients and in making his living.

acceptance	acp	offer	O
affirmed	aff	offeree	OE
answer	ans	offeror	OR
assumption of risk	a/r	ordinance	ord
attorney	atty	pain and suffering	p/s
beyond a reasonable doubt	b/r/d	parol evidence	p/e
bona fide purchaser	BFP	plaintiff	P
breach of contract	br/k	prima facie	p/f
cause of action	c/a	probable cause	p/c
common law	c/l	proximate cause	px/c
Constitution	Con	real property	r/p
constitutional	con	reasonable doubt	r/d
contract	K	reasonable man	r/m
contributory negligence	c/n	rebuttable presumption	rb/p
cross	x	remanded	rem
cross-complaint	x/c	res ipsa loquitur	RIL
cross-examination	x/ex	respondeat superior	r/s
cruel and unusual punishment	c/u/p	Restatement	RS
defendant	D	reversed	rev
dismissed	dis	Rule Against Perpetuities	RAP
double jeopardy	d/j	search and seizure	s/s
due process	d/p	search warrant	s/w
equal protection	e/p	self-defense	s/d
equity	eq	specific performance	s/p
evidence	ev	statute	S
exclude	exc	statute of frauds	S/F
exclusionary rule	exc/r	statute of limitations	S/L
felony	f/n	summary judgment	s/j
freedom of speech	f/s	tenancy at will	t/w
good faith	g/f	tenancy in common	t/c
habeas corpus	h/c	tenant	t
hearsay	hr	third party	TP
husband	H	third party beneficiary	TPB
injunction	inj	transferred intent	TI
in loco parentis	ILP	unconscionable	uncon
inter vivos	I/v	unconstitutional	unconst
joint tenancy	j/t	undue influence	u/e
judgment	judgt	Uniform Commercial Code	UCC
jurisdiction	jur	unilateral	uni
last clear chance	LCC	vendee	VE
long-arm statute	LAS	vendor	VR
majority view	maj	versus	v
meeting of minds	MOM	void for vagueness	VFV
minority view	min	weight of authority	w/a
Miranda rule	Mir/r	weight of the evidence	w/e
Miranda warnings	Mir/w	wife	W
negligence	neg	with	w/
notice	ntc	within	w/i
nuisance	nus	without	w/o
obligation	ob	without prejudice	w/o/p
obscene	obs	wrongful death	wr/d

Table of Cases

Introduction

Quick Reference Rules of Law

Allen v. Bissinger & Co.

Official reporter of government commission (P) v. Recipient of commission's report (D)

Utah Sup. Ct., 62 Utah 226, 219 P. 539 (1923).

NATURE OF CASE: Appeal from judgment for plaintiff in action to recover monies under an alleged contract.

FACT SUMMARY: Bissinger & Co. (D) contended that no contract had been formed between it and Allen (P), the official reporter for the Interstate Commerce Commission (Commission), for copies of the Commission's official hearings related to freight, contending that there was a lack of mutual assent between the parties. Allen (P) contended that a contract had been formed because Bissinger (D) accepted his offer for copies of the reports.

🏛 RULE OF LAW
A contract is formed where, applying a reasonableness standard, an acceptance, although not exactly mirroring the language of an offer, clearly refers to the subject matter of the offer, so that the parties manifest an intention to agree on the same thing.

FACTS: Allen (P), the official reporter of the Interstate Commerce Commission (Commission), sent notices to major shippers, including Bissinger & Co. (D), of Commission hearing regarding freight matters. Along with the notice was an offer for copies of the official reports of the hearings. Bissinger (D) wrote to Allen (P), stating "We will be interested in your official report of the different changes in the handling of freight and would ask you to put our name down for a copy of same." Based on Bissinger's (D) letter, Allen (P) had a copy of the hearings up to August 17 prepared and shipped to Bissinger (D). Then, a copy of the official report for some subsequent hearings was sent to Bissinger (D) in October. A few days after receiving this second report, Bissinger (D) wrote Allen (P), informing him that the reports were useless to Bissinger (D), requesting that Allen (P) take back the reports, and agreeing to pay a reasonable charge for the cost of the reports already sent. Allen (P) responded that the Commission would accept a cancellation for reports prepared for hearings held after September 27, but could not do so for reports for hearings held through September 27, as a copy of the report for hearings up to that point had already been prepared. Allen (P) sent that copy in November and invoiced Bissinger (D) for $1,047.50, representing 12.5 cents per page for the 8,380 pages sent to Bissinger (D). Bissinger (D), expressing surprise at the per-page cost, as well as the number of pages sent to it, refused to pay. In response, Allen (P) informed Bissinger (D) that the per-page rate was one set by the Commission that had been in effect for 10 years, and that it was not possible to know ahead of time how extensive the hearings, and therefore the reports,

would be. Allen (P) sued to recover the monies billed for the reports, and the trial court granted judgment in Allen's (P) favor. The state's highest court granted review.

ISSUE: Is a contract formed where, applying a reasonableness standard, an acceptance, although not exactly mirroring the language of an offer, clearly refers to the subject matter of the offer, so that the parties manifest an intention to agree on the same thing?

HOLDING AND DECISION: (Cherry, J.) Yes. A contract is formed where, applying a reasonableness standard, an acceptance, although not exactly mirroring the language of an offer, clearly refers to the subject matter of the offer, so that the parties manifest an intention to agree on the same thing. Bissinger (D) argues that there was no meeting of the minds because the language in Allen's (P) offer—"a copy of the hearings"—was not mirrored by the language in Bissinger's (D) letter—"official report of the different changes in the handling of freight." From this, Bissinger (D) argues that the parties did not refer to the same thing in the transaction, and never agreed upon the subject-matter of the contract. This line of argument must be rejected, however, because, under the circumstances, applying a reasonableness standard, viewed in light of Allen's (P) offer, Bissinger's (D) reply is responsive and relevant. Allen (P) described and offered only one official report, and Bissinger (D) referred to and requested a copy of "your official report," etc., which phrase in ordinary commercial practice would be understood to sufficiently identify the matter referred to. The additional descriptive words used, "of different changes in the handling of freight," while lacking in precision, reasonably can be seen as referring to the subject of Allen's (P) offer. This is especially true, since there was no other official report known to the parties to which the acceptance could refer. Under the circumstances, the parties' communications manifest an intention to agree upon the same thing. The evidence was thus sufficient, as a matter of law, to support the finding of the trial court that Allen's (P) offer was accepted by Bissinger (D). Affirmed.

▶ ANALYSIS

The court in this case also made clear the principle that absent fraud or misconduct on the offeror's part, once an offeree has accepted the offer, it will not be relieved of its bargain merely because the bargain turns out to be burdensome or unprofitable. Thus, the court here did not find a lack of a contract based on Bissinger's (D) assertion that

Continued on next page.

the reports were "absolutely useless" and that it had not expected to receive a "library."

■≡■

Quicknotes

CONTRACT An agreement pursuant to which a party agrees to act, or to forbear from acting, in exchange for performance on the part of the other party.

FRAUD A false representation of facts with the intent that another will rely on the misrepresentation to his detriment.

MUTUAL ASSENT A requirement of a valid contract that the parties possess a mutuality of assent as manifested by the terms of the agreement and not by a hidden intent.

■≡■

Feldman v. Google, Inc.

Internet advertiser (P) v. Internet ads provider (D)

513 F. Supp. 2d 229 (E.D. Pa. 2007).

NATURE OF CASE: Summary judgment motions as to the enforceability of an internet clickwrap agreement.

FACT SUMMARY: Feldman (P) contended that an online agreement he must have clicked on before he could place internet ads through Google, Inc. (D) was not binding because he did not have notice of and did not assent to the terms of the agreement, and, therefore, there was no "meeting of the minds." He also contended the agreement was unenforceable because it lacked definite essential terms as to price.

🏛 **RULE OF LAW**
An online clickwrap agreement is binding where an online user has been given reasonable notice of the agreement's terms and it is clear that by clicking on an acceptance "button" the user agrees to be bound by those terms, notwithstanding that the agreement does not include a specific price term, but describes with sufficient definiteness a practicable process by which price is determined.

FACTS: Feldman (P), a lawyer, purchased advertising from Google, Inc.'s (D) "AdWords" Program to attract potential clients. Whenever an internet user searched on the internet search engine, Google.com, for keywords or "Adwords" purchased by Feldman (P), his ads would appear. If the searcher clicked on his ad, Google (D) would charge him for each click made on the ad. Feldman (P) believed that he was the victim of "click fraud," which occurs when entities or persons, such as competitors or pranksters, without any interest in an advertiser's services, click repeatedly on the advertiser's ad, the result of which drives up his advertising cost and discourages him from advertising. Feldman (P) brought suit in federal district court in Pennsylvania, contending that 20 to 30 percent of all clicks for which he was charged were fraudulent, and that Google (D) had means to track and prevent such fraud. Google (D) moved to dismiss and to transfer the case to court in California, asserting that a forum selection clause in the AdWords online agreement—which Feldman (P) must have clicked on before he could place ads through Google (D)—required disputes to be resolved in Santa Clara County, California. Feldman (P) did not deny that he clicked on this online agreement, which was preceded by the notice, in bold, "Carefully read the following terms and conditions. If you agree with these terms, indicate your assent below." Also, the first few paragraphs of the contract were visible on the computer window, and an advertiser had the ability to read the entire contract, by scrolling through it. The preamble, visible at first impression, stated

that consent to the terms listed in the Agreement constituted a binding agreement with Google (D). A link to a printer-friendly version of the contract was also offered for those advertisers who wanted a printed copy. Feldman (P) asserted that he had no notice of the agreement's terms and that there was no mutual assent to the agreement. He also asserted that the agreement was unenforceable because it lacked definite essential terms as to price and as to when the contract was entered into. The court treated Google's (D) motions collectively as a motion for summary judgment. Feldman (P) also moved for summary judgment, and the court rendered its opinion as to these cross-motions.

ISSUE: Is an online clickwrap agreement binding where an online user has been given reasonable notice of the agreement's terms and it is clear that by clicking on an acceptance "button" the user agrees to be bound by those terms, notwithstanding that the agreement does not include a specific price term, but describes with sufficient definiteness a practicable process by which price is determined?

HOLDING AND DECISION: (Giles, J.) Yes. An online clickwrap agreement is binding where an online user has been given reasonable notice of the agreement's terms and it is clear that by clicking on an acceptance "button" the user agrees to be bound by those terms, notwithstanding that the agreement does not include a specific price term, but describes with sufficient definiteness a practicable process by which price is determined. As a threshold matter, federal law governs in the determination of the effect given to a forum selection clause in diversity cases, since the issue is one of procedural law rather than substantive law. Applying federal law leads to the conclusion that the AdWords agreement was enforceable. Under traditional contract principles applicable here, a written contract will be enforceable if the parties had reasonable notice of its terms and assented thereto (a clickwrap agreement, although digital, is considered a writing because it can be printed and stored). Absent a showing of fraud, failure to read an enforceable clickwrap agreement, as with any binding contract, will not excuse compliance with its terms. The AdWords agreement gave reasonable notice of its terms. In order to activate an AdWords account, the user had to visit a webpage which displayed the agreement in a scrollable text box. The text of the AdWords agreement was immediately visible to the user, as was a prominent admonition in boldface to read the terms and conditions carefully, and

Continued on next page.

with instruction to indicate assent if the user agreed to the terms. Without such assent, the user could not proceed to set up his account. A reasonably prudent internet user would have known of the existence of terms in the AdWords agreement, and, here, Feldma (P) must have had reasonable notice of the terms. By clicking on "Yes, I agree to the above terms and conditions" button, he indicated assent to the terms. Therefore, the requirements of an express contract for reasonable notice of terms and mutual assent are satisfied. Additionally, Feldman's (P) argument that the agreement is unenforceable because of a failure to supply a definite, essential term as to price is without merit. Under both California and Pennsylvania law, the price term is an essential term of a contract and must be supplied with sufficient definiteness for a contract to be enforceable. However, a contract is not invalid for lack of definiteness where the parties have agreed on a practicable method of determining the price in the contract with reasonable certainty. Here, the AdWord agreement sets forth a practicable method of determining the market price with reasonable certainty. Google's (D) motion to transfer is granted and Feldman's (P) summary judgment motion is denied.

▶ ANALYSIS

At first, Feldman (P) asserted that there was an express contract between the parties. Then, in an amended complaint, he "changed his tune" and argued that no express contract existed because the agreement was not valid. Withdrawing his express contract allegations, Feldman (P) advanced the theory of implied contract because he argued he did not have notice of and did not assent to the terms of the agreement and therefore there was no "meeting of the minds." Contracts are "express" when the parties state their terms and "implied" when the parties do not state their terms. The distinction is based not on the contracts' legal effect but on the way the parties manifest their mutual assent. There cannot be an implied-in-fact contract if there is an express contract that covers the same subject matter. Because the court here found there was an express contract, it effectively ruled there could not be an implied contract between Feldman (P) and Google (D), and that the express contract's terms reflected the parties' agreement.

■■■

Quicknotes

EXPRESS CONTRACT A contract the terms of which are specifically stated; may be oral or written.

FRAUD A false representation of facts with the intent that another will rely on the misrepresentation to his detriment.

IMPLIED CONTRACT An agreement between parties that may be inferred from their general course of conduct.

IMPLIED-IN-FACT CONTRACT Refers to conditions which arise by physical or moral inference: (a) prerequisites

or circumstances which a reasonable person would assume necessary to render or receive performance; and (b) the good-faith cooperation of the promisee in receiving the performance of the promisor.

MOTION FOR SUMMARY JUDGMENT Judgment rendered by a court in response to a motion by one of the parties, claiming that the lack of a question of material fact in respect to an issue warrants disposition of the issue without consideration by the jury.

SUMMARY JUDGMENT Judgment rendered by a court in response to a motion made by one of the parties, claiming that the lack of a question of material fact in respect to an issue warrants disposition of the issue without consideration by the jury.

■■■

Mutual Assent and Consideration

Quick Reference Rules of Law

Ray v. William G. Eurice & Bros., Inc.

Engineer (P) v. Builder (D)

Md. Ct. App., 201 Md. 115, 93 A.2d 272 (1952).

NATURE OF CASE: Appeal from denial of damages for breach of contract.

FACT SUMMARY: The trial court found a mistake precluded a meeting of the minds between the parties, and thus no contract existed to be breached.

🏛 RULE OF LAW
A party is bound to a signed document which he has read with the capacity to understand it, absent fraud, duress, and mutual mistake.

FACTS: Ray (P), an engineer, presented architect's plans to Eurice (D) to solicit a bid for the construction of a house. Eurice (D), an experienced builder, rendered an estimate based upon revisions to the plans. Revised plans were attached to a contract which was read and signed by Eurice (D). Subsequently, Eurice (D) refused to perform, and Ray (P) sued for breach. Eurice (D) contended he never saw the specifications referred to by the contract and believed the contract referred to his own standard specifications. Thus a mistake precluded a meeting of the minds preventing the formation of a contract. The trial court found for Eurice (D), and Ray (P) appealed.

ISSUE: Is a party bound to his signed document if he has read it, has the capacity to understand it, and there is no fraud, duress, or mutual mistake?

HOLDING AND DECISION: (Hammond, J.) Yes. A party is bound to a signed document which he has read with the capacity to understand, and in the absence of fraud, duress, or mutual mistake. The contractor was very experienced and had no logical basis for assuming the specifications were his rather than those referred to in the contract. His mistake was unilateral rather than mutual. Thus, the contract was enforceable and was breached. The proper measure of damages is the cost in excess of the contract price that would be incurred by Ray (P) in having the house built. That amount is ascertainable with sufficient definiteness here, and equals $5,993.40. Reversed.

▶ ANALYSIS

Only a mutual mistake will prevent a meeting of the minds and thereby defeat the existence of an enforceable contract. A party's outward manifestations of an intent to contract are sufficient to bind him to the agreement. A party who is damaged by his lack of diligence in reviewing the contract has no remedy.

Quicknotes

DURESS Unlawful threats or other coercive behavior by one person that causes another to commit acts that he would not otherwise do.

FRAUD A false representation of facts with the intent that another will rely on the misrepresentation to his detriment.

MUTUAL MISTAKE A mistake by both parties to a contract, who are in agreement as to what the contract terms should be, but the agreement as written fails to reflect that common intent; such contracts are voidable or subject to reformation.

UNILATERAL MISTAKE Occurs when only one party to an agreement makes a mistake and is generally not a basis for relief by rescission or reformation.

■▬■

Lonergan v. Scolnick

Interested potential buyer (P) v. Seller (D)

Cal. Dist. Ct. App., 129 Cal. App. 2d 179, 276 P.2d 8 (1954).

NATURE OF CASE: Appeal from judgment for defendant in action for specific performance/damages.

FACT SUMMARY: After Lonergan (P) made several inquiries concerning some advertised land, it was sold to another.

🏛 RULE OF LAW

There is no meeting of the minds, and, therefore, no enforceable contract, where communications between the parties do not evidence a definite offer and acceptance.

FACTS: Lonergan (P) read about some property being offered for sale. Lonergan (P) wrote Scolnick (D), the seller, requesting additional information. Lonergan (P) later wrote for a legal description and whether a certain escrow company would be satisfactory to Scolnick (D). Scolnick (D) informed Lonergan (P) that if he wanted the property he would have to act fast, as Scolnick (D) expected to sell the property to a third party in a week. Lonergan (P) sent a letter one week later stating that he wanted the property. Scolnick (D) had already sold it several days before. Lonergan (P) brought suit for specific performance and/or damages alleging that a valid contract had been formed. Scolnick (D) alleged that the parties had merely negotiated, no offer and acceptance had occurred, and there had been no meeting of the minds as to forming a valid contract. The trial court rendered judgment for Scolnick (D). The state appellate court granted review.

ISSUE: Is there a meeting of the minds, and, therefore, an enforceable contract, where communications between the parties do not evidence a definite offer and acceptance?

HOLDING AND DECISION: (Barnard, J.) No. There is no meeting of the minds, and, therefore, no enforceable contract, where communications between the parties do not evidence a definite offer and acceptance. Until there is a definite offer and acceptance, the parties are merely in a negotiation stage, which creates no binding relationship between them. The meeting of the minds is normally evidenced by an offer and acceptance. The ad herein was merely the solicitation of offers for the property. None of the letters, on either side, constituted an offer and acceptance. Scolnick's (D) final letter made it clear that he would accept the first valid offer tendered. Lonergan (P) could not arbitrarily change negotiations into a contract unless Scolnick (D) had made a firm offer, a fact not established by the evidence. From Scolnick's (D) statement in his letter, alone, Lonergan (P) knew or should have known that he was not being given time in which to accept an offer that was being made, but that some further assent on the part of Scolnick (D) was required. Under the language used, Lonergan (P) was not being given a right to act within a reasonable time after receiving the letter. Because there was no offer, there could not be an acceptance, and, therefore, there was no meeting of the minds of the parties. Consequently, no enforceable contract was formed. Affirmed.

▶ ANALYSIS

In *Fairmount Glass Works v. Crunden-Martin Woodenware*, 106 Ky. 659, 51 S.W. 196 (1899), the plaintiff inquired as to the defendant's lowest price on ten loads of Mason jars. The reply was "$4.50 and $5.00 for immediate acceptance." The defendant refused to fill plaintiff's order. The court held that defendant's reply "was not a quotation of prices, but a definite order to sell." In *Harvey v. Facey*, A.C. 552 (1893), plaintiff telegraphed defendant, "Will you sell us Bumper Hall Pen? Telegraph lowest price." The defendant replied, "Lowest price for Bumper Hall Pen 900 Pounds." Plaintiff responded, "We agree to buy Bumper Hall Pen for 900 Pounds." The court held that there was no contract.

Quicknotes

ACCEPTANCE Assent to the specified terms of an offer, resulting in the formation of a binding agreement.

FIRM OFFER Under the Uniform Commercial Code, refers to a signed, written offer to enter into a contract for the sale of goods that is irrevocable for a specified period of time, or if no time is stated then for a reasonable time period not exceeding three months.

OFFER A proposed promise to undertake performance of an action, or to refrain from acting, that is to become binding upon acceptance by the offeree.

SPECIFIC PERFORMANCE An equitable remedy whereby the court requires the parties to perform their obligations pursuant to a contract.

Izadi v. Machado (Gus) Ford, Inc.

Buyer (P) v. Car dealer (D)

Fla. Dist. Ct. App., 550 So. 2d 1135 (1989).

NATURE OF CASE: Appeal from defense judgment in suit by buyer against car dealer, alleging breach of contract, fraud, and statutory violations involving misleading advertising.

FACT SUMMARY: Izadi (P) attempted to purchase a 1988 Ford Ranger Pick-Up by offering Machado Ford (D) $3,595 in cash and an unspecified trade-in for which he expected to be credited with a value of $3,000 pursuant to a Machado Ford (Machado) (D) advertisement placed in the Miami Herald. Machado (D) refused Izadi's (P) offer and his interpretation of their advertisement, and Izadi (P) sued Machado Ford (D) claiming breach of contract, fraud, and statutory violations involving misleading advertising.

🏛 RULE OF LAW
If an offer is conveyed by the objective reading of an advertisement, it does not matter that the advertiser may subjectively have not intended for its chosen language to constitute a binding offer.

FACTS: Izadi (P) attempted to purchase a 1988 Ford Ranger Pick-Up, a vehicle referred to at the foot of an ad, by tendering to Machado Ford (Machado) (D) $3,595 in cash and an unspecified trade-in. The proposal was made on the basis of Izadi's (P) belief that the ad offered $3,000 as a "minimum trade-in allowance" for any vehicle, regardless of its actual value. The putative grounds for this understanding were that the $3,000 trade-in figure was prominently referred to at the top of the ad, apparently as a portion of the consideration needed to "buy a new Ford," and that it was also designated as the projected deduction from the $7,095 gross cost for the Ranger Pick-Up. Machado (D), however, refused to recognize this interpretation of its advertisement and turned Izadi (P) down. In doing so, it relied instead on "the infinitesimally small print" under the $3,000 figure which indicated it applied only toward the purchase of "any New '88 Eddie Bauer Aerostar or Turbo T-Bird in stock," neither of which was mentioned in the remainder of the ad, and the statements in the individual vehicle portions that the offer was based on a trade-in that was "worth $3,000." Izadi (P) brought suit based on claims of breach of contract, fraud, and statutory violations involving misleading advertising. The trial court found in favor of Machado Ford (D), and Izadi (P) appealed.

ISSUE: If an offer is conveyed by the objective reading of an advertisement, does it matter that the advertiser may subjectively have not intended for its chosen language to constitute a binding offer?

HOLDING AND DECISION: (Schwartz, C.J.) No. If an offer is conveyed by the objective reading of an advertisement, it does not matter that the advertiser may subjectively have not intended for its chosen language to constitute a binding offer. An allegedly binding offer must be viewed as a whole, and it must be decided whether to disregard inconsistent or conflicting provisions. Here, such review could involve disregarding both the superfine print and apparent qualification as to the value of the trade-in as contradictory to the far more prominent thrust of the ad, which was that $3,000 would be credited for any trade-in on any Ford. Such review could also lead to the conclusion that the ad contained just an unqualified $3,000 offer, which Izadi (P) accepted. From the carefully chosen language and arrangement of the ad itself, it could be concluded that Machado (D), although it did not intend to honor the $3,000 trade-in representation, affirmatively, but wrongly, sought to make the public believe that it would be honored—a classic "bait and switch" situation. Given how tiny the print of the exclusionary clause was, it is difficult to reach any other conclusion. This situation invokes the applicability of a line of persuasive authority that a binding offer may be implied from the very fact that deliberately misleading advertising intentionally leads the reader to the conclusion that one exists. Affirmed in part, reversed in part, and remanded.

▶ ANALYSIS

As made clear in the *Izadi* decision, the test of the true interpretation of an offer or acceptance is not what the party making it thought it meant or intended it to mean, but what a reasonable person in the position of the parties would have thought it meant. The court did, nevertheless, emphasize that Izadi's (P) ability eventually to recover in this case depended on the showing that he was, in fact, led or misled into a genuine, even if unjustified, belief that such an offer had indeed been made. If he were merely attempting to take a knowing advantage of imprecise language in the advertisement and did not, in fact, rely upon it, he could not recover. In this regard, Restatement (Second) of Contracts § 167 comment a (1981) states, "A misrepresentation is not a cause of a party's making a contract unless he relied on the misrepresentation in manifesting his assent."

Continued on next page.

Quicknotes

BREACH OF CONTRACT   Unlawful failure by a party to perform its obligations pursuant to contract.

OFFER   A proposed promise to undertake performance of an action, or to refrain from acting, that is to become binding upon acceptance by the offeree.

■═■

Normile v. Miller

Purchaser (P) v. Seller (D)

N.C. Sup. Ct., 313 N.C. 98, 326 S.E.2d 11 (1985).

NATURE OF CASE: Appeal from denial of summary judgment motion for specific performance.

FACT SUMMARY: Normile (P) sought specific performance for the sale of Miller's (D) property after he accepted Miller's (D) counteroffer (which did not specify a time of acceptance) within the time period set for acceptance in his original offer, but after Miller (D) sold the property to Segal (P), thus revoking her counteroffer.

🏛 RULE OF LAW
A prospective purchaser does not have the power to accept a counteroffer after receiving notice of its revocation by accepting the counteroffer within the time period specified in the prospective purchaser's original offer.

FACTS: Miller (D) placed real estate for sale. Normile (P) completed a form purchase offer, and through brokers, presented it to Miller (D). The form had a set expiration period and called for other particulars of the sale. Miller (P) made changes in the terms—i.e., a counteroffer—and returned the form to Normile (P), who erroneously believed he was free to wait and think about the proposed counteroffer terms until the time set forth in the original offer that he had submitted to Miller (D). The counteroffer did not specify a time of acceptance. Prior to the expiration period on the original offer, Miller (D) accepted Segal's (P) offer to purchase the property, thus revoking her counteroffer. This revocation was communicated to Normile (P) by his broker, but Normile (P) attempted to accept the counteroffer, after being informed of its revocation, within the period for acceptance specified in the original offer. After this attempt was rejected, Normile (P) sued for specific performance and moved for summary judgment. However, the trial court granted Segal (P) summary judgment, and Normile (P) appealed the denial of his summary judgment motion. The state's highest court granted review.

ISSUE: Does a prospective purchaser have the power to accept a counteroffer after receiving notice of its revocation by accepting the counteroffer within the time period specified in the prospective purchaser's original offer?

HOLDING AND DECISION: (Frye, J.) No. A prospective purchaser does not have the power to accept a counteroffer after receiving notice of its revocation by accepting the counteroffer within the time period specified in the prospective purchaser's original offer. The original offer and its terms were rejected when Miller (D) made her qualified or conditional acceptance, which became a counteroffer. Although Normile (P) controlled the time for acceptance of his original offer, he could not control the time for acceptance of the counteroffer, since the counteroffer was a completely new offer and did not incorporate the original offer's time-of-acceptance term. If the terms of an offer are changed or qualified, there is no meeting of the minds, and, therefore, no contract. Here, Miller (D) did not accept the original offer, and her counteroffer did not include either a time limitation or a valid option supported by consideration, whereby it would remain open. Thus, when Miller (D) sold the property to Segal (P), she revoked her counteroffer to Normile (P), and Normile (P) was put on notice of this revocation by his broker. Normile's (P) failure to accept the counteroffer prior to its revocation precluded him from creating an enforceable contract based on the counteroffer. Affirmed as modified.

▶ ANALYSIS

Offers must be accepted entirely or the conditional acceptance constitutes a counteroffer. The offer grants the offeree the power to enter into an enforceable contract through acceptance. Acceptance of an offer, when supported by valuable consideration, creates an enforceable contract.

Quicknotes

ACCEPTANCE Assent to the specified terms of an offer, resulting in the formation of a binding agreement.

COUNTEROFFER A statement by the offeree which has the legal effect of rejecting the offer and of proposing a new offer to the offeror.

OFFER A proposed promise to undertake performance of an action, or to refrain from acting, that is to become binding upon acceptance by the offeree.

REVOCATION The cancellation or withdrawal of some authority conferred or an instrument drafted, such as the withdrawal of a revocable contract offer prior to the offeree's acceptance.

SPECIFIC PERFORMANCE An equitable remedy whereby the court requires the parties to perform their obligations pursuant to a contract.

Petterson v. Pattberg

Executor (P) v. Holder of mortgage (D)

N.Y. Ct. App., 248 N.Y. 86, 161 N.E. 428 (1928).

NATURE OF CASE: Appeal from affirmance of judgment for plaintiff in action for breach of contract.

FACT SUMMARY: Pattberg (D) offered to discount the mortgage on J. Petterson's estate on the condition that it be paid on a certain date. Pattberg (D) then sold the mortgage before Petterson (P), as executor of the estate, had paid him.

🏛 RULE OF LAW
An offer to enter into a unilateral contract may be withdrawn at any time prior to performance of the act requested to be done.

FACTS: Pattberg (D) held a mortgage on property belonging to J. Petterson's estate. Petterson (P) was executor of that estate. Pattberg (D) offered to discount the amount of the mortgage on the condition that it be paid on a certain date. Before that date Petterson (P) went to Pattberg's (D) home and offered to pay him the amount of the mortgage. Pattberg (D) told Petterson (P) that he had already sold the mortgage to a third person.

ISSUE: Can an offer to enter into a unilateral contract be withdrawn prior to performance of the act requested to be done?

HOLDING AND DECISION: (Kellogg, J.) Yes. An offer to enter into a unilateral contract may be withdrawn at any time prior to performance of the act requested to be done. Here, Pattberg's (D) offer proposed to Petterson (P) the making of a unilateral contract, the gift of a promise (to discount the mortgage) in exchange for the performance of an act (payment by a certain date). Pattberg (D) was free to revoke his offer any time before Petterson (P) accepted by performing the act. He revoked the offer by informing Petterson (P) that he had sold the mortgage. An offer to sell property may be withdrawn before acceptance without any formal notice to the person to whom the offer is made. It is sufficient if that person has actual knowledge that the person who made the offer has done some act inconsistent with the continuance of the offer, such as selling the property to a third person. Reversed.

DISSENT: (Lehman, J.) Until the act requested by Pattberg (D)—the payment of the mortgage at a discount on a date certain—was performed, Pattberg (D) had the right to revoke his offer. Petterson (P) was unable to perform here because Pattberg (D) did not agree to such payment when Petterson (P) presented it. "It is a principle of fundamental justice that if a promisor is himself the cause of the failure of performance either of an obligation due him or of a condition upon which his own liability depends, he cannot take advantage of the failure." The law should not be that Pattberg's (D) promise is not binding on him merely because he chose not to perform, notwithstanding that Petterson (P) fulfilled all conditions demanded by Pattberg (D). Because Pattberg (D) made a binding promise that was conditioned on Petterson's (P) performance, he could not revoke it after Petterson (P) had, in good faith acceptance of Pattberg's (D) offer, tendered payment.

▶ ANALYSIS

Other facts in *Petterson* which do not appear in the opinion may have influenced the court. The trial record shows that Pattberg (D) was prevented from testifying as to a letter sent to J. Petterson, in which the offer was revoked. The record also suggests that Petterson (P) knew of the sale of the mortgage. Note, 1928, 14 Cornell L.Q. 81. The Restatement of Contracts (Second) provides, "Where an offer invites an offeree to accept by rendering performance, an option contract is created when the offeree begins performance." Actual performance is necessary. Preparations to perform, though they may be essential to performance, are not enough. However, they may constitute justifiable reliance sufficient to make the offeror's promise binding under § 90.

■■■■

Quicknotes

REVOCATION The cancellation or withdrawal of some authority conferred or an instrument drafted, such as the withdrawal of a revocable contract offer prior to the offeree's acceptance.

UNILATERAL CONTRACT An agreement pursuant to which a party agrees to act, or to forbear from acting, in exchange for performance on the part of the other party.

■■■■

Cook v. Coldwell Banker/Frank Laiben Realty Co.

Former salesperson (P) v. Employer (D)

Mo. Ct. App., 967 S.W.2d 654 (1998).

NATURE OF CASE: Appeal from a jury verdict and judgment for plaintiff for damages for breach of a bonus agreement contract.

FACT SUMMARY: Cook (P), a former employee of Coldwell Banker (D), alleged that she had accepted Coldwell's (D) offer of a bonus by substantial performance.

🏛 RULE OF LAW
In the context of an offer for a unilateral contract, the offer may not be revoked when the offeree has accepted the offer by substantial performance.

FACTS: Cook (P) worked for Coldwell (D) as a licensed real estate broker. In March 1991, Coldwell (D) announced a bonus program in order to retain its agents. The bonuses awarded for commissions earned by the brokers were to be paid at the end of each year. In September, Coldwell (D) indicated that the bonuses would be paid in March of the following year instead. Cook (P) had earned a $500 bonus which was paid to her in September and was also entitled to another bonus, staying with Coldwell (D) until the end of the year in reliance on its promise of that bonus. In January, 1992, Cook (P) accepted a position with another firm and was told she would not be receiving her bonus from Coldwell (D). Cook (P) sent a demand letter to Coldwell (D), who refused to pay. Cook (P) then filed an action for breach of a bonus contract and sought damages, which a jury awarded her. Coldwell Banker (D) appealed.

ISSUE: In the context of an offer for a unilateral contract, may the offer be revoked when the offeree has accepted the offer by substantial performance?

HOLDING AND DECISION: (Crane, J.) No. In the context of an offer for a unilateral contract, the offer may not be revoked when the offeree has accepted the offer by substantial performance. An offer to make a unilateral contract is accepted when the requested performance is rendered. A promise to pay a bonus in return for an at-will employee's continued employment is an offer for a unilateral contract which becomes enforceable when accepted by the employee's performance. Part performance or tender may furnish consideration for the implied subsidiary promise that the offeror will not revoke his offer if part of the requested performance is given. In this case, there was evidence that, before the offer was modified in September, 1991, Cook (P) had remained with Coldwell (D) and had earned enough in commissions to be eligible for the offered bonus. This evidence was sufficient to make a submissible case for breach of a unilateral contract. Affirmed.

▶ ANALYSIS

The holding of this case reflects a modern expansion of the concept of a unilateral contract. In a unilateral contract, an offeree's performance is considered to be both the acceptance of, and the consideration for, the offeror's promise to pay. The revised Restatement of Contracts abandoned the distinction between unilateral and bilateral contracts.

■▬■

Quicknotes

SUBSTANTIAL PERFORMANCE Performance of all the essential obligations pursuant to an agreement.

UNILATERAL CONTRACT An agreement pursuant to which a party agrees to act, or to forbear from acting, in exchange for performance on the part of the other party.

■▬■

Walker v. Keith

Lessor (D) v. Lessee (P)

Ky. Ct. App., 382 S.W.2d 198 (1964).

NATURE OF CASE: Appeal from declaratory judgment for plaintiff lessee in action for breach of an option to renew a lease clause.

FACT SUMMARY: Walker (D), the lessor, contended that the option provision in his lease with Keith (P), the lessee, did not fix rent with sufficient certainty to constitute an enforceable contract between the parties.

🏛 **RULE OF LAW**
▉▅▉ Where essential terms such as price are not contained in an option contract, and no standards are included whereby such terms may be judicially determined, no contract exists.

FACTS: Walker (D), the lessor, entered into a ten-year lease with Keith (P), the lessee. The contract gave Keith (P) an option to renew the lease for ten additional years. The parties were to agree on a fair rental at that time to be fixed based on the "comparative basis of rental values at the date of renewal with rental values at this time reflected by the comparative business conditions of the two periods." Keith (P) attempted to renew his lease, but Walker (D) refused. Keith (P) brought suit for damages or specific performance. The trial court fixed the reasonable rental value at $125 per month. Walker (D) appealed, alleging that there was no way to fix the price and that, therefore, no contract existed. The intermediate court of appeals granted review.

ISSUE: Where essential terms such as price are not contained in an option contract, and no standards are included whereby such terms may be judicially determined, does a contract exist?

HOLDING AND DECISION: (Clay, Commn.) No. Where essential terms such as price are not contained in an option contract, and no standards are included whereby such terms may be judicially determined, no contract exists. The price term is essential in a lease contract. The option clause fails to fix it or to provide any standard whereby the court could fix it. Equity cannot rewrite a contract supplying essential terms which the parties failed to provide. Reasonable rent to one party may be unreasonable to the other. The parties herein have merely agreed to agree. Their failure to agree renders the option/offer incapable of being accepted. No contract was ever formed. Reversed.

▶ *ANALYSIS*

A number of courts have tried to supply missing terms, even essential ones by making "reasonable" judgments as to value, rental, etc. *Hull v. Weatherford*, 32 Ariz. 370 (1927).

Courts feel that "reasonable" rental can be determined by comparison with the rental of similar property, for a similar period of time and a similar use. *Edwards v. Tobin*, 132 Or. 38 (1930). In *Walker*, the court focuses on whether a contract exists. Only if one is found to exist may the court supply terms.

▉▅▉

Quicknotes

LEASE An agreement or contract which creates a relationship between a landlord and tenant (real property) or lessor and lessee (real or personal property).

MATERIAL TERMS OF CONTRACT A fact without the existence of which a contract would not have been entered.

▉▅▉

Quake Construction, Inc. v. American Airlines, Inc.

Construction subcontractor (P) v. Owner (D)

Ill. Sup. Ct., 141 Ill. 2d 281, 565 N.E.2d 990 (1990).

NATURE OF CASE: Appeal from reversal of dismissal of suit for damages resulting from alleged breach of contract.

FACT SUMMARY: When American Airlines (D) canceled its agreement with the general contractor for construction of an expansion of its airport facilities, Quake (P), a subcontractor, alleged that the letter of intent it had received from the general contractor constituted an enforceable, binding contract.

> ## 🏛 RULE OF LAW
> Although letters of intent may be enforceable, such letters are not necessarily enforceable unless the parties intend them to be contractually binding.

FACTS: American Airlines (D) hired a general contractor to prepare and accept bids and award contracts for construction of the expansion of American's (D) facilities at O'Hare International Airport. Quake Construction (P) was invited by the general contractor to bid on the employee facilities and automotive maintenance shop projects. Quake (P) was orally informed that it had been awarded the contract for the project. To induce Quake (P) and its subcontractors to provide their license numbers, the general contractor sent Quake (P) a letter of intent stating that the formal contract agreement was being prepared and would be available for signature shortly. The letter also contained a cancellation clause. American (D) later terminated Quake's (P) involvement with the project, and Quake (P) sued for the damages it had allegedly suffered in procuring the contract, preparing to perform under the contract, as well as its loss of anticipated profit from the contract. The circuit court held that the letter was not an enforceable contract and dismissed the complaint. The appellate court found the letter ambiguous regarding the parties' intent to be bound by it and remanded. American Airlines (D) appealed.

ISSUE: Although letters of intent may be enforceable, are such letters necessarily enforceable if the parties do not intend them to be contractually binding?

HOLDING AND DECISION: (Calvo, J.) No. Although letters of intent may be enforceable, such letters are not necessarily enforceable unless the parties intend them to be contractually binding. It is settled law in Illinois regarding letters of intent that the intent of the parties is controlling. A circuit court must initially determine, as a question of law, whether the language of a purported contract is ambiguous as to the parties' intent. If the terms of an alleged contract are ambiguous or capable of more than one interpretation, parol evidence is admissible to ascertain the parties' intent. The cancellation clause here exhibited the parties' intent to be bound by the letter because no need would exist to provide for the cancellation of the letter unless the letter had some binding effect. The cancellation clause could also, however, be interpreted to mean that the parties did not intend to be bound until they entered into a formal agreement. Therefore, the appellate court correctly concluded that the letter was ambiguous regarding the parties' intent to be bound by it. Affirmed.

CONCURRENCE: (Stamos, J.) Because dismissal is unwarranted unless clearly no set of facts can be proved under the pleadings that will entitle a plaintiff to recover, the circuit court should not have dismissed. The letter of intent is just ambiguous enough for Quake's (P) complaint to survive a motion to dismiss. Drafters of letters of intent would be well advised to avoid ambiguity on the point of whether the issuers are bound, if they want to avoid further litigation and undesired contractual obligations.

▶ ANALYSIS

An "agreement to agree" is a type of incomplete bargaining. In such a case, only one or two terms may be left for future agreement, and the parties have reached agreement on most other matters. Under the Uniform Commercial Code § 2-204(3), a contract for sale does not fail for indefiniteness if the parties have intended to make a contract and there is a reasonably certain basis for giving an appropriate remedy.

Quicknotes

AMBIGUITY Language that is capable of more than one interpretation.

CONSTRUCTION CONTRACT A contract containing provisions that specify the terms pursuant to which a building is to be constructed.

CONTRACT An agreement pursuant to which a party agrees to act, or to forbear from acting, in exchange for performance on the part of the other party.

PAROL EVIDENCE RULE Doctrine precluding parties to an agreement from introducing evidence of prior or contemporaneous agreements in order to repudiate or alter the terms of a written contract.

Hamer v. Sidway

Assignor of nephew (P) v. Executor (D)

N.Y. Ct. App., 124 N.Y. 538, 27 N.E. 256 (1891).

NATURE OF CASE: Appeal from denial of damages in an action for breach of contract.

FACT SUMMARY: Sidway's (D) decedent promised to pay $5,000 to Hamer's (P) assignor if he would forbear from the use of liquor, tobacco, swearing, or playing cards or billiards for money until his 21st birthday.

> **🏛 RULE OF LAW**
> In general, a waiver of any legal right at the request of another party is a sufficient consideration for a promise.

FACTS: Story, of whose estate Sidway (D) was executor, agreed with his nephew, William, that he, Story, would pay him $5,000 if he refrained from drinking liquor, using tobacco, swearing, or playing cards or billiards for money until his 21st birthday. Upon turning 21, William wrote Story saying that he had fulfilled his part of this deal and was entitled to the money. Story replied that William had in fact earned the money, but because Story feared that William might squander it, Story told William that he would keep the money set aside for him at interest. William agreed to this arrangement. Story died 12 years later without having paid the $5,000. William assigned his right in the money to his wife who, in turn, assigned her right to Hamer (P), who brought this action for breach of contract when Sidway (D) refused to pay on the ground that William gave no consideration nor did he suffer a detriment, but rather that his health and habits were benefited. Hamer (P) appealed judgment for Sidway (D).

ISSUE: Generally, is a waiver of any legal right at the request of another party a sufficient consideration for a promise?

HOLDING AND DECISION: (Parker, J.) Yes. Generally, a waiver of any legal right at the request of another party is a sufficient consideration for a promise. Valuable consideration may consist of either some right, interest, profit, or benefit accruing to the one party, for whom forbearance, detriment, loss, or responsibility is given, suffered, or undertaken by the other. To follow Sidway's (D) contention would be to leave open to controversy whether a consideration was erased by the degree a detriment is given by a promisee also benefited him. Second, the letter to William stating that the money would be set aside, coupled with his assent to that arrangement, changed the relationship of Story and William from debtor-creditor to trustee-beneficiary. If before a declaration of trust a party was a mere debtor, a subsequent agreement recognizing the fund as already in his hands and stipulating for its investment on the creditor's account will have the effect to create a trust. While the word "trust" was never used, the language of the letter assured William that the money would be set apart and kept without interference until he was capable of managing it himself. Reversed.

▶ ANALYSIS

The trust question was raised above because a pure contract action would have been barred by the running of the statute of limitations while an action on a trust would not have been so barred. "Consideration means not so much that one party is profiting as that the other abandons some legal right in the present or limits his legal freedom of action in the future as an inducement for the promise of the first." Pollock, Contracts, 166. Abstinence from liquor or giving up the use of liquor has independently been held to be sufficient consideration for a promise.

■═■

Quicknotes

CONSIDERATION Value given by one party in exchange for performance, or a promise to perform, by another party.

TRUST The holding of property by one party for the benefit of another.

■═■

Pennsy Supply, Inc. v. American Ash Recycling Corp. of Pennsylvania

Subcontractor (P) v. Materials supplier (D)

Pa. Super. Ct., 895 A.2d 595 (2006).

NATURE OF CASE: Appeal from grant of demurrer dismissing an action for breach of contract, breach of implied and express warranties of merchantability, breach of warranty of fitness for a particular purpose, and promissory estoppel.

FACT SUMMARY: Pennsy Supply, Inc. (Pennsy) (P) contended that its disposal of a hazardous material it had obtained for free from American Ash Recycling Corp. of Pennsylvania (American Ash) (D) constituted consideration necessary to support various breach of contract, warranty and merchantability claims.

RULE OF LAW
Relief of a manufacturer's legal obligation to dispose of a material classified as hazardous waste, such that the manufacturer avoids the costs of disposal, constitutes sufficient consideration to ground contract and warranty claims brought by the disposer.

FACTS: Pennsy Supply, Inc. (Pennsy) (P), a paving subcontractor, obtained paving material, known as Treated Ash Aggregate (TAA) or AggRite, for free from American Ash Recycling Corp. of Pennsylvania (American Ash) (D). Pennsy (P) used the material for driveways and a parking lot in a school district construction project. When the paving started to crack extensively, Pennsy (P) remedied at no cost to the district. The scope and cost of the remedial work included the removal and appropriate disposal of the AggRite, which the state classified as a hazardous waste material. Pennsy (P) requested American Ash (D) to arrange for the removal and disposal of the AggRite, but American Ash (D) refused. Pennsy (P) provided notice to American Ash (D) of its intention to recover costs, and then filed suit for breach of contract; breach of implied warranty of merchantability; breach of express warranty of merchantability; breach of warranty of fitness for a particular purpose; and promissory estoppel. American Ash (D) demurred, and the trial court sustained its demurrers on the basis of its finding that any alleged agreement between the parties was unenforceable for lack of consideration. The trial court found that there was no evidence that disposal costs were part of any bargaining process or that American Ash (D) offered the AggRite with an intent to avoid disposal costs. The state's intermediate court of appeals granted review.

ISSUE: Does relief of a manufacturer's legal obligation to dispose of a material classified as hazardous waste, such that the manufacturer avoids the costs of disposal,

constitute sufficient consideration to ground contract and warranty claims brought by the disposer?

HOLDING AND DECISION: (Orie Melvin, J.) Yes. Relief of a manufacturer's legal obligation to dispose of a material classified as hazardous waste, such that the manufacturer avoids the costs of disposal, constitutes sufficient consideration to ground contract and warranty claims brought by the disposer. Consideration—a benefit to the promisor or a detriment to the promisee—is an essential element of an enforceable contract and must be bargained for as an exchange for a promise. It is not enough, however, that the promisee has suffered a legal detriment at the request of the promisor. The detriment incurred must be the "quid pro quo," or the "price" of the promise, and the inducement for which it was made. If the promisor merely intends to make a gift to the promisee upon the performance of a condition, the promise is gratuitous and the satisfaction of the condition is not consideration for a contract. Here, the facts alleged do not show only that American Ash (D) made a conditional gift of the AggRite to Pennsy (P). Pennsy (P) alleged that American Ash (D) gave away the AggRite in an effort to have others dispose of it so that American Ash (D) could avoid incurring disposal costs. Thus, here, American Ash's (D) promise to supply AggRite free of charge induced Pennsy (P) to assume the detriment of collecting and taking title to the material, and it was this detriment that induced American Ash (D) to make the promise to provide free AggRite for the project. Moreover, the lack of an actual bargaining process between the parties is unnecessary to establish consideration; the facts, if proven, need merely show that the promise induced the detriment and the detriment induced the promise. Therefore, Pennsy (P) alleged facts that, if proven true, would indicate sufficient consideration to support breach of contract, breach of warranty, and promissory estoppel claims. Reversed and remanded.

▶ ANALYSIS

As this case demonstrates, the distinction between conduct that constitutes consideration and conduct that is a condition to a gift is not a clear one because the very same conduct may be consideration or a condition to a gift depending on how the parties treat the conduct. As indicated in 17A Am. Jur. 2d § 104 (2004 & 2005 Supp.), "[a]n

Continued on next page.

aid, though not a conclusive test, in determining which construction of the promise is more reasonable is an inquiry into whether the occurrence of the condition would benefit the promisor. If so, it is a fair inference that the occurrence was requested as consideration. On the other hand, if the occurrence of the condition is no benefit to the promisor but is merely to enable the promisee to receive a gift, the occurrence of the event on which the promise is conditional, though brought about by the promisee in reliance on the promise, is not properly construed as consideration."

■≡■

Quicknotes

BREACH OF CONTRACT Unlawful failure by a party to perform its obligations pursuant to contract.

BREACH OF EXPRESS WARRANTY The breach of an express promise made by one party to a contract on which the other party may rely, relieving that party from the obligation of determining whether the fact is true and indemnifying the other party from liability if that fact is shown to be false.

BREACH OF WARRANTY The breach of a promise made by one party to a contract on which the other party may rely, relieving that party from the obligation of determining whether the fact is true and indemnifying the other party from liability if that fact is shown to be false.

CONSIDERATION Value given by one party in exchange for performance, or a promise to perform, by another party.

DEMURRER The assertion that the opposing party's pleadings are insufficient and that the demurring party should not be made to answer.

IMPLIED WARRANTY An implied promise made by one party to a contract that the other party may rely on a fact, relieving that party from the obligation of determining whether the fact is true and indemnifying the other party from liability if that fact is shown to be false.

PROMISSORY ESTOPPEL A promise that is enforceable if the promisor should reasonably expect that it will induce action or forbearance on the part of the promisee, and does in fact cause such action or forbearance, and it is the only means of avoiding injustice.

WARRANTY OF FITNESS An implied promise made by a merchant in a contract for the sale of goods that such goods are suitable for the purpose for which they are purchased.

WARRANTY OF MERCHANTABILITY An implied promise made by a merchant in a contract for the sale of goods that such goods are suitable for the purpose for which they are purchased.

■≡■

Dougherty v. Salt

Minor and guardian (P) v. Executor (D)

N.Y. Ct. App., 227 N.Y. 200, 125 N.E. 94 (1919).

NATURE OF CASE: Appeal from reinstatement of verdict for plaintiff in breach of contract action.

FACT SUMMARY: The trial court dismissed Dougherty's (P) action to recover on a note finding no consideration supported the note.

🏛 RULE OF LAW
 A note that is not supported by consideration is unenforceable.

FACTS: Dougherty (P), a minor, was visited by his aunt who indicated she wished to take care of him. The note was a preprinted form and carried no indication of consideration. Dougherty's (P) guardian was the sole witness who testified the aunt wanted to take care of the child, and thus was motivated to execute the note payable at her death. After her death, suit was brought to enforce the note, which was dismissed, although the jury found the note was supported by consideration. The appellate court reversed, finding sufficient consideration and holding the trial court erred in overruling the jury. Salt (D), the executor, appealed.

ISSUE: Is a note that is not supported by consideration enforceable?

HOLDING AND DECISION: (Cardozo, J.) No. A note that is not supported by consideration is unenforceable. The only evidence available indicated the note was given out of the generosity of the maker. The payee was not a creditor and was not owed support by the maker. Thus, the note was not supported by consideration and was unenforceable. Reversed.

▶ ANALYSIS

The note in this case was labeled an executory gift, one which is to be performed or executed in the future. The triggering event here was the death of the aunt. No consideration was found despite the fact the preprinted form stated value had been received. Thus, the court looked to the substance rather than the appearance of the note.

■━■

Quicknotes

CONSIDERATION Value given by one party in exchange for performance, or a promise to perform, by another party.

GIFT A transfer of property to another person that is voluntary and which lacks consideration.

■━■

Batsakis v. Demotsis

Greek resident lender (P) v. Borrower (D)

Tex. Ct. Civ. App., 226 S.W.2d 673 (1949).

NATURE OF CASE: Appeal from action to recover on a promissory note.

FACT SUMMARY: Batsakis (P) loaned Demotsis (D) 500,000 drachmae (which, at the time, had a total value of $25 in American money) in return for Demotsis's (D) promise to repay $2,000 in American money.

 **RULE OF LAW**
Mere inadequacy of consideration will not void a contract.

FACTS: During World War II, Batsakis (P), a Greek resident, loaned Demotsis (D), also a Greek resident, the sum of 500,000 drachmae which, at the time, had a distressed value of only $25 in American money. In return, Demotsis (D), eager to return to the United States, signed an instrument in which she promised to repay Batsakis (P) $2,000 of American money. When Demotsis (D) refused to repay, claiming that the instrument was void at the outset for lack of adequate consideration, Batsakis (P) brought an action to collect on the note and recovered a judgment for $750 (which, at the time, after the war, reflected the rising value of drachmae), plus interest. Batsakis (P) appealed on the ground that he was entitled to recover the stated sum of the note—$2,000—plus interest.

ISSUE: Will mere inadequacy of consideration void a contract?

HOLDING AND DECISION: (McGill, J.) No. Mere inadequacy of consideration will not void a contract. Only where the consideration for a contract has no value whatsoever will the contract be voided. A plea of want of consideration amounts to a contention that the instrument never became a valid obligation in the first instance. As a result, mere inadequacy of consideration is not enough. Here, the trial court obviously placed a value on the consideration—the drachmae—by deeming them to be worth $750. Thus, the trial court felt that there was consideration of value for the original transaction. Furthermore, the 500,000 drachmae was exactly what Demotsis (D) bargained for. It may not have been a good bargain, but she nonetheless agreed to repay Batsakis (P) $2,000. Accordingly, Batsakis (P) is entitled to recover $2,000, and not just $750, plus interest. Affirmed as reformed.

▶ *ANALYSIS*

Official comment (e) to the Restatement (Second) of Contracts, § 81, states, "gross inadequacy of consideration may be relevant in the application of other rules (such as) . . . lack of capacity, fraud, duress, undue influence, or mis-

take." Section 234 provides for the avoidance of a contract which, at the time it is made, contains an unconscionable term. The official comment (c) to this section states that "gross disparity in the values exchanged . . . may be sufficient ground, without more, for denying specific performance."

Quicknotes

SPECIFIC PERFORMANCE An equitable remedy whereby the court requires the parties to perform their obligations pursuant to a contract.

UNCONSCIONABILITY Rule of law whereby a court may excuse performance of a contract, or of a particular contract term, if it determines that such term(s) are unduly oppressive or unfair to one party to the contract.

Plowman v. Indian Refining Co.

Employer (P) v. Oil company (D)

20 F. Supp. 1 (E.D. Ill. 1937).

NATURE OF CASE: Action for breach of contract.

FACT SUMMARY: Plowman (P) and others sought to enforce a benefit agreement between them and their former employer, Indian Refining (Indian) (D).

RULE OF LAW
Past services are not sufficient consideration to support the enforceability of a contract to provide continuing payments to former employees.

FACTS: Plowman (P) and others were employed by Indian (D) for several years. They were told, orally and in writing, that because of their past service to the company they would be retired at half-pay. The length of such payments was not established at trial. The payments were conditioned upon the recipients' picking up their checks at the factory. The payments were made for approximately one year and then summarily discontinued. The employees sued, contending there was an enforceable contract created. Indian (D) defended on the basis of a lack of consideration, rendering any agreement unenforceable.

ISSUE: Are past services sufficient consideration to support an enforceable contract?

HOLDING AND DECISION: (Lindley, J.) No. Past services are not sufficient consideration to support an enforceable contract. The only consideration for the promise to pay was the company's purported concern over its employees who had to be laid off. This concern was a reward for past services and thus the promise was unsupported by consideration. The requirement that the checks be picked up was merely a condition. Thus no enforceable agreement existed.

ANALYSIS

Consideration consists of a voluntary detriment or forbearance by the party in return for a promise. If the detriment already has been performed, it could not be in exchange for the promise, and thus could not be considered consideration. Thus, "past consideration" cannot support an enforceable contract.

■═■

Quicknotes

CONDITION Requirement; potential future occurrence upon which the existence of a legal obligation is dependent.

PAST CONSIDERATION Consideration made before a contract is created and is usually not legally sufficient consideration to support a contract.

■═■

Marshall Durbin Food Corp. v. Baker

Former employer (D) v. Former employee (P)

Miss. Ct. App., 909 So. 2d 1267 (2005).

NATURE OF CASE: Appeal from judgment awarding former employee payments in action to enforce a severance contract.

FACT SUMMARY: Marshall Durbin Food Corp. (D) contended that a contract that purported to pay Baker (P), a former employee, his salary for five years upon the happening of certain triggering events, was invalid for want of consideration.

🏛 RULE OF LAW
An agreement is supported by sufficient consideration to create an enforceable contract where one party has made an illusory promise, the second party has made a promise of a unilateral contract that is contingent on the first party's performance, and the first party has performed to fulfillment of the contingency.

FACTS: Baker (P) had been an employee of Marshall Durbin Food Corp. (the "Company") (D), which was controlled by Mr. Durbin. During a period where the Company (D) was experiencing hardship and chaos, Baker (P) obtained from Mr. Durbin an agreement that upon certain triggering events, Baker (P) would be entitled to five years of his then-current salary. One of those triggering events was Mr. Durbin's incapacity. The agreement specified how the payments would be calculated, specified an "effective date," and recited that it was not intended to create a contract of employment, which remained at-will. The agreement also recited that it was entered into for consideration of $10 and other valuable consideration, the receipt of which was acknowledged. The Company's (D) board ratified this agreement. Around a year and a half later, Mr. Durbin was diagnosed with malignant cancer, and Baker (P) took over as the Company's (D) president. About a month later, Mr. Durbin was judicially declared incapacitated, whereupon Baker (P) informed the Company (D) that the agreement had been triggered and that he would no longer be working as an employee, but would continue to do work for the Company (D) as a contractor. The following month, Mr. Durbin died and a new board was elected. Baker (P) sued for specific performance of the agreement, and was informed by the Company (D) that the new board, believing the agreement was invalid, had repudiated it. In answer to Baker's (P) suit, the Company (D) asserted the agreement was invalid for lack of consideration. The trial court, determining that the agreement had been entered into to retain top management, including Baker (P), at a time the Company (D) was experiencing difficulties, and that Baker (P), in reliance on the agreement, had not sought employment elsewhere, held for Baker (P). The state's intermediate appellate court granted review.

ISSUE: Is an agreement supported by sufficient consideration to create an enforceable contract where one party has made an illusory promise, the second party has made a promise of a unilateral contract that is contingent on the first party's performance, and the first party has performed to fulfillment of the contingency?

HOLDING AND DECISION: (Barnes, J.) Yes. An agreement is supported by sufficient consideration to create an enforceable contract where one party has made an illusory promise, the second party has made a promise of a unilateral contract that is contingent on the first party's performance, and the first party has performed to fulfillment of the contingency. As a threshold matter, the agreement's recital of consideration creates a rebuttable presumption that consideration actually existed. Here, the Company (D) has failed to present sufficient evidence to rebut the presumption by a clear preponderance of the evidence. That unrebutted presumption is sufficient to affirm the trial court's decision as to the existence of consideration. Nonetheless, the parties' arguments about the issue will be addressed. First, the Company (D) argues that both Baker's (P) promise and the Company's (D) promise were illusory, since their relationship remained at-will. This argument, while valid as to Baker (P), must be rejected as to the Company (D). Baker's (P) promise was illusory because he had the right to look for other employment at any time, so he did not give anything up when he promised to stay with the Company (D). In turn, the Company's (D) promise was that if Baker (P) continued his employment until the happening of a triggering event, the Company (D) would compensate him as set forth in the contract. The Company's (D) promise, although contingent, was not illusory. Accordingly, Baker (P) could, and did, supply consideration for the Company's (D) promise by "an act other than a promise"—Baker's (P) act of continuing to work for the Company (D) and the Company's (D) corresponding receipt of benefit from his services. Here, the contingency (Baker (P) being employed during the triggering event of Mr. Durbin's incapacity) has been fulfilled. Thus, Baker's (P) consideration was not supplied by a promise but by his actual performance during the fulfillment of the contingency. Additionally, the Company (D) argues that Baker's (P) forbearance from seeking other employment was not a

Continued on next page.

legal detriment and cannot constitute consideration because Baker (P) had the legal right to look for other employment, since his employment was at will. This issue need not be addressed because the trial court found—and the evidence supports its finding—that Baker (P) experienced detriment in forbearing from seeking or accepting other employment, and the Company (D) benefitted from retaining his services. It is established law that a benefit to the promisor or detriment to the promisee is sufficient consideration for a contract. This may consist either in some interest, right, profit or benefit accruing to the one party, or some forbearance, detriment, loss or responsibility given, suffered or undertaken by the other. For all these reasons, the trial court correctly determined there to be consideration for the contract. Affirmed as to this issue. [The court reversed as to the agreement's effective date.]

▶ *ANALYSIS*

This case illustrates the principle that the presence of an illusory promise does not destroy the possibility of a contract. Instead, it may create a unilateral contract, and the promisor who made the illusory promise (here, Baker (P)) can accept the contract by performance. Other courts, however, hold that an illusory promise by one party renders the return promise unenforceable, unless some other consideration is present.

■≡■

Quicknotes

AT-WILL EMPLOYMENT The rule that an employment relationship is subject to termination at any time, or for any cause, by an employee or an employer in the absence of a specific agreement otherwise.

ILLUSORY PROMISE A promise that is not legally enforceable because performance of the obligation by the promisor is completely within his discretion.

REBUTTABLE PRESUMPTION A rule of law, inferred from the existence of a particular set of facts, that is conclusive in the absence of contrary evidence.

SEVERANCE Dividing or separating; setting aside one or more claims in a lawsuit to be tried separately.

SPECIFIC PERFORMANCE An equitable remedy whereby the court requires the parties to perform their obligations pursuant to a contract.

UNILATERAL CONTRACT An agreement pursuant to which a party agrees to act without an express exchange for performance on the part of the other party.

■≡■

Jannusch v. Naffziger

Business seller (P) v. Business buyer (D)

Ill. Ct. App., 379 Ill. App. 3d 381, 883 N.E.2d 711 (2008).

NATURE OF CASE: Appeal from judgment for defendants in action for breach of contract.

FACT SUMMARY: The Jannusches (P) owned Festival Foods, a concessions business. The Jannusches (P) contended that they had an enforceable oral contract with the Naffzigers (D) to buy Festival Foods because essential terms were identified, i.e., price and the goods to be conveyed, and that the Naffzigers (D) breached that contract.

🏛 RULE OF LAW
Under the Uniform Commercial Code (U.C.C.), a contract that is primarily for the sale of goods is enforceable where, although many terms are missing, essential terms, including price and the identification of the goods to be sold, have been agreed upon.

FACTS: The Jannusches (P) owned and operated Festival Foods, a concessions business that owned a truck and servicing trailer and equipment such as refrigerators and freezers, roasters, chairs and tables, fountain service and signs and lighting equipment. The Naffzigers (D) expressed interest in purchasing the business, and, after meeting several times, the parties orally agreed on a $150,000 purchase price, in exchange for which the Naffzigers (D) would receive the truck and trailer, all necessary equipment, and the opportunity to work at event locations secured by the Jannusches (P). The Naffzigers (D) paid $10,000 immediately and took possession of Festival Foods the next day. They operated the business for the remainder of the season, i.e., for over four months. Throughout this period, the Naffzigers (D) received the income from the business, purchased inventory, replaced equipment, paid taxes on the business and paid employees. At the end of the season, unhappy with the income the business was generating, the Naffzigers (D) returned Festival Foods to the storage facility where it previously had been stored. The Jannusches (P) sued for breach of contract. The Naffzigers (D) testified they had agreed only to run the business while they pursued buying it. They also testified they had rejected putting their agreement into writing because they had not received the bank loan. However, the following week, the Naffzigers (D) consulted with an attorney regarding the legal aspects of buying and owning a business, and asked the attorney to prepare a contract for the purchase. Ultimately, the bank approved the loan. The Jannusches (P) testified that the Naffzigers (D) hired them as consultants during some of the events and paid for their lodging. There was other, conflicting, testimony as to the train of events. Ultimately, the trial court held that even though a contract had been formed, the evidence was insufficient to establish by a preponderance of the evidence that there was a meeting of the minds as to what that agreement was. Accordingly, the court rendered judgment for the Naffzigers (D). The state's intermediate appellate court granted review.

ISSUE: Under the U.C.C., is a contract that is primarily for the sale of goods enforceable where, although many terms are missing, essential terms, including price and the identification of the goods to be sold, have been agreed upon?

HOLDING AND DECISION: (Cook, J.) Yes. Under the U.C.C., a contract that is primarily for the sale of goods is enforceable where, although many terms are missing, essential terms, including price and the identification of the goods to be sold, have been agreed upon. First, the trial court correctly determined that the contract at issue is governed by the U.C.C.. Where a contract is for both goods and services, the "predominant purpose" test is applied to determine if the contract falls within U.C.C. Article 2 governing the sale of goods. This test is generally a question of fact. Here, significant tangible assets were involved, so that the evidence presented was sufficient to support the conclusion that the proposed agreement was predominantly one for the sale of goods. Second, under the U.C.C., a contract for the sale of goods worth over $500 must be in writing unless certain exceptions apply. Here, two exceptions apply: (1) the party against whom enforcement is sought admits in his pleading, testimony, or otherwise in court that a contract for sale was made (the Naffzigers (D) so admitted) and (2) an oral contract for the sale of goods which has been partially performed is enforceable. Thus, the key question is whether a binding contract was formed. The Naffzigers (D) argue that nothing was said in the contract about many terms that are customarily in—and essential to—contracts for the sale of a business, including terms relating to allocating a price for good will, a covenant not to compete, allocating a price for the equipment, how to release liens, what would happen if there was no loan approval, and other issues. This argument is unpersuasive. Although the Naffzigers (D) are correct that a contract that is missing essential terms is unenforceable, the essential terms of the contract at issue were agreed upon. The purchase price was $150,000, and the items to be transferred were specified. No essential terms remained to be agreed upon; the only action remaining was the performance of the contract. The

Continued on next page.

Naffzigers (D) took possession of the items to be transferred and used them as their own, and they paid $10,000 of the purchase price. Merely because they were disappointed with the income the business generated while they operated it does negate the existence of a contract. Although the parties had different subjective ideas as to what occurred in their course of dealing, their objective conduct indicated an agreement to the essential terms. Parties discussing the sale of goods do not transfer those goods and allow them to be retained for a substantial period before reaching agreement. The Naffzigers (D) replaced equipment, reported income, paid taxes, and paid the Jannusches (P) as consultants, all of which is inconsistent with the idea that the Naffzigers (D) were only "pursuing buying the business." Moreover, the fact the parties did not enter a written contract is not dispositive; the fact that a formal written document is anticipated does not preclude enforcement of a specific preliminary promise. At issue was not an agreement to enter into an agreement; there was more. Although the agreement could have been fleshed out with additional terms, the essential terms were agreed upon. Therefore, the Naffziger's (D) return of the goods at the end of the season was not a rejection of the Jannusches (P) offer to sell, it was a breach of contract. Reversed and remanded.

▎▶ *ANALYSIS*

The U.C.C., as opposed to common law, does not ask whether there was mutual assent to a contract. Instead, as in this case, the U.C.C. focuses the inquiry on the parties' intent to be bound, notwithstanding that some (non-essential) terms have not been addressed.

■═■

Quicknotes

BREACH OF CONTRACT   Unlawful failure by a party to perform its obligations pursuant to contract.

ORAL CONTRACT   A contract that is not reduced to written form.

■═■

E.C. Styberg Engineering Co. v. Eaton Corp.

Components manufacturer (P) v. Parts producer (D)

492 F.3d 912 (7th Cir. 2007).

NATURE OF CASE: Appeal from judgment for defendant in action for breach of contract.

FACT SUMMARY: E.C. Styberg Engineering Co. (Styberg) (P), a components manufacturer, contended that Eaton Corp. (D), an automobile parts producer, and Styberg (P) had a contract for Eaton (D) to purchase 13,000 transmission components from Styberg (P).

🏛 RULE OF LAW
Under the Uniform Commercial Code (U.C.C.), a contract for the sale of goods in not formed where the parties' communications evidence ongoing negotiations, but no agreement, as to key terms, such as price, quantity, and monthly production volume.

FACTS: E.C. Styberg Engineering Co. (Styberg) (P) manufactured components. Eaton Corp. (D), an automobile parts producer, purchased various components from Styberg (P). For a two-year period, Styberg (P) manufactured an automobile transmission component known as the I-brake, which Eaton (D) used in certain transmissions it produced. At first, Styberg (P) began selling prototype I-brake units to Eaton (D), and Eaton (D) began purchasing limited quantities of I-brakes so it could test the product in the marketplace. Subsequently, Eaton (D) decided to pursue full production of I-brakes, and the parties began negotiating an agreement under which Styberg (P) would produce large quantities of I-brakes for Eaton (D). Getting a minimum unit commitment from Eaton (D) was important to Styberg (P) because it had to expend significant capital to mass-produce the custom-designed parts. The parties went back and forth with various proposals, in e-mails, phone calls, letters, and meetings. On July 8, 1999, Styberg (P) sent Eaton (D) a proposal for a 60,000 unit order. According to the proposal, the first 13,000 units sold would have an average price of $544.88, with the initial price of the units being $595, but progressively decreasing as Styberg (P) tweaked and perfected its manufacturing process. The proposal also requested $343,000 in "tooling money" to assist Styberg (P) in acquiring materials for its customized production and set forth a production schedule. On July 29, 1999, Eaton (D) communicated to Styberg (P) that it would purchase 13,000 units at $544.88 each and provide $293,000 for tooling. On August 9, 1999, Styberg (P) thanked Eaton (D) for its July 29 commitment, but also communicated to Eaton (D)—as it had previously—that it needed a minimum commitment of between 25,000 and 30,000 units to cover its capital expenditures. On September 1, 1999, employees from both parties participated in a conference call. Styberg (P) again indicated to Eaton

(D) that a 13,000 unit commitment was not enough to cover its costs, and that it needed a minimum 30,000 commitment. Eaton's (D) notes from the call said, "Styberg will come back w/capacity + quotes for 13K flat out." On September 9, 1999, Styberg (P) sent Eaton (D) a production schedule that included a detailed break-down of Styberg's (P) anticipated monthly production capacity for 13,000 units as well as a quote for an initial unit price of $595 plus $31 per unit until a certain part became available. Allegedly, on September 27, 1999, Eaton (D) confirmed that this was acceptable, but there was also evidence that such a communication never occurred. Eaton (D) did not issue a specific purchase order for 13,000 I-brakes, nor did Styberg (P) send a purchase order acknowledgment for 13,000 I-brakes. In April 2000, Eaton (D) notified Styberg (P) that it expected delivery of 240 units. Styberg (P) shipped the units under an existing purchase order, and Eaton (D) paid for the units. On May 8, 2000, Eaton (D) requested another 240 units for shipment, which were to be delivered the following month. Three days later, however, Eaton (D) cancelled the request. After May 11, 2000, Eaton (D) neither ordered nor paid for any I-brakes. In May 2003, Styberg (P) sued Eaton (D) in district court for breach of contract, seeking approximately $3.4 million in damages. The district court, concluding that no contract had been formed for the purchase by Eaton (D) of 13,000 I-brakes, rendered judgment for Eaton (D). In reaching its conclusion, the court characterized the e-mail, telephone, and letter exchanges as evidence of continuing negotiations in which the parties could not agree on key terms like quantity, price, and monthly production volume. The court of appeals granted review.

ISSUE: Under the U.C.C., is a contract for the sale of goods formed where the parties' communications evidence ongoing negotiations, but no agreement, as to key terms, such as price, quantity, and monthly production volume?

HOLDING AND DECISION: (Flaum, J.) No. Under the U.C.C., a contract for the sale of goods in not formed where the parties' communications evidence ongoing negotiations, but no agreement, as to key terms, such as price, quantity, and monthly production volume. Styberg's (P) appeal challenges the district court's factual findings and the legal conclusions that flow therefrom. However, the evidence and relevant case law shows that the district court's conclusions were not clearly erroneous. Under U.C.C. § 2-204, a contract for the sale of goods may be made in any manner sufficient to show agreement,

Continued on next page.

including conduct by both parties which recognizes the existence of such a contract. This is a liberal view of what is required to create a contract for the sale of goods. Notwithstanding this liberal approach, for a contract for the sale of goods to be formed, its essential terms must be agreed upon. Styberg (P) contends that there was agreement as to such essential terms. It argues that the parties agreed that Eaton (D) would purchase 13,000 I-brakes from Styberg (P) at an average unit price of $544.88. Styberg (P) identifies three possible sources for the alleged contract: 1) Eaton's July 29, 1999 letter; 2) Styberg's (P) September 9, 1999 schedule; and 3) Eaton's (D) request for I-brakes in 2000. Styberg (P) argues that the July 29 letter was either an acceptance of Styberg's (P) July 8 offer to supply Eaton (D) with 13,000 I-brakes or an offer to purchase I-brakes that Styberg (P) accepted on August 9, 1999 by saying "thank you." Then, according to Styberg (P), although the parties had a contract with the price and quantity terms firmly in place, they continued to negotiate about larger orders and other open terms. Eaton (D), on the other hand, characterized the July 29 letter as part of a series of ongoing negotiations, during which Eaton (D) and Styberg (P) could not agree on the essential terms, with Styberg (P) wanting a minimum commitment of 20,000 I-brakes to justify its capital investment, and Eaton (D) not wanting to be bound by such a large commitment. Case law provides that a price quotation is considered an invitation for an offer, rather than an offer to form a binding contract. Thus, Styberg's (P) July 8 letter was an invitation for an offer; if it was not, then Eaton's (D) July 29 letter could not have constituted an acceptance of that offer. However, even assuming that the July 29 letter was an offer in response to the price quotation, the district court did not clearly err in finding that Styberg (P) rejected the offer and continued to push for a higher minimum-unit commitment. After all, the parties had a conference call on September 1, during which Styberg (P) again indicated that a 13,000 unit commitment was not enough. The district court also did not clearly err in finding that Eaton (D) did not communicate on September 27 an acceptance of Styberg's (P) September 9 proposed schedule, as conflicting evidence and the district court's judgment of witnesses' veracity supported such a finding. Finally, the district court did not clearly err in rejecting Styberg's (P) argument that the parties' conduct manifested the existence of a contract. Two 240-unit orders at the price specified in Styberg's (P) quotes was insufficient to prove an agreement for the sale of 13,000 units. Courts finding contracts based on parties' conduct have typically done so either where there was repeated and ongoing conduct manifesting an agreement or where the parties had an established course of dealing to which they adhered. Here, Eaton's (D) two requests for 240 I-brakes, one of which was cancelled, did not come close to the repeated, ongoing dealing necessary to establish a course of dealing required to prove the existence of a contract. Affirmed.

▶ ANALYSIS

This case illustrates the potentially fact-heavy nature of cases involving ongoing negotiations where the formation of a contract is at issue. As in this case, the outcome in such cases typically is not clear-cut. Here, the district court accepted Eaton's (D) interpretation of ambiguous evidence, and the court of appeals affirmed because the district court's choice between two reasonable interpretations of that evidence was not clearly erroneous. In all fairness to Styberg (P), it seems Styberg (P) had some strong arguments why it was led to believe that Eaton (D) had agreed to the minimum 13,000 unit purchase.

Quicknotes

BREACH OF CONTRACT Unlawful failure by a party to perform its obligations pursuant to contract.

DAMAGES Monetary compensation that may be awarded by the court to a party who has sustained injury or loss to his person, property or rights due to another party's unlawful act, omission or negligence.

Princess Cruises, Inc. v. General Electric Co.

Shipowner (P) v. Ship repairer (D)

143 F.3d 828 (4th Cir. 1998).

NATURE OF CASE: Appeal by General Electric (D) from federal district court's refusal to grant its motion for summary judgment to vacate the jury's award in favor of Princess Cruises (P) for incidental and consequential damages for breach of contract.

FACT SUMMARY: In October, 1994, Princess Cruises, Inc. (Princess) (P) issued a Purchase Order and scheduled its SS Sky Princess for routine inspection services and repairs to be done in December by General Electric Co. (GE) (D), the original manufacturer of the ship's main turbines, for a proposed contract price of $260,000. Upon inspection of the ship, GE (D) found additional work needed to be done, and, as a result, Princess (P) canceled a ten-day Christmas cruise. Princess (P) paid the full amount of the contract. At trial, Princess (P) alleged the repairs had not been properly done and it had been forced to cancel a ten-day Easter cruise. In April 1996, Princess (P) filed a complaint against GE (D) alleging breach of contract, breach of express and implied maritime warranty, and negligence.

🏛 **RULE OF LAW**
When the predominant purpose of a maritime or land-based contract is the rendering of services rather than the furnishing of goods, the Uniform Commercial Code (U.C.C.) is inapplicable, and courts must draw on common-law doctrines when interpreting the contract.

FACTS: Princess Cruises, Inc. (Princess) (P) and General Electric Company (GE) (D) entered into a maritime contract for inspection and repair services relating to Princess's (P) cruise ship, the SS Sky Princess. A jury found GE (D) liable for breach of contract and awarded Princess (P) $4,577,743.00 in damages. On appeal, GE (D) contended that the district court erred in denying its renewed motion for judgment as a matter of law, which had requested that the court vacate the jury's award of incidental and consequential damages. Specifically, GE (D) argued that the district court erroneously applied U.C.C. principles rather than common-law principles to a contract primarily for services. Although Princess's (P) fine-print terms and conditions mentioned the sale of goods, Princess's (P) actual purchase description requested a GE (D) "service engineer" to perform service functions: the opening of valves for survey and the inspection of the ship's port main turbine. GE's (D) Final Price Quotation also contemplated service functions, stating in large print on every page that it was a "Quotation for Services." The Final Price Quotation's first page noted that GE (D) was offering a quotation for

"engineering services." GE's (D) Quotation further specified that the particular type of service offered was "Installation/Repair/Maintenance." The Final Price Quotation then listed the scope of the contemplated work (opening, checking, cleaning, inspecting, disassembling), in short, service functions. Although GE's (D) materials list showed that GE (D) planned to manufacture a small number of parts for Princess (P), Princess (P) appeared to have had most of the needed materials already onboard.

ISSUE: When the predominant purpose of a maritime or land-based contract is the rendering of services rather than the furnishing of goods, must courts draw on common-law doctrines when interpreting the contract rather than looking to the U.C.C.?

HOLDING AND DECISION: (Goodwin, J.) Yes. When the predominant purpose of a maritime or land-based contract is the rendering of services rather than the furnishing of goods, the U.C.C. is inapplicable, and courts must draw on common-law doctrines when interpreting the contract. Here, in analyzing a mixed maritime contract for goods and services, the court must first determine whether the predominant purpose of the transaction is the sale of goods, and, once this initial analysis has been performed, the court then may properly decide whether the common law, the U.C.C., or other statutory law governs the transaction. In the instant case, the contract for inspection and repair of the ship was predominantly for services, not goods, and the contract thus was governed by common-law doctrines rather than the U.C.C.. The purchase description and the final price quotation contemplated a provision of services, and, although the repairer was known to manufacture goods, its correspondence and quotations came from its service engineering department. It is plain that the GE-Princess transaction principally concerned the rendering of services, specifically, the routine inspection and repair of the SS Sky Princess, with incidental, albeit expensive, parts supplied by GE (D). The language of both the Purchase Order and the Final Price Quotation indicated that although GE (D) planned to supply certain parts, the parts were incidental to the contract's predominant purpose, which was inspection, repair, and maintenance services. As a matter of law, the jury should only have awarded damages consistent with the terms and conditions of GE's Final Price Quotation under common-law doctrines of contract law and should not have awarded incidental or consequential damages. Reversed and remanded.

Continued on next page.

▶ *ANALYSIS*

As noted in the *Princess Cruises* decision, before applying the U.C.C., courts generally examine the transaction to determine whether the sale of goods predominates. In this regard, the test for inclusion or exclusion is not whether the transaction is for both sales and services, but granting that it is, whether the predominant factor of the transaction—its thrust, its purpose—reasonably stated, is the rendition of service, with goods incidentally involved (e.g., contract with artist for painting) or is a transaction of sale, with labor incidentally involved (e.g., installation of a water heater in a bathroom). As an aid in the making of this determination, the Fourth Circuit has deemed the following factors significant in determining the nature of the contract: (1) the language of the contract, (2) the nature of the business of the supplier, and (3) the intrinsic worth of the materials.

■══■

Quicknotes

BREACH OF CONTRACT Unlawful failure by a party to perform its obligations pursuant to contract.

CONSEQUENTIAL DAMAGES Monetary compensation that may be recovered in order to compensate for injuries or losses sustained as a result of damages that are not the direct or foreseeable result of the act of a party, but that nevertheless are the consequence of such act and which must be specifically pled and demonstrated.

INCIDENTAL DAMAGES Those damages reasonably incurred and arising from the subject matter of a claim for actual damages; such damages generally arise from activities undertaken by the nonbreaching party as a result of the breach.

■══■

Brown Machine, Inc. v. Hercules, Inc.

Seller of trim press (P) v. Buyer (D)

Mo. Ct. App., 770 S.W.2d 416 (1989).

NATURE OF CASE: Appeal from award of damages for indemnification.

FACT SUMMARY: Hercules (D), which purchased a trim press from Brown (P) through an exchange of boilerplate forms, refused to indemnify Brown (P) in a lawsuit brought by a Hercules (D) employee who was injured while using the trim press, claiming that Brown's (P) boilerplate language of indemnification was only a counteroffer.

🏛 RULE OF LAW
An offeree's reply that purports to accept an offer but makes acceptance conditional on the offeror's assent to terms not contained in the original offer is a counteroffer rather than an acceptance.

FACTS: During negotiations for sale of a trim press to Hercules (D), Brown (P) submitted a proposal to which it attached a boilerplate form containing an indemnity provision. Hercules (D) then sent a written purchase order on its own boilerplate form, which contained no indemnity provision. After Hercules (D) purchased the machine from Brown (P), an employee of Hercules (D), who sustained injuries while operating the trim press, filed suit against Brown (P). Brown (P) demanded that Hercules (D) defend the suit, but Hercules (D) refused. Brown (P) filed suit against Hercules (D) for indemnification of the settlement amount paid, claiming that a condition of the original sales contract for the trim press required that Hercules (D) indemnify Brown (P) for any claims arising from operation or misuse of the trim press. The jury awarded damages plus interest to Brown (P), and Hercules (D) appealed.

ISSUE: Is an offeree's reply which purports to accept an offer but makes acceptance conditional on the offeror's assent to terms not contained in the original offer a counteroffer rather than an acceptance?

HOLDING AND DECISION: (Stephan, J.) Yes. An offeree's reply which purports to accept an offer but makes acceptance conditional on the offeror's assent to terms not contained in the original offer is a counteroffer rather than an acceptance. The general rule is that a price quotation is not an offer but rather an invitation to enter into negotiations or a mere suggestion to induce offers by others. However, price quotes, if sufficiently detailed, can amount to an offer creating the power of acceptance; to do so, it must reasonably appear from the price quote that assent to the quote is all that is needed to ripen the offer into a contract. In this case Hercules (D) could not have reasonably believed that Brown's (P) quotation was

intended to be an offer but rather an offer to enter into negotiations for the trim press. Even if the quotation were construed as an offer, there was no timely acceptance. Under these circumstances, the purchase order, not the price quotation, is treated as the offer since the purchase order did not create an enforceable contract. The question then was whether Brown's (P) acknowledgment containing the indemnity provision constituted a counteroffer or an acceptance of Hercules's (D) offer with additional or different terms. The general view held by the majority of states is that, to convert an acceptance to a counteroffer under Uniform Commercial Code (U.C.C.) § 2-207(1), the conditional nature of the acceptance must be clearly expressed in a manner sufficient to notify the offeror that the offeree is unwilling to proceed with the transaction unless the additional or different terms are included in the contract. Brown's (P) acknowledgment was not "expressly made conditional" on Hercules's (D) assent to the additional or different terms as provided for under § 2-207(1). Since Brown's (P) order acknowledgment was not a counteroffer, it operated as acceptance with additional or different terms from the offer since the purchase order contained no indemnity provision. Hercules's (D) purchase order here expressly limited acceptance to the terms of its offer. Given such an express limitation, the additional terms, including the indemnification provision, failed to become part of the contract between the parties. Reversed.

▶ ANALYSIS

Under U.C.C. § 2-207(1), an offeree's response to an offer operates as a valid acceptance of the offer even though it contains terms additional to, or different from, the terms of the offer, unless the "acceptance is expressly made conditional" on the offeror's assent to the additional or different terms. Where the offeree's acceptance is made "expressly conditional" on the offeror's assent, the response operates not as an acceptance but as a counteroffer, which must be accepted by the original offeror. Under § 2-207(2), additional terms become a part of the contract between merchants unless (a) the offer expressly limits acceptance to the terms of the offer; (b) they materially alter it; or (c) notification of objection to them has already been given or is given within a reasonable time after notice of them is given.

■=■

Continued on next page.

Quicknotes

ACCEPTANCE Assent to the specified terms of an offer, resulting in the formation of a binding agreement.

COUNTEROFFER A statement by the offeree which has the legal effect of rejecting the offer and of proposing a new offer to the offeror.

U.C.C. § 2-207(1) Provides that a valid contract may exist where the acceptance contains additional terms not present in the offer, unless the offer specifically limits acceptance from including additional terms.

■═■

Paul Gottlieb & Co., Inc. v. Alps South Corp.

Fabrics producer (P) v. Medical device manufacturer (D)

Fla. Ct. App., 985 So. 2d 1 (2007).

NATURE OF CASE: Appeal from judgment for defendant/counterclaim plaintiff in action for contract damages.

FACT SUMMARY: Paul Gottlieb & Co., Inc. (Gottlieb) (P) contended that a limitation of liability clause on the back of its standardized finished goods contract did not materially alter the contract it had with Alps South Corp. (Alps) (D), so that the clause should not, as a matter of law, have been excluded from the contract, and, therefore, the clause served to limit Gottlieb's (P) liability to Alps (D) for consequential damages.

🏛 RULE OF LAW
Under Uniform Commercial Code (U.C.C.) § 2-207, a limitation of liability clause found on the back of a standardized contract for the sale of goods between merchants does not materially alter the contract where it does not, as a matter of law, cause unreasonable surprise or hardship.

FACTS: Paul Gottlieb & Co., Inc. (Gottlieb) (P) produced specialty fabrics. Alps South Corp. (Alps) (D) was a medical device manufacturer that produced liners that amputees used to attach prosthetic devices. Alps (D) began testing various high-tech fabrics to enhance the durability and stability of its liners; Gottlieb (P) supplied some of the fabrics. Eventually, Alps (D) settled on Gottlieb's (P) "Coolmax" fabric, which initially was well-received by Alps' (D) customers. Six months later, however, Alps (D) rejected some fabric samples Gottlieb (P) submitted because of unacceptable inconsistencies in both color and texture. Alps (D) sent a letter promptly notifying Gottlieb (P) of the product deficiencies and stating that any future commercial relationship mandated that Gottlieb (P) provide a more consistent product. However, the letter failed to inform Gottlieb (P) of the possibility that Alps (D) could incur substantial additional costs as a result of using a different fabric. Also, Alps (D) did not disclose the specialized use of the fabric to Gottlieb (P). Gottlieb (P) agreed to rework the fabric before delivering it to Alps (D). Then, Gottlieb (P) exhausted the yarn used to make the Coolmax fabric, and, without notifying Alps (D), Gottlieb (P) substituted a similar fabric. The new fabric did not stretch nearly as well as the Coolmax fabric, but this defect was not easily detected by Alps (D), which eventually started receiving complaints from its customers about the liners using the substitute fabric. Eventually, Alps (D) was forced to recall and destroy the liners using the substitute fabric. After Alps (D) and Gottlieb (P) discovered that the cause of the defective products was the undisclosed

substitute yarn, Alps (D) refused to pay Gottlieb (P) for a submitted bill. Gottlieb (P) then brought suit for damages from the nonpayment. Alps (D) counterclaimed for damages it asserted were caused by Gottlieb's (P) breach of warranty. In regard to Alps' (D) counterclaim, Gottlieb (P) had used a standardized finished goods contract that had on its back a limitations of liability clause that purported to limit consequential damages (the contract was one of a series of six that had similar clauses on the forms). The trial court considered the language of this clause to be an affirmative defense to Alps' (D) counterclaim, but ultimately held that the clause materially altered the contract, so that the clause was excluded from the contract under U.C.C. § 2-207. The trial court awarded nonpayment damages (around $29,000) to Gottlieb (P) and consequential damages (around $695,000) to Alps (D). The state's intermediate appellate court granted review.

ISSUE: Under U.C.C. § 2-207, does a limitation of liability clause found on the back of a standardized contract for the sale of goods between merchants materially alter the contract where it does not, as a matter of law, cause unreasonable surprise or hardship?

HOLDING AND DECISION: (Casanueva, J.) No. Under U.C.C. § 2-207, a limitation of liability clause found on the back of a standardized contract for the sale of goods between merchants does not materially alter the contract where it does not, as a matter of law, cause unreasonable surprise or hardship. In reaching its decision to exclude the limitation of liability clause, the trial court reasoned that if the clause were given effect, the limitation of liability "would allow Gottlieb to substitute a product without notice to Alps that would affect the final marketability of the final product." This reasoning was flawed. Gottlieb's (P) substitution of fabric, resulting in a breach of the contract, is an undisputed fact that does not bear on the construction of the clause, and the trial court should have determined only whether the clause, as a matter of law, materially altered the contract. Under U.C.C. § 2-207(1), a timely acceptance serves as an acceptance notwithstanding that it states terms additional to or different from those offered or agreed upon, unless acceptance is expressly made conditional on assent to the additional or different terms. Where there are such additional terms, they become part of the contract unless, inter alia, they materially alter the contract. The only issue before the court is whether the clause on the back of Gottlieb's (P) form contract materially altered the contract. The burden is on the party seeking

Continued on next page.

to exclude the additional terms to prove material alteration, here, Alps (D). To determine whether an additional term materially alters a contract, courts typically use some alternative of a "surprise or hardship" test. Some courts have removed hardship from the analysis and look solely for surprise. As to surprise, Alps (D) must prove that, under the circumstances, it cannot be presumed that a reasonable merchant would have consented to the additional term. However, Alps (D) has not done so. The only surprise came to Alps (D) because it did not read the contract—never an excuse that lets a party out of a contract. Moreover, the type of clause at issue is not one that the U.C.C. deems as one that would involve unreasonable surprise. Alps (D) also failed to adduce evidence of hardship as a result of surprise. Gottlieb (P) never represented that, in the event of a breach, it would reimburse Alps (D) for any or all consequential damages it sustained resulting from the breach. Instead, Alps (D) previously had returned a sample of nonconforming fabric to Gottlieb (P) with a letter insisting on conforming goods. This letter did not mention or make claim for additional costs or damages resulting from Gottlieb's (P) prior breach of performance. Additionally, Alps (D) never informed Gottlieb (P) of any consequences other than discontinuing their relationship, or of the specific manner in which the subject fabric would be used or what product would be crafted. Thus, Gottlieb (P) could not foresee the greater extent of its potential liability upon breach. Because Alps (D) failed to inform Gottlieb (P) of the larger consequences of the breach, Alps (D) cannot maintain that incorporating the limitation of liability clause would result in a severe economic hardship. Thus, Alps (D) failed to carry the burden of proof on material alteration, and the limitation of liability clause is part of the contract between the parties. That clause, however, only limits consequential damages, including lost profits. An additional ground for precluding lost profits damages is that Alps (D) failed to carry its burden of proving lost profits with reasonable certainty. Alps (D) may still pursue non-consequential damages, such as direct and incidental damages, which the trial court should determine on remand. Reversed and remanded.

▶ ANALYSIS

This dispute arises from the common, but risky, commercial practice where the seller and buyer negotiate a contract involving goods by exchanging one another's standardized forms. This practice is sometimes referred to as the "battle of the forms" and is governed by § 2-207, which is intended to end the battle by eliminating the uncertainty that often results from the exchange of conflicting purchase order forms and acknowledgement and acceptance forms. The battle lines are frequently created where, as here, the seller's form contains terms different from or additional to those set forth in the buyer's form. Despite the differences in the forms, the parties proceed with the commercial transactions and, as

in this case, fight the battle in court after the transaction concludes.

■═■

Quicknotes

BURDEN OF PROOF The duty of a party to introduce evidence to support a fact that is in dispute in an action.

CONSEQUENTIAL DAMAGES Monetary compensation that may be recovered in order to compensate for injuries or losses sustained as a result of damages that are not the direct or foreseeable result of the act of a party, but that nevertheless are the consequence of such act and which must be specifically pled and demonstrated.

COUNTERCLAIM An independent cause of action brought by a defendant to a lawsuit in order to oppose or deduct from the plaintiff's claim.

■═■

Hines v. Overstock.com, Inc.

Consumer (P) v. Online closeout retailer (D)

668 F. Supp. 2d 362 (E.D.N.Y 2009).

NATURE OF CASE: Motion to dismiss, stay for arbitration, or transfer in purported class action for, inter alia, breach of contract.

FACT SUMMARY: Hines (P), a consumer, brought a purported class action challenging a restocking fee charged by Overstock.com, Inc. (Overstock) (D), contending that the fee had never been disclosed. Overstock (D) asserted that the contract governing the transaction required arbitration of all disputes, as well as a transfer to a different forum. Hines (P) claimed she had no notice of the terms and conditions setting forth the arbitration or that a reasonable user of the website would have seen the terms, so that those terms were unenforceable.

🏛 RULE OF LAW
Terms and conditions of an online contract are not enforceable where a particular user does not have actual notice of the terms and conditions, and a reasonable user of the website would not have seen the terms and conditions.

FACTS: Hines (P), a consumer, bought a vacuum cleaner from Overstock.com, Inc. (Overstock) (D), an on-line "closeout" retailer. She returned the machine and was reimbursed the entire purchase minus a $30 restocking fee. Hines (P) brought in federal district court in New York a purported class action for breach of contract, fraud, and other grounds, challenging the restocking fee. She claimed that she had been advised that she could return the vacuum without incurring any costs, and that the fee had never been disclosed. Overstock (D) asserted that all purchases were made online and were governed by its terms and conditions, which required arbitration of all disputes, as well as a transfer to a different forum (state court in Utah). Accordingly, Overstock (D) moved to dismiss, stay for arbitration, or transfer. Hines (P) claimed she had no notice of the terms and conditions setting forth the arbitration or the transfer provision, and that a reasonable user of the website would not have seen the terms, so that those terms were unenforceable. She explained that those terms were observable to a user only after scrolling down the online page(s), and that there was no need for her to scroll down to the end of the page(s) because she was directed each step of the way to click on to a bar to take her to the next step to complete the purchase. The district court ruled on the motion.

ISSUE: Are terms and conditions of an online contract enforceable where a particular user does not have actual notice of the terms and conditions, and a reasonable user of the website would not have seen the terms and conditions?

HOLDING AND DECISION: (Johnson, J.) No. Terms and conditions of an online contract are not enforceable where a particular user does not have actual notice of the terms and conditions, and a reasonable user of the website would not have seen the terms and conditions. To decide whether the arbitration terms are enforceable, it must be determined whether, as a matter of state law, the underlying arbitration agreement is valid. Regardless of whether New York or Utah law is controlling, Overstock (D) has failed to meet its burden of showing that there was a valid arbitration agreement under either state's law because it has shown neither that Hines (P) had notice of the terms and conditions, nor that a reasonable user of the website would have. For a contract to be binding, there must be "mutual assent" and a "meeting of the mind." The type of agreement at issue in this case is a "browsewrap agreement." Such an agreement is one where website terms and conditions of use are posted on the website typically as a hyperlink at the bottom of the screen, and it does not require the user to manifest assent to the terms and conditions expressly; instead, a party gives his assent simply by using the website. In ruling upon the validity of a browse-wrap agreement, courts consider primarily whether a website user has actual or constructive knowledge of a site's terms and conditions prior to using the site. Here, Hines (P) had no actual notice of the terms and conditions of use, and Overstock (D) had not produced any evidence to the contrary. Unlike in other cases where courts have upheld browsewrap agreements, the notice that "Entering this Site will constitute your acceptance of these Terms and Conditions," was only available within the terms and conditions. Hines (P), therefore, lacked notice of the terms and conditions because she was not prompted to review them and because the link to them was not prominently displayed so as to provide reasonable notice of them. Accordingly, there was no valid arbitration agreement, and the motion to stay for arbitration is denied. Similarly, the motion to transfer is denied because Hines (P) did not have notice of the forum selection portions of the terms and conditions, and a reasonable user would not have had notice of them. In sum, Overstock (D) has failed to explain how Hines (P) and its other customers were "advised" of the terms and conditions, or to cite a single case that suggests that merely posting such terms on a different part of a website constitutes reasonable communication of a forum selection clause. [The court also determined that

Continued on next page.

Overstock (D) failed to meet its burden of showing that another venue would be proper under a forum non conveniens theory.] Motion denied.

▶ *ANALYSIS*

As this case shows, the making of contracts over the internet has not fundamentally changed the principles of contract, and those principles will be applied to online contracts. On the internet, the primary means of forming a contract are the so-called "clickwrap" (or "click-through") agreements, in which website users typically click an "I agree" box after being presented with a list of terms and conditions of use, and the "browsewrap" agreements, such as the one at issue in this case, where website terms and conditions of use are posted on the website typically as a hyperlink at the bottom of the screen. Courts have used traditional contract principles, such as "meeting of the minds" and "manifestation of mutual assent," as the starting point for determining whether such online contracts are enforceable.

■══■

Quicknotes

ARBITRATION An alternative resolution process where a dispute is heard and decided by a neutral third party, rather than through legal proceedings.

BREACH OF CONTRACT Unlawful failure by a party to perform its obligations pursuant to contract.

CLASS ACTION A suit commenced by a representative on behalf of an ascertainable group that is too large to appear in court, who shares a commonality of interests and who will benefit from a successful result.

FORUM NON CONVENIENS An equitable doctrine permitting a court to refrain from hearing and determining a case when the matter may be more properly and fairly heard in another forum.

INTER ALIA Among other things.

MOTION TO DISMISS Motion to terminate an action based on the adequacy of the pleadings, improper service or venue, etc.

■══■

DeFontes v. Dell, Inc.

Consumer (P) v. Computer seller (D)

R.I. Sup. Ct., 984 A.2d 1061 (2009).

NATURE OF CASE: Appeal from denial of motion to stay proceedings and compel arbitration in putative class action for violation of the Deceptive Trade Practices Act.

FACT SUMMARY: Dell, Inc. and various affiliates (collectively, "Dell") (D) contended that consumers (P) who bought computers from Dell (D) were bound by the arbitration provisions in Dell's (D) terms and conditions, which Dell (D) contended the consumers (P) had accepted by accepting delivery of the computers. The consumers (P) countered that even though they had three separate opportunities to review the terms and conditions, none was sufficient to give rise to a contractual obligation.

🏛 RULE OF LAW

Terms and conditions included with consumer goods are not binding on consumers who accept the goods and do not return the goods where, because of the ambiguity of the terms and conditions requiring inferences on the part of the consumer, it would not be reasonably apparent to a reasonably prudent consumer that he or she could reject the terms and conditions simply by returning the goods.

FACTS: Consumers (P) who bought computers from Dell and its affiliates (collectively, "Dell") (D), brought a putative class action against Dell (D) for violation of the Deceptive Trade Practices Act on the grounds that Dell (D) had charged them a tax on service contracts they had purchased when no such tax was required by their state. Dell (D) moved to stay proceedings and compel arbitration on the grounds that the consumers (P) were bound by the arbitration provisions in Dell's (D) terms and conditions, which Dell (D) contended the consumers (P) had accepted by accepting delivery of the computers. Dell (D) asserted that the consumers (P) had three opportunities to review the terms and conditions: by selecting a hyperlink on the Dell (D) website, by reading the terms that were included in the acknowledgment/invoice that was sent to plaintiffs sometime after they placed their orders, or by reviewing the copy of the terms Dell (D) included in the packaging of its computer products. The trial court, applying Texas law and the Uniform Commercial Code (U.C.C.), held that the consumers (P) were not bound by Dell's (D) terms and conditions. The court found that the hyperlink on Dell's (D) website was inconspicuously located at the bottom of the webpage and insufficient to place customers on notice of the terms and conditions. As to the acknowledgements sent to the consumers (P) after their purchases and the

copy of the terms included in the computer packaging, the court observed that courts will ordinarily enforce such "shrinkwrap" agreements provided they contain an express disclaimer that explains to consumers that they can reject the proposed terms and conditions by returning the product. The trial court saw expressed the crucial test as whether a reasonable person would have known that return of the product would serve as rejection of those terms. Looking at the language of the terms and conditions, the court concluded that it was insufficient to give a reasonable consumer notice of the method of rejection. The language admonished the consumers (P) to carefully read the terms and conditions; informed them that the terms and conditions contained a dispute resolution clause; informed them that they would be bound to the terms by accepting the computers; and that the terms and conditions were subject to change without prior written notice at any time, in Dell's (D) sole discretion. The court found that Dell's (D) failure to include an express disclaimer meant that Dell (D) could not prove that the consumers (P) knowingly consented to the terms and conditions of the agreement. Accordingly, the court ruled that the consumers (P) could not be compelled to enter arbitration. The state's highest court granted review.

ISSUE: Are terms and conditions included with consumer goods binding on consumers who accept the goods and do not return the goods where, because of the ambiguity of the terms and conditions requiring inferences on the part of the consumer, it would not be reasonably apparent to a reasonably prudent consumer that he or she could reject the terms and conditions simply by returning the goods?

HOLDING AND DECISION: (Williams, C.J. (ret.)) No. Terms and conditions included with consumer goods are not binding on consumers who accept the goods and do not return the goods where, because of the ambiguity of the terms and conditions requiring inferences on the part of the consumer, it would not be reasonably apparent to a reasonably prudent consumer that he or she could reject the terms and conditions simply by returning the goods. This case, involving interstate commerce, invokes the Federal Arbitration Act (FAA), which requires enforcement of privately negotiated arbitration agreements "save upon such grounds as exist at law or in equity for the revocation of any contract." Thus, the question becomes whether, under state law (here, Texas) and the U.C.C., the consumers (P) are bound by the terms and conditions

Continued on next page.

agreement. Under U.C.C. § 2-204, contracts for the sale of goods may be formed in any manner sufficient to show agreement. The U.C.C. assumes that the buyer is the offeror and the seller is the offeree. However, the modern trend is to place the power of acceptance with the consumer, after he or she receives goods containing a standard form statement of additional terms and conditions, provided the buyer retains the power to accept or return the product. Judge Frank Easterbrook has authored what are widely considered to be the two leading cases on shrink-wrap agreements. In *ProCD, Inc. v. Zeidenberg*, 86 F.3d 1447 (7th Cir. 1996), the court challenged the traditional understanding of offer and acceptance in consumer transactions by holding that a buyer of software was bound by an agreement that was included within the packaging and later appeared when the buyer first used the software. In *ProCD*, Judge Easterbrook held that U.C.C. § 2-207, which addresses the treatment of additional terms in an exchange of forms between merchants, is inapplicable in the consumer setting because only one form is involved. He reasoned that under § 2-204 "[a] vendor, as master of the offer, may invite acceptance by conduct, and may propose limitations on the kind of conduct that constitutes acceptance. A buyer may accept by performing the acts the vendor proposes to treat as acceptance." Judge Easterbrook expanded this holding in *Hill v. Gateway 2000, Inc.,* 105 F.3d 1147 (7th Cir. 1997) beyond transactions involving software where the consumer is prompted to accept or decline the terms when he first uses the program. He determined that when a merchant delivers a product that includes additional terms and conditions, but expressly provides the consumer the right to either accept those terms or return the product for a refund within a reasonable time, a consumer who retains the goods beyond that period may be bound by the contract. Although not all courts have accepted *ProCD's* reasoning, it is clearly the majority position. The *ProCD* line of cases is better reasoned and more consistent with contemporary consumer transactions. It is simply unreasonable to expect a seller to apprise a consumer of every term and condition at the moment he or she makes a purchase. "A modern consumer neither expects nor desires to wade through such minutia, particularly when making a purchase over the phone, where full disclosure of the terms would border on the sadistic." Consumers are aware that with delivery comes a multitude of standard terms attendant to nearly every consumer transaction. Accordingly, formation occurs when the consumer accepts the full terms after receiving a reasonable opportunity to refuse them. Nonetheless, the seller has the burden of showing that the buyer accepted the seller's terms after delivery. Thus, the crucial question here becomes whether Dell (D) reasonably invited acceptance by making clear in the terms and conditions agreement that by accepting its product the consumer (P) was accepting the terms and conditions contained within and that the consumer (P) could reject the terms and conditions by returning the product. Dell (D) has failed to do so. The language of its terms and

conditions did not make clear a period beyond which consumer would have indicated their assent to those terms. "Acceptance of goods" has a technical meaning not easily discernable to the average consumer, and many consumers believe they are bound by the terms simply by opening the package. More significantly, the terms and conditions did not make clear that consumers could reject the terms simply by returning the goods. Here, there was no explicit disclaimer advising consumers of their right to reject the terms. Thus, it is possible that the consumers (P) were unaware of both their power to reject and the method with which to do so. Too many inferential steps were required of the consumers (P) and too many of the relevant provisions were left ambiguous. It is not clear that a reasonably prudent offeree would understand that by keeping the Dell (D) computer he or she was agreeing to be bound by the terms and conditions agreement and retained, for a specified time, the power to reject the terms by returning the product. Affirmed.

▌ *ANALYSIS*

Those courts that reject the reasoning of *ProCD* and *Hill* find that a consumer's acceptance of goods and not returning them is consistent with a contract being formed at the time that the order was placed and cannot be construed as acquiescing in the terms and conditions later submitted to the consumer, whether they are included with the invoice or acknowledgment or with the packaging. These court reasons that if the contract was formed at the time the order was placed, the terms and conditions are additional term of the contract under § 2-207. Thus, these terms and conditions do not become part of the contract but a proposal to add additional terms, which can only become part of the contract through the consumer's express agreement.

■═■

Quicknotes

CLASS ACTION A suit commenced by a representative on behalf of an ascertainable group that is too large to appear in court, who shares a commonality of interests and who will benefit from a successful result.

INTERSTATE COMMERCE Commercial dealings between two parties located in different states or located in one state and accomplished through a point in another state or a foreign country; commercial dealings transacted between two states.

■═■

Promissory Estoppel and Restitution

Quick Reference Rules of Law

Kirksey v. Kirksey

Sister (P) v. Donor of land (D)

Ala. Sup. Ct., 8 Ala. 131 (1845).

NATURE OF CASE: Appeal from judgment for plaintiff in action to recover damages for breach of a promise.

FACT SUMMARY: Kirksey (D) promised "Sister Antillico" (P) a place to raise her family on the condition that "you come down and see me."

🏛 RULE OF LAW
A promise on the condition "If you will come down and see me" is not given as a bargained exchange for the promisee's "coming down and seeing" the promisor so that the executory promise is not sufficiently supported by bargained-for consideration to be enforceable.

FACTS: Kirksey (D) wrote to "Sister Antillico" (P) a letter containing the following clause: "If you will come down and see me, I will let you have a place to raise your family." "Sister Antillico" (P) moved sixty miles to Kirksey's (D) residence where she remained for over two years. Kirksey (D) then required her to leave although her family was not yet "raised." "Sister Antillico" (P) contends that the loss which she sustained in moving was sufficient consideration to support Kirksey's (D) promise to furnish her with "a place" until she could raise her family.

ISSUE: Is a promise on the condition "If you will come down and see me" given as a bargained exchange for the promisee's "coming down and seeing" the promisor so that the executory promise is sufficiently supported by bargained-for consideration to be enforceable?

HOLDING AND DECISION: (Ormond, J.) No. A promise on the condition "If you will come down and see me" is not given as a bargained exchange for the promisee's "coming down and seeing" the promisor so that the executory promise is not sufficiently supported by bargained-for consideration to be enforceable. Such a promise is a promise to make a gift. Any expenses incurred by the promisee in "coming down and seeing" are merely conditions necessary to acceptance of the gift. In this case, Kirksey (D) did not appear to be bargaining either for "Sister Antillico's" presence or for her sixty-mile move. Instead, Kirksey (D) merely wished to assist her out of what he perceived as a grievous and difficult situation. Reversed.

▌ ANALYSIS

This well-known case demonstrates the court's insistence on finding a bargained-for exchange before it will enforce an executory promise. A promise to make a gift is generally not legally binding until it is executed. Compare Williston's famous hypothetical in which a benevolent man says to a tramp: "If you go around the corner to the clothing shop there, you may purchase an overcoat on my credit." This hypo highlights the conceptual problem of the present case in that it is unreasonable to construe the walk around the corner as the price of the promise, yet it is a legal detriment to the tramp to make the walk. Perhaps a reasonable (though not conclusive) guideline is the extent to which the happening of the condition will benefit the promisor. The present case might be decided differently today under the doctrine of promissory estoppel which had not yet been developed in 1845.

■≡■

Quicknotes

CONDITION Requirement; potential future occurrence upon which the existence of a legal obligation is dependent.

GIFT A transfer of property to another person that is voluntary and which lacks consideration.

PROMISSORY ESTOPPEL A promise that is enforceable if the promisor should reasonably expect that it will induce action or forbearance on the part of the promisee, and does in fact cause such action or forbearance, and it is the only means of avoiding injustice.

■≡■

Harvey v. Dow

Daughter (P) v. Parent (D)

Maine Sup. Ct., 962 A.2d 322 (2008). *Appeal after remand*, 11 A.3d 308 (2011).

NATURE OF CASE: Appeal from judgment for defendants in action to compel conveyance of land, or for damages.

FACT SUMMARY: Harvey (P), the Dows' (D) daughter, claimed that the Dows (D) were promissorily estopped from conveying a deed to a parcel of land on which she had built a house, contending that their general promises to transfer some of their land to her, as well as actions by her father, Jeffrey Sr. (D), including approving the site of her house, obtaining a building permit for it, and then building a substantial part of it himself at that location, supported a claim for promissory estoppel.

🏛 RULE OF LAW
When considering a claim of promissory estoppel, a court must consider the alleged promisor's conduct as well as any generalized promises the promisor has made in determining if all of the promisor's actions, taken together, constitute a "promise" to the claimant.

FACTS: Ever since Harvey (P) was a child, her parents, the Dows (D), had been making general promises to her and her brother that the Dows (D) would at some point in the future convey some or all of the Dows' (D) 125 acres of land to the children. After Harvey (P) got married, she and her husband decided to build a house on the Dows' (D) property, with the Dows' (D) permission. Initially, the financing was to come from the Dows' (D) home equity line of credit, but, after Harvey's (D) husband died in an accident, Harvey (D) decided to use the proceeds from the husband's life insurance proceeds. Harvey's father, Jeffrey Sr. (D), approved the site of the new house, obtained a building permit for it, and then built a substantial part of it himself at that location. Subsequently, the relationship between Harvey (P) and the Dows (D) began to deteriorate. After Harvey (P) moved into the house once it was completed, at around a $200,000 cost to her, she began to ask Jeffrey Sr. (D) for a deed so that she could obtain a mortgage to finance other projects. After a period of discussion, it became clear that the Dows (D) were not going to execute a deed. Harvey (P) brought suit to compel the Dows (D) to convey unspecified real property to her, or for damages, as well as other claims. One her theories of recovery was promissory estoppel. The Dows (D) counterclaimed for a declaratory judgment that Harvey (P) had no rights in their property. At trial, there was conflicting evidence as to whether either of the Dows (D) had promised to deed any of their land to Harvey (P). The trial court concluded that Harvey (P) had failed to make out a claim

of promissory estoppel, finding that the Dows' (D) statements were not promises that could be enforced even if they were the subject of detrimental reliance, as the promises were too indefinite and there was no agreement on basic elements such as the boundaries or size of the property involved. Harvey (P) appealed, arguing that the trial court had erred by failing to look beyond the Dows' (D) generalized statements to determine whether she had made out a promissory estoppel claim. The state's highest court granted review.

ISSUE: When considering a claim of promissory estoppel, must a court consider the alleged promisor's conduct as well as any generalized promises the promisor has made in determining if all of the promisor's actions, taken together, constitute a "promise" to the claimant?

HOLDING AND DECISION: (Mead, J.) Yes. When considering a claim of promissory estoppel, a court must consider the alleged promisor's conduct as well as any generalized promises the promisor has made in determining if all of the promisor's actions, taken together, constitute a "promise" to the claimant. Promissory estoppel applies to promises that are otherwise unenforceable, and is used to enforce such promises to avoid injustice. Thus, a promise is an essential of a promissory estoppel claim. Here, the trial court was correct in finding that the Dows (D) had made only generalized promises to Harvey (P) to convey land to her, and that those promises were not enforceable express promises due to indefinites as to key terms, such as identification of a specific parcel's size, boundaries, etc. If that is all the Dows (D) did, the trial court would have been correct in concluding that Harvey's (P) promissory estoppel claim had to fail. However, the Dows (D) did more than just make generalized promises to convey unspecified land at some unspecified point in time. They also acquiesced in, supported, and encouraged Harvey's (P) construction of a house n their property. Against the backdrop of the parties' general understanding that Harvey (P) would one day receive property as a gift or inheritance from her parents, Jeffrey Sr. (D) agreed to the location, obtained a building permit to allow construction at that site, and not only acquiesced in the house being built, but built a large portion of it himself. In a promissory estoppel analysis, the promise relied on by the promisee need not be express but may be implied from a party's conduct. Here, such a promise could be implied from Jeffrey Sr.'s (D) conduct. Given that Harvey's (P) reliance on such a promise, if proved, has resulted in her owning an

Continued on next page.

immobile $200,000 asset on the Dow's (D) land, refusal to enforce the promise would work an injustice on Harvey (P). Accordingly, such a promise can be enforced despite the lack of consideration. The Restatement (Second) of Contracts supports this position, defining a promise as "a manifestation of intention to act or refrain from acting in a specified way," where such a manifestation justifies the promisee's comprehending that the promisor has made a certain commitment. Here, Jeffrey Sr.' (D) actions could be construed as a manifestation of his intent to confirm his general promise to convey land to Harvey (P) and to direct it to that specific parcel. As regards promises to make a gift, the Restatement provides that such promises are enforceable only where it is foreseeable and reasonable that the promisee will rely on the promise. Here, given the Dows' (D) generalized statements and actions, it is arguable that Harvey's (P) reliance on these manifestations of intention to act was eminently foreseeable and reasonable. Accordingly, the trial court erred in failing to consider the Dows' (D) actions, in conjunction with their generalized statements, in determining whether the existence of promissory estoppel was established on these facts. The case is remanded to the trial court to make such considerations. Vacated and remanded.

▶ ANALYSIS

On remand, the trial court again found for the Dows (D). The trial court did not make any new findings, and concluded that the Dows' (D) actions, as well as their generalized promises, were insufficient to support a claim of promissory estoppel. Harvey (P) appealed again, and the state's highest court, while concluding that the trial court had all the facts it needed for a proper promissory estoppel analysis, held that the trial court's legal conclusion was erroneous. The court held that, as a matter of law, Dows' (D) acquiescence, support, and encouragement of Harvey's construction of a house on a parcel of their land conclusively demonstrated their intention to make a present conveyance of that property. Accordingly, the court vacated the trial court's judgment and remanded for entry of a judgment in favor of Harvey (P), but remanded once again for a determination of the appropriate remedy, admonishing the trial court to keep in mind that a promise binding under promissory estoppel is a contract, and full-scale enforcement by normal remedies is often appropriate.

■══■

Quicknotes

COUNTERCLAIM An independent cause of action brought by a defendant to a lawsuit in order to oppose or deduct from the plaintiff's claim.

DAMAGES Monetary compensation that may be awarded by the court to a party who has sustained injury or loss to his person, property or rights due to another party's unlawful act, omission or negligence.

DECLARATORY JUDGMENT A judgment of the court establishing the rights of the parties.

DEED A signed writing transferring title to real property from one person to another.

DETRIMENTAL RELIANCE Action by one party, resulting in loss, which is based on the conduct or promises of another.

PROMISSORY ESTOPPEL A promise that is enforceable if the promisor should reasonably expect that it will induce action or forbearance on the part of the promisee, and does in fact cause such action or forbearance, and it is the only means of avoiding injustice.

REAL PROPERTY Land, an interest in land, or anything attached to the land that is incapable of being removed.

■══■

King v. Trustees of Boston University

Estate administratrix (P) v. Charity (D)

Mass. Sup. Jud. Ct., 420 Mass. 52, 647 N.E.2d 1196 (1995).

NATURE OF CASE: Appeal from a judgment for defendant in suit alleging conversion.

FACT SUMMARY: Coretta Scott King (P), in her capacity as administratrix of the estate of her late husband, Dr. Martin Luther King, Jr., sued Boston University (BU) (D) for conversion, alleging that the estate (P), and not BU (D), held title to Dr. King's papers housed in BU's (D) library.

🏛 **RULE OF LAW**
Where donative intent is sufficiently clear, the court will give effect to that intent to the extent possible without abandoning basic contract principles such as reliance.

FACTS: Coretta Scott King (P) sued Boston University (BU) (D) for conversion of papers that Dr. Martin Luther King, Jr., an alumnus of BU (D), had deposited with BU (D). The jury determined that Dr. King made a promise to give absolute title to his papers to BU (D) in a letter signed by him, and that the promise was enforceable as a charitable pledge supported by consideration or reliance. The jury also determined that the letter promising the papers was not a contract. The trial court denied King's (P) motion for judgment notwithstanding the verdict. King (P) appealed, alleging that BU (D) could not reasonably rely on his statement of donative intent because of Dr. King's initial retention of legal ownership, and that one statement in the letter amounted to a will and was therefore unenforceable because it failed to comply with formal requirements for a will.

ISSUE: If donative intent is sufficiently clear, will the court give effect to that intent to the extent possible without abandoning basic contract principles such as reliance?

HOLDING AND DECISION: (Abrams, J.) Yes. Where donative intent is sufficiently clear, the court will give effect to that intent to the extent possible without abandoning basic contract principles such as reliance. The bailor-bailee relationship established in the letter could be viewed by a rational factfinder as a security for the promise to give a gift in the future of the bailed property, and thus as evidence in addition to the statement in the letter of an intent of the donor to be bound. The statute of wills does not prevent a person from making a contract or a promise to take effect at his death. The letter could have been read to contain a promise supported by consideration or reliance and the issue of the transfer of ownership was properly submitted to the jury. Affirmed.

▶ **ANALYSIS**

A pledge is defined as a bailment of personal property to secure an obligation of the bailor. To enforce a charitable subscription or a charitable pledge in Massachusetts, a party must establish that there was a promise to give some property to a charitable institution and that the promise was supported by consideration or reliance. This court reviewed whether there was sufficient evidence for the case to have been properly submitted to the jury.

■■■

Quicknotes

BAILMENT The delivery of property to be held in trust and which is designated for a particular purpose, following the satisfaction of which the property is either to be returned or disposed of as specified.

CONSIDERATION Value given by one party in exchange for performance, or a promise to perform, by another party.

DONATIVE INTENT Donor's intent to make a gift.

WILL An instrument setting forth the distribution to be made of an individual's estate upon his death; since a will is not effective until the death of its maker, it is revocable during his life.

■■■

Katz v. Danny Dare, Inc.

Employee (P) v. Employer (D)

Mo. Ct. App., 610 S.W.2d 121 (1980).

NATURE OF CASE: Appeal from denial of pension benefits.

FACT SUMMARY: Dare (D) contended that Katz (P) did not give up anything of value in return for pension benefits, and that, thus, it's promise to pay such benefits was unenforceable.

🏛 **RULE OF LAW**
The application of the doctrine of promissory estoppel does not require the relinquishment of a legal interest.

FACTS: Katz (P) had worked for Dare (D) for over 25 years. He suffered personal injuries and became ineffective in his job. Dare (D), through its president, sought to induce his retirement by paying him pension benefits. Katz (P) could accept the pension or be fired, and after 13 months of negotiations, he retired. The retirement was specifically in reliance upon the promise to pay the pension. Dare (D) paid the pension for a period of time and then unilaterally reduced, then eliminated it. Katz (P) sued, contending Dare (D) was estopped from denying the enforceability of the agreement. Dare (D) contended Katz (P) did not give up anything by retiring, as his alternative was to be fired. The trial court denied recovery, and Katz (P) appealed.

ISSUE: Must a party relinquish a legal right to apply promissory estoppel?

HOLDING AND DECISION: (Turnage, J.) No. The application of the doctrine of promissory estoppel does not require the relinquishment of a legal right. It requires a promise, detrimental reliance, and that injustice cannot be otherwise avoided. In this case, admittedly a promise to pay benefits was made, and Katz relied on such promise in retiring. Dare (D) could have terminated him, yet chose to negotiate for more than a year over the pension. Thus, the retirement was voluntary. Therefore, Dare (D) is estopped from failing to recognize its obligations. Reversed and remanded.

▶ ANALYSIS

The general understanding is that all promises must be supported by consideration to be enforceable. However, other promises may be enforceable in the absence of consideration based upon promissory estoppel. In this case, it was the detrimental reliance reasonably based on the promise to pay which enforced the pension agreement. Clearly, no consideration was given by Katz (P) for the promise.

■━■

Quicknotes

DETRIMENTAL RELIANCE Action by one party, resulting in loss that is based on the conduct or promises of another.

PROMISSORY ESTOPPEL A promise that is enforceable if the promisor should reasonably expect that it will induce action or forbearance on the part of the promisee, and does in fact cause such action or forbearance, and it is the only means of avoiding injustice.

■━■

Aceves v. U.S. Bank, N.A.

Mortgagor (P) v. Mortgagee (D)

Cal. Ct. App., 120 Cal. Rptr. 3d 507 (2011).

NATURE OF CASE: Appeal from judgment for defendant in action, inter alia, for promissory estoppel and to set aside the sale of a foreclosed house.

FACT SUMMARY: Aceves (P), who defaulted on her mortgaged house, contended that the mortgagee, U.S. Bank, N.A. (U.S. Bank) (D) was promissorily estopped from foreclosing on her house because, in detrimental reliance on U.S. Bank's (D) promise to work with her to reinstate and modify her loan, she forewent the opportunity to save her home by converting a chapter 7 bankruptcy case to a chapter 13 case. Instead, U.S. Bank (D) foreclosed on the house without ever commencing negotiations toward a possible loan solution.

🏛 **RULE OF LAW**
A mortgagor in default states a claim of promissory estoppel where the mortgagor has, in reliance on the mortgagee's promise to reinstate and modify the mortgage, foregone the opportunity to save the mortgagor's home by converting a chapter 7 bankruptcy case to a chapter 13 case.

FACTS: Aceves (P) mortgaged her house with a lender, and the lender, in turn, transferred its entire interest under the mortgage to U.S. Bank, N.A. (U.S. Bank) (D). Aceves (P) became unable to pay the mortgage payments, and, shortly thereafter, she filed for bankruptcy protection under chapter 7 of the Bankruptcy Code, imposing an automatic stay on the foreclosure proceedings. Aceves (P) contacted U.S. Bank (D) and was told that, once her loan was out of bankruptcy, the bank "would work with her on a mortgage reinstatement and loan modification." She was asked to submit documents to U.S. Bank (D) for its consideration, which she did. Aceves (P) intended to convert her chapter 7 bankruptcy case to a chapter 13 case and to rely on the financial resources of her husband "to save her home" under chapter 13. In general, chapter 7 permits a debtor to discharge unpaid debts, but a debtor who discharges an unpaid home loan cannot keep the home. However, under chapter 13, a homeowner in default is permitted to reinstate the original loan payments, pay the arrearages over time, avoid foreclosure, and retain the home. U.S. Bank (D) filed a motion in the bankruptcy court to lift the stay so it could proceed with a nonjudicial foreclosure. When Aceves (P) approached the company servicing the loan about modifying the loan, she was told they could not speak to her before the motion to lift the bankruptcy stay had been granted. In reliance on U.S. Bank's (D) promise to work with her to reinstate and modify the loan, Aceves (P) did not oppose the motion

to lift the bankruptcy stay and decided not to seek bankruptcy relief under chapter 13. The bankruptcy court lifted the stay, and, five days later, although neither U.S. Bank (D) nor the servicing company had contacted Aceves (P) to discuss the reinstatement and modification of the loan, U.S. Bank (D) scheduled Aceves's home for public auction a month later. A day later, Aceves (P) sent documents to the servicing company related to reinstating and modifying the loan. Around two weeks later, the servicing company informed Aceves (P) that a "negotiator" would contact her on or before a date that was four days after the scheduled auction of her house. Although the negotiator called, neither the servicing company nor U.S. Bank (D) ever worked with Aceves (P) to reinstate and modify her loan. The auction took place as scheduled, and U.S. Bank (D) bought the house. Two months later, U.S. Bank (D) served Aceves (P) with a three-day notice to vacate the premises and, a month later, filed an unlawful detainer action against her and her husband. Apparently, Aceves (P) and her husband vacated the premises during the eviction proceedings. Aceves (P) brought suit against U.S. Bank (D), claiming, inter alia, promissory estoppel and seeking to set aside the foreclosure sale of her house and to void the deed upon the sale of the home. The trial court entered judgment for U.S. Bank (D), and the state's intermediate appellate court granted review.

ISSUE: Does a mortgagor in default state a claim of promissory estoppel where the mortgagor has, in reliance on the mortgagee's promise to reinstate and modify the mortgage, foregone the opportunity to save the mortgagor's home by converting a chapter 7 bankruptcy case to a chapter 13 case?

HOLDING AND DECISION: (Mallano, J.) Yes. A mortgagor in default states a claim of promissory estoppel where the mortgagor has, in reliance on the mortgagee's promise to reinstate and modify the mortgage, foregone the opportunity to save the mortgagor's home by converting a chapter 7 bankruptcy case to a chapter 13 case. All the elements necessary to state a claim of promissory estoppel are present. These are: (1) a promise clear and unambiguous in its terms; (2) reliance by the party to whom the promise is made; (3) the reliance must be both reasonable and foreseeable; and (4) the party asserting the estoppel must be injured by her reliance. As to the first element, U.S. Bank (D) agreed to work with Aceves (P) on a mortgage reinstatement and loan modification if she no longer pursued relief in the bankruptcy court. This was a clear

Continued on next page.

and unambiguous promise that indicated that U.S. Bank (D) would not foreclose on Aceves's (P) home without first engaging in negotiations with her to reinstate and modify the loan on mutually agreeable terms. U.S. Bank's (D) promise was to negotiate with Aceves (P), not necessarily to reach agreement on a reinstated loan. U.S. Bank (D) failed to fulfill its unambiguous promise by failing to negotiate. As to the second element, Aceves (P) relied on U.S. Bank's (D) promise by declining to convert her chapter 7 bankruptcy proceeding to a chapter 13 proceeding, and by not opposing U.S. Bank's (D) motion to lift the bankruptcy stay. As to the third element, Aceves (P) reasonably relied on U.S. Bank's (D) promise, as modification of her loan would have been more beneficial to her than pursuing chapter 13 bankruptcy protections. By promising to work with Aceves to *modify* the loan in addition to reinstating it, U.S. Bank (D) thus presented Aceves (P) with a compelling reason to opt for negotiations with the bank instead of seeking bankruptcy relief. Aceve's (P) reasonable reliance was thus also foreseeable and expected by U.S. Bank (D). As to fourth element, Aceves (P) detrimentally relied on U.S. Bank's (D) promise because she gave up an opportunity to avoid foreclosure on her residence. Under chapter 13, a debtor get to keep the residence only if she cures the default by making the payments required under the loan; the loan is reinstated, but not modified. Therefore, the mortgagee's interests are not diminished under chapter 13. Aceves (P) gave up various chapter 13 rights, including reinstating the loan to predefault conditions; obtaining a maximum of five years to make up the arrearages; and preventing U.S. Bank (D) from foreclosing on the property (by using her husband's resources). Accordingly, Aceves (P) has state a claim for promissory estoppel. U.S. Bank (D) argues that an oral promise to postpone either a loan payment or a foreclosure is unenforceable. While this general principle is true, a written contract may be modified by oral agreement or promissory estoppel. Finally, a promissory estoppel claim generally entitles a plaintiff to the damages available on a breach of contract claim. Because Aceves (P) did not pay the needed to reinstate the loan before the foreclosure, promissory estoppel does not provide a basis for voiding the deed of sale or otherwise invalidating the foreclosure. Additionally, the elements of fraud are similar to the elements of promissory estoppel, with the additional requirements that a false promise be made and that the promisor know of the falsity when making the promise. Aceves (P) has adequately pleaded the facts necessary to make out a claim of fraud. Reversed as to claims of promissory estoppel and fraud. Affirmed as to all remaining claims. Affirmed in part and reversed in part.

▶ *ANALYSIS*

In this case, the reliance element of promissory estoppel was strong, and the court ruled that Aceves' (P) reliance was both reasonable and foreseeable. Instances of

reliance will be deemed neither foreseeable nor reasonable where a plaintiff's misguided belief or guileless action results in reliance on a statement on which no reasonable person would rely; the conduct of the plaintiff in light of her own intelligence and information is manifestly unreasonable; or where the plaintiff has a mere hopeful expectation. None of these instances can be equated with justifiable reliance, and no relief will be granted.

■═■

Quicknotes

CHAPTER 7 BANKRUPTCY A legal proceeding whereby a debtor, who is unable to pay his debts as they become due, is relieved of his obligation to pay his creditors by liquidation and distribution of his remaining assets.

CHAPTER 13 BANKRUPTCY Debtor may modify plan at any time before the completion of the payments under such plan.

DETRIMENTAL RELIANCE Action by one party, resulting in loss, which is based on the conduct or promises of another.

EVICTION The removal of a person from possession of property.

INTER ALIA Among other things.

PROMISSORY ESTOPPEL A promise that is enforceable if the promisor should reasonably expect that it will induce action or forbearance on the part of the promisee, and does in fact cause such action or forbearance, and it is the only means of avoiding injustice.

■═■

James Baird Co. v. Gimbel Bros., Inc.

Contractor (P) v. Linoleum supplier (D)

64 F.2d 344 (2d Cir. 1933).

NATURE OF CASE: Appeal from judgment for defendant in action for breach of a contract for the sale of goods.

FACT SUMMARY: Gimbel (D) offered to supply linoleum to various contractors who were bidding on a public construction contract. Baird (P), relying on Gimbel's (D) quoted prices, submitted a bid and later the same day received a telegraphed message from Gimbel (D) that its quoted prices were in error. Baird's (P) bid was accepted.

RULE OF LAW

(1) Where an offer is withdrawn before it is accepted, and the offer language does not indicate a contrary intention, a contract is not formed.

(2) The doctrine of promissory estoppel is not applicable where an offer is made for an exchanged act or promise and no consideration has been received by the offeror.

FACTS: Gimbel (D), having heard that bids were being taken for a public building, had an employee obtain the specifications for linoleum required for the building and submitted offers to various possible contractors, including Baird (P), of two prices for linoleum depending upon the quality used. The offer was made in ignorance of a mistake as to the actual amount of linoleum needed, causing Gimbel's (D) prices to be about half the actual cost. The offer concluded as follows: "If successful in being awarded this contract, it will be absolutely guaranteed . . . and . . . we are offering these prices for reasonable (sic) prompt acceptance after the general contract has been awarded." Baird (P) received this on the 28th, the same day on which Gimbel (D) discovered its mistake, and telegraphed all contractors of the error, but the communication was received by Baird (P) just after Baird (P) submitted its lump sum bid relying on Gimbel's (D) erroneous prices. Baird's (P) bid was accepted on the 30th. Baird (P) received Gimbel's (D) written confirmation of the error on the 31st but sent an acceptance despite this two days later. Gimbel (D) refused to recognize a contract.

ISSUE:

(1) Where an offer is withdrawn before it is accepted, and the offer language does not indicate a contrary intention, is a contract formed?

(2) Is the doctrine of promissory estoppel applicable where an offer is made for an exchanged act or promise and no consideration has been received by the offeror?

HOLDING AND DECISION: (Hand, J.)

(1) No. Where an offer is withdrawn before it is accepted, and the offer language does not indicate a contrary intention, a contract is not formed. First, looking at the language of Gimbel's (D) offer, Gimbel's (D) use of the phrase "if successful in being awarded this contract" clearly shows Gimbel's (D) intent of not being bound simply by a contractor relying or acting upon the quoted prices. This is reinforced by the phrase "prompt acceptance after the general contract has been awarded." No award had been made at the time and reliance on the prices cannot be said to be an award of the contract. If a relying contractor had been awarded the contract and then repudiated it, Gimbel (D) would not have had any right to sue for breach, nor, had the relying contractor gone bankrupt, could Gimbel (D) have gone against his bankruptcy estate. The contractors could have protected themselves by insisting on a contract guaranteeing the prices before relying upon them. However, the court will not strain to find a contract in aid of one who fails to protect himself. Thus, based on the offer language, no bilateral contract was formed.

(2) No. The doctrine of promissory estoppel is not applicable where an offer is made for an exchanged act or promise and no consideration has been received by the offeror. The theory of promissory estoppel is not available here. Ordinarily, it is appropriate in donative or charitable cases where harsh results to the promisee arising from the promisor's breaking his relied-upon promise are to be protected against. However, an offer for an exchange, either being an act or another promise, is not meant to become a promise until a consideration is received. Here, the linoleum was to be delivered for the contractor's acceptance, not his bid. Moreover, the offer could not be considered an option, giving Baird (P) the right to accept the offer if its bid was accepted, but not binding it to do so if it could get a better price elsewhere. There was nothing in the offer language indicating that Gimbel (D) intended to be bound by such a one-sided deal. If it had so bound itself, promissory estoppel might have been applicable, since in such an instance, Baird (P) could have claimed reliance on Gimbel's (D) offer. Affirmed.

Continued on next page.

▶ *ANALYSIS*

Later cases have held the doctrine of promissory estoppel not to be as narrow. The majority of courts which have considered the issue hold that justifiable detrimental reliance on an offer renders it irrevocable. Naturally, the contractor must have something upon which to justifiably rely. The court in its decision notes that Restatement (Second) § 90 follows its view. However, Restatement (Second) § 90 has expanded the section so as to enlarge its scope according to the more modern viewpoint. It must be shown that the offeror foresaw that his promise would reasonably induce forbearance or action. The first inkling of this doctrine probably arose in the well-known *Hamer v. Sidway*, 27 N.E. 256 (1891), where an uncle promised to pay his nephew $5,000 for refraining from the use of liquor, swearing, and other activities until his 21st birthday, and reached full maturity in J. Traynor's decision in *Drennan v. Star Paving Company*, 51 Cal. 2d 409, 333 P.2d 757 (1958). Generally, this case is a good example of the manner in which the court will examine the words and actions of the parties in order to determine their intent and, hence, the existence of a contract. It appears that Gimbel (D) could have used the defense of unilateral mistake based upon a clerical error as seen in *M.F. Kemper Construction Co. v. City of Los Angeles*, 235 P.2d 7 (1951).

■≡■

Quicknotes

DETRIMENTAL RELIANCE Action by one party, resulting in loss that is based on the conduct or promises of another.

IRREVOCABLE OFFER An offer that may not be retracted by the promisor without the assent of the offeree.

PROMISSORY ESTOPPEL A promise that is enforceable if the promisor should reasonably expect that it will induce action or forbearance on the part of the promisee, and does in fact cause such action or forbearance, and it is the only means of avoiding injustice.

■≡■

Drennan v. Star Paving Co.

General contractor (P) v. Subcontractor (D)

Cal. Sup. Ct., 51 Cal. 2d 409, 333 P.2d 757 (1958).

NATURE OF CASE: Appeal of an award of damages for breach of contract.

FACT SUMMARY: Drennan (P) sued Star (D) to recover damages when Star (D) could not perform the paving work at the price quoted in its subcontracting bid.

🏛 **RULE OF LAW**
Reasonable reliance on a promise binds an offeror even if there is no other consideration.

FACTS: In formulating a bid to the Lancaster School District, Drennan (P), a general contractor, solicited bids for subcontracting work. Star (P), a paving company, submitted the lowest paving bid, and Drennan (P) used that bid in formulating its bid to the school district. Using Star's (D) subcontracting bid of $7,131.60, Drennan (P) was awarded the general contract. Star (D) then told Drennan (P) that it made a mistake and could not do the work for less than $15,000. Star (D) refused to do the work, and Drennan (P) found a substitute company that did the work for $10,948.60. Drennan (P) sued Star (D) for the difference, claiming that Drennan (P) had reasonably relied on Star's (D) offer. Star (D) claimed that it had made a revocable offer. The trial court ruled in favor of Drennan (P) on the grounds of promissory estoppel, and Star (D) appealed.

ISSUE: Does reasonable reliance on a promise bind the offeror if there no other consideration?

HOLDING AND DECISION: (Traynor, J.) Yes. Reasonable reliance on a promise binds the offeror even if there is no other consideration. Section 90 of the Restatement of Contracts provides that when a promise is made that induces action or forbearance of the promisee, the promissor is bound if injustice would result from nonenforcement. In the case of a unilateral offer, the offeror is bound to the promise if it produces reasonable reliance. Star (D) made a promise to Drennan (P) of a certain price. Star's (D) bid was the lowest, and Drennan (P) reasonably relied on it in formulating its bid and winning the contract. As a result, Drennan (P) was obligated to do the work at the price quoted and even had to put up a bond. Star (D) should have known such a result would occur if Star's (D) bid was accepted. The absence of consideration is not fatal to Star's (D) initial promise, as Drennan (P) substantially changed its position in reliance on Star (D). Injustice can only be avoided by the enforcement of Star's (D) subcontracting promise. Affirmed.

▶ **ANALYSIS**

Such reasonable reliance cases are often called firm offers. Firm offers can sometimes be implied promises to hold an offer open and have received criticism on the grounds that one party (the subcontractor) is bound while the other party (the general contractor) is not. Nonetheless, the modern trend is to enforce such promises.

■■■

Quicknotes

CONSIDERATION Value given by one party in exchange for performance, or a promise to perform, by another party.

FIRM OFFER Under the Uniform Commercial Code, refers to a signed, written offer to enter into a contract for the sale of goods that is irrevocable for a specified period of time, or if no time is stated then for a reasonable time period not exceeding three months.

PROMISSORY ESTOPPEL A promise that is enforceable if the promisor should reasonably expect that it will induce action or forbearance on the part of the promisee, and does in fact cause such action or forbearance, and it is the only means of avoiding injustice.

RELIANCE Dependence on a fact that causes a party to act or refrain from acting.

REVOCABLE OFFER An offer that may be retracted by the promisor without the assent of the offeree.

■■■

Berryman v. Kmoch

Owner of land (D) v. Real estate agent (P)

Kan. Sup. Ct., 221 Kan. 304, 559 P.2d 790 (1977).

NATURE OF CASE: Appeal from summary judgment denying the validity of an option contract.

FACT SUMMARY: Kmoch (P) claimed his expenditures of time and money in attempting to attract buyers constituted consideration to support the enforceability of an option on Berryman's (D) land.

🏛 RULE OF LAW
An agreement that lacks consideration may be enforceable based on promissory estoppel when: (1) the promisor reasonably expected the promisee to rely on the promise; (2) the promisee reasonably relied on the promise; and (3) a failure to enforce the promise would result in perpetuation of fraud or result in other injustice.

FACTS: Berryman (D) entered into an agreement giving Kmoch (P), a real estate agent who wrote the agreement, an option to purchase his land, yet the recited consideration was never paid. Berryman (D) expressed to Kmoch (P) his desire to be released from the agreement and sold the property to a third party. Subsequently, Kmoch (P) sought to exercise the option, and Berryman (D) sued to have the option declared void for lack of consideration. Kmoch (P) contended his expenditures of time and money in attempting to find a buyer for the land constituted detrimental reliance and the failure to enforce the promise will perpetuate fraud or result in other injustice on the agreement rendering it enforceable without consideration based on promissory estoppel. The trial court entered summary judgment for Berryman (D), and Kmoch (P) appealed.

ISSUE: May an agreement that lacks consideration be enforceable based on promissory estoppel when: (1) the promisor reasonably expected the promisee to rely on the promise; (2) the promisee does in fact act in reliance on the promise; and (3) the failure to enforce the promise will perpetuate fraud or result in other injustice?

HOLDING AND DECISION: (Fromme, J.) Yes. An agreement that lacks consideration may be enforceable based on promissory estoppel when: (1) the promisor reasonably expected the promisee to rely on the promise; (2) the promisee reasonably relied on the promise; and (3) a failure to enforce the promise would result in perpetuation of fraud or result in other injustice. In this case, Kmoch (P) was a real estate agent and personally wrote the agreement. Therefore, he knew it was not a contract to sell, and he knew that unless the consideration was paid the agreement was merely a continuing offer subject to revoca-

tion at any time prior to acceptance. Therefore, he did not reasonably rely on the agreement as a contract to purchase the land in expending the time and money to attract buyers. Accordingly, promissory estoppel cannot be applied to enforce the option. The agreement was merely a revocable offer which was revoked by Berryman's (D) expressed desire to do so occurring prior to Kmoch's (P) acceptance. Affirmed.

▶ ANALYSIS

The primary distinction between promises supported by promissory estoppel and those supported by consideration is that consideration is bargained for while promissory estoppel is not. The detriment suffered as a consequence of the promise does not induce the promise. Courts generally will analyze a contract for the presence of consideration, and only in its absence will the elements of promissory estoppel be determined. Some jurisdictions limit the applicability of promissory estoppel to certain types of fact patterns such as promises to make a gift of land, or charitable subscriptions. However, the modern view extends the doctrine to any case meeting the requirements of promissory estoppel.

■■■■■

Quicknotes

CONSIDERATION Value given by one party in exchange for performance, or a promise to perform, by another party.

PROMISSORY ESTOPPEL A promise that is enforceable if the promisor should reasonably expect that it will induce action or forbearance on the part of the promisee, and does in fact cause such action or forbearance, and it is the only means of avoiding injustice.

RELIANCE Dependence on a fact that causes a party to act or refrain from acting.

■■■■■

Pop's Cones, Inc. v. Resorts International Hotel, Inc.

Franchisee (P) v. Lessor (D)

N.J. Super. Ct., App. Div., 307 N.J. Super. 461, 704 A.2d 1321 (1998).

NATURE OF CASE: Appeal from summary judgment for defendant in a suit seeking damages based on a theory of promissory estoppel.

FACT SUMMARY: Pop's (P), a TCBY franchisee operating in Margate, after discussions with Resorts International Hotel (D) on the possibility of leasing space in its hotel, relied on Resorts' (D) assurances that the deal would be approved, and did not renew its lease on its Margate location.

🏛 RULE OF LAW

A promise which the promisor should reasonably expect to induce action or forbearance on the part of the promisee or a third person, and which does induce such action or forbearance, is binding if injustice can be avoided only by enforcement of the promise.

FACTS: Pop's (P), a vendor of frozen yogurt products, negotiated with Resorts (D) to lease a location in its resort hotel. Relying on Resorts' (D) advice and assurances that an agreement had been reached, Pop's (P) ended its lease at its other location, placed its equipment in temporary storage, and retained an attorney to finalize the terms of the lease. When Resorts (D) later withdrew its offer, Pop's (P) could not return to its former location, which had been relet, and incurred further expenses until it found another suitable location one year later. Pop's (P) sued Resorts (D) for damages resulting from its detrimental reliance upon promises made during the contract negotiations. When Resorts' (D) motion for summary judgment was granted, Pop's (P) appealed.

ISSUE: Is a promise which the promisor should reasonably expect to induce action or forbearance on the part of the promisee or a third person, and which does induce such action or forbearance, binding if injustice can be avoided only by enforcement of the promise?

HOLDING AND DECISION: (Kleiner, J.) Yes. A promise which the promisor should reasonably expect to induce action or forbearance on the part of the promisee or a third person, and which does induce such action or forbearance, is binding if injustice can be avoided only by enforcement of the promise. Recent cases relaxing the strict requirement of a "clear and definite promise" in making a prima facie case of promissory estoppel are persuasive. Whether Pop's (P) reliance upon Resorts' (D) assurances was reasonable is a question for the jury. Since Pop's (P) is not seeking enforcement of the lease, nor speculative lost profits, but merely its out-of-pocket expenses, its complaint should not have been summarily dismissed. Reversed and remanded.

▶ ANALYSIS

The court in this case overruled earlier New Jersey cases requiring a "clear and definite promise" for a promissory estoppel action. Since the contract itself was not involved, and Pop's (P) only requested damages resulting from its detrimental reliance on promises made, despite the ultimate failure of the contract negotiations, the court followed the Restatement (Second) of Contracts § 90 approach. Under this approach, a more equitable analysis designed to avoid injustice has eroded the earlier stricter adherence to proof of a clear and definite promise.

Quicknotes

DETRIMENTAL RELIANCE Action by one party, resulting in loss that is based on the conduct or promises of another.

EQUITABLE Just; fair.

PROMISSORY ESTOPPEL A promise that is enforceable if the promisor should reasonably expect that it will induce action or forbearance on the part of the promisee, and does in fact cause such action or forbearance, and it is the only means of avoiding injustice.

Credit Bureau Enterprises, Inc. v. Pelo

Credit bureau (P) v. Debtor (D)

Iowa Sup. Ct., 608 N.W.2d 20 (2000).

NATURE OF CASE: Appeal by debtor from judgment taken against him by creditor.

FACT SUMMARY: In the early morning of January 8, 1995, Russell Pelo (D) argued with his wife, left the home and checked into a motel. He (D) then called his wife and threatened to buy a gun and harm himself. Pelo (D) was later taken to a private hospital by the police. At the hospital he was asked, but refused to sign a payment release form, although later, under duress, he signed. The hospital sought payment for the services provided to Pelo (D) during his stay, but Pelo (D) refused to pay.

RULE OF LAW
Requiring a patient who is involuntarily committed to a private hospital to pay for medical services which the patient receives does not violate the patient's right to due process or constitutional right to contract.

FACTS: Russell Pelo (D) left his marital residence after having an argument with his wife and checked into a motel. He telephoned his wife "making threats of self harm" and purchased a shotgun. Pelo (D) was subsequently taken to a hospital by the police. Pursuant to statutory emergency hospitalization procedures, a magistrate found probable cause that Pelo (D) was seriously mentally impaired and likely to physically injure himself. The magistrate thus entered an emergency hospitalization order requiring that Pelo (D) be detained in custody at the hospital's psychiatric unit for examination and care. The hospitalization referee found that Pelo suffered from bipolar disorder, an illness from which Pelo had suffered for many years. In addition, the referee concluded that although Pelo (D) was in need of and would benefit from treatment for his serious mental illness, the required elements for involuntary hospitalization were lacking and that further involuntary hospitalization was not authorized. Pelo was released from the hospital and court jurisdiction. Subsequently, the hospital sought compensation from Pelo in the amount of $2,775.79 for the medical services provided to him. Pelo (D) refused to pay the bill or authorize his health insurance carrier to do so. The hospital later assigned its claim to Credit Bureau Enterprises, Inc. (D) for collection. Credit Bureau (P) sued Pelo (D) in district court, winning a judgment on the hospital bill, and Pelo (D) appealed.

ISSUE: Does requiring a patient who is involuntarily committed to a private hospital to pay for medical services which the patient receives violate the patient's right to due process or constitutional right to contract?

HOLDING AND DECISION: (McGiverin, C.J.) No. Requiring a patient who was involuntarily committed to a private hospital to pay for medical services he received did not violate his right to due process or his constitutional right to contract. Historically, quasi-contracts were not true contracts and, therefore, constitutional provisions concerning the right to contract did not apply. Here, Pelo (D) did not assert that the emergency hospitalization or involuntary commitment proceedings were constitutionally invalid, and preliminary factual findings of the magistrate and hospitalization referee found that Pelo (D) was, in fact, seriously mentally impaired so as to warrant the hospitalization. Pelo (D) was involuntarily committed to the private hospital based upon his threats of self harm made to his wife and his purchase of a shotgun. He was liable for the payment of the hospital bill under the theory of contract implied in law, or quasi-contract, since the hospitalization was of medical benefit to him and such services were provided by the hospital in good faith and not gratuitously. Pelo (D) did not challenge the factual basis for his hospitalization, nor was it likely that such a challenge would have been successful given the fact that the necessary probable cause findings concerning emergency hospitalization by the magistrate and involuntary commitment procedures by the hospitalization referee were made. These fact-finding requirements were in place to guarantee a patient's liberty and due process interests when the state exercises its authority through emergency hospitalization and involuntary commitment proceedings. Pelo (D) also did not challenge the hospitalization referee's finding that he suffered from bipolar disorder, nor did he challenge the district court's finding that $2,775.79 was the reasonable cost of services provided to him during his hospitalization. Affirmed.

▶ ANALYSIS

As noted in the Credit Bureau decision, the Restatement of Restitution § 2 states that a person who officiously confers a benefit upon another is not entitled to restitution. Under this rule, recovery is denied so that one will not have to pay for a benefit forced upon one against one's will or for which one did not request or knowingly accept. "Officiousness," as here used, means interference in the affairs of others not justified by the circumstances under which the interference takes place. [Restatement of Restitution § 2 Comment a.] In certain circumstances, however, restitution for services performed will be required even though the recipient did not request or voluntarily consent to

Continued on next page.

receive such services. For example, § 116 of the Restatement of Restitution provides that a person who has supplied things or services to another, although acting without the other's knowledge or consent, is entitled to restitution from the other if: (a) he acted unofficiously and with intent to charge therefor, and (b) the things or services were necessary to prevent the other from suffering serious bodily harm or pain, and (c) the person supplying them had no reason to know that the other would not consent to receiving them, if mentally competent; and (d) it was impossible for the other to give consent or, because of extreme youth or mental impairment, the other's consent would have been immaterial.

■≡■

Quicknotes

RESTITUTION The return or restoration of what the defendant has gained in a transaction to prevent the unjust enrichment of the defendant.

RIGHT TO CONTRACT Article 4 § 10 of the United States Constitution guarantees the right to contract and prohibits any State from passing any law that impairs this right, or impairs the obligations tendered by contractual agreement.

■≡■

Commerce Partnership 8098 Limited Partnership v. Equity Contracting Co.

Property owner (D) v. Subcontractor (P)

Fla. Dist. Ct. App., 695 So. 2d 383 (1997) (en banc).

NATURE OF CASE: Appeal from judgment for plaintiff in a construction contract claim.

FACT SUMMARY: Equity Contracting Co. (P), a subcontractor on a construction job who was not paid by the general contractor, alleged that Commerce Partnership 8098 Limited Partnership (D) had been unjustly enriched, and sought payment for the work it had performed.

RULE OF LAW
Where an owner has given consideration for the subcontractor's work by paying out the contract price for the work, an unpaid subcontractor's claim that the owner has been unjustly enriched must fail.

FACTS: Commerce Partnership 8098 Limited Partnership (Commerce) (D) contracted with a general contractor to perform improvements on its office building. Equity Contracting Co. (Equity) (P) was the stucco and surfacing subcontractor for the job, and completely performed its work. The general contractor did not pay Equity (P) for the work it had performed, and later filed for bankruptcy. Equity (P) then sued Commerce (D), alleging unjust enrichment. In an answer, Commerce (D) asserted that it had paid the general contractor in full. The trial court entered judgment in favor of Equity (P), and Commerce (D) appealed.

ISSUE: Where an owner has given consideration for the subcontractor's work by paying out the contract price for the work, must an unpaid subcontractor's claim that the owner has been unjustly enriched fail?

HOLDING AND DECISION: (Gross, J.) Yes. Where an owner has given consideration for the subcontractor's work by paying out the contract price for the work, an unpaid subcontractor's claim that the owner has been unjustly enriched must fail. A subcontractor's quasi-contract action against an owner must prove two elements to establish that the enrichment of the owner was unjust. The subcontractor must have exhausted all remedies against the general contractor and still remain unpaid, and the owner must not have given consideration to any person for the improvements furnished by the subcontractor. An unjust enrichment cannot exist where payment has been made for the benefit conferred. In this case, Equity (P) did not prove at trial that Commerce (D) had not made payment to any party for the benefits conferred on the property by Equity (P). On remand, Equity (P) will bear the burden of proving that Commerce (D) did not pay the general contractor. Reversed and remanded.

ANALYSIS

Though valid, the holding in this case has been rejected by many other courts. Proof of unjust enrichment is necessary for recovery in restitution. Unjust enrichment is an equitable concept.

Quicknotes

MECHANICS' LIEN A lien enforceable pursuant to statute in structures and/or improvements constructed in order to secure payment for the value of labor performed or materials furnished.

RESTITUTION The return or restoration of what the defendant has gained in a transaction to prevent the unjust enrichment of the defendant.

UNJUST ENRICHMENT The unlawful acquisition of money or property of another for which both law and equity require restitution to be made.

Watts v. Watts

Cohabitant (P) v. Cohabitant (D)

Wis. Sup. Ct., 137 Wis. 2d 506, 405 N.W.2d 303 (1987).

NATURE OF CASE: Appeal from dismissal of action for unjust enrichment.

FACT SUMMARY: Sue Anne Watts (P), upon the termination of her nonmarital cohabitation with James Watts (D), sought an order for an accounting of the personal and business assets accumulated during the parties' cohabitation and a determination of her share of that property.

🏛 RULE OF LAW
Unmarried cohabitants may raise claims based upon unjust enrichment following the termination of their relationships where one of the parties attempts to retain an unreasonable amount of the property acquired through the efforts of both.

FACTS: Sue Anne Evans Watts (P) and James Watts (D) accumulated property during their nonmarital cohabitation relationship, which lasted 12 years and produced two children. She was 19 when they met, living with her parents, and working full time as a nurse's aide in preparation for a nursing career. Shortly after they met, he persuaded her to quit her job and move into an apartment paid for by him. During their relationship, she contributed child-care and homemaking services. Additionally, she contributed personal property to the relationship, worked in his office as a receptionist, typist, and assistant bookkeeper, and also started a business from which he barred her after she moved out of their home. Sue Anne (P) sought an accounting of the personal and business assets accumulated during the cohabitation and to determine her share of those assets. Her claim was based on five theories, one of which was unjust enrichment. The trial court dismissed the action for failure to state a claim on which relief may be granted, and this appeal followed.

ISSUE: May unmarried cohabitants raise claims based upon unjust enrichment following the termination of their relationships where one of the parties attempts to retain an unreasonable amount of the property acquired through the efforts of both?

HOLDING AND DECISION: (Abrahamson, J.) Yes. Unmarried cohabitants may raise claims based upon unjust enrichment following the termination of their relationships where one of the parties attempts to retain an unreasonable amount of the property acquired through the efforts of both. A claim of unjust enrichment does not arise out of an agreement entered into by the parties but is grounded on the moral principle that one who has received a benefit has a duty to make restitution where retaining such a benefit would be unjust. An action for unjust enrichment is based upon proof of three elements: (1) a benefit conferred on the defendant by the plaintiff, (2) appreciation or knowledge by the defendant of the benefit, and (3) acceptance or retention of the benefit by the defendant under circumstances making it inequitable for the defendant to retain the benefit. The facts alleged are sufficient to state a claim based upon unjust enrichment. Reversed and remanded.

▶ ANALYSIS

The court noted that because no express or implied-in-fact agreement usually exists between the parties in cohabitation termination cases, recovery based upon unjust enrichment is sometimes referred to as "quasi-contract," or contract "implied in law" rather than "implied in fact." Quasi-contracts are obligations created by law to prevent injustice. Many courts have recognized that when a court refuses to enforce contract and property rights between unmarried cohabitants, the result is that one party keeps all or most of the assets accumulated during the relationship, while the other party is deprived of property which he or she helped to accumulate. Such a result is contrary to the principles of equity.

■═■

Quicknotes

QUASI-CONTRACT An implied contract created by law to prevent unjust enrichment.

RESTITUTION The return or restoration of what the defendant has gained in a transaction to prevent the unjust enrichment of the defendant.

■═■

Mills v. Wyman

Nurse-caretaker (P) v. Parent (D)

Mass. Sup. Jud. Ct., 20 Mass. (3 Pick.) 207 (1825).

NATURE OF CASE: Action on appeal to recover upon alleged promise.

FACT SUMMARY: Mills (P) took care of Wyman's (D) son without being requested to do so and for so doing was promised compensation for expenses arising out of the rendered care by Wyman (D). Wyman (D) later refused to compensate Mills (P).

> ## 🏛 RULE OF LAW
> A moral obligation is insufficient as consideration for a promise.

FACTS: Mills (P) nursed and cared for Levi Wyman, the son of Wyman (D). Upon learning of Mills's (P) acts of kindness toward his son, Wyman (D) promised to repay Mills (P) his expenses incurred in caring for Levi Wyman. Later, Wyman (D) refused to compensate Mills (P) for his expenses. Mills (P) filed an action in the court of common pleas where the Wyman (D) was successful in obtaining a nonsuit against Mills (P). Mills (P) appealed.

ISSUE: Is a moral obligation sufficient consideration for a promise?

HOLDING AND DECISION: (Parker, C.J.) No. It is said a moral obligation is sufficient consideration to support an express promise. However, the universality of the rule cannot be supported. Therefore, there must be some other preexisting obligation which will suffice as consideration. Affirmed.

▶ ANALYSIS

In cases such as this one, the nearly universal holding is that the existing moral obligation is not a sufficient basis for the enforcement of an express promise to render the performance that it requires. The general statement is that it is not sufficient consideration for the express promise. The difficulties and differences of opinion involved in the determination of what is a moral obligation are probably much greater than those involved in determining the existence of a legal obligation. This tends to explain the attitude of the majority of courts on the subject and justifies the generally stated rule.

■═■

Quicknotes

CONSIDERATION Value given by one party in exchange for performance, or a promise to perform, by another party.

EXPRESS PROMISE The expression of an intention to act, or to forbear from acting, granting a right to the promisee to expect and enforce its performance.

■═■

Webb v. McGowin

Good Samaritan (P) v. Estate (D)

Ala. Ct. App., 27 Ala. App. 82, 168 So. 196 (1935), *cert. denied*, 232 Ala. 374, 168 So. 199 (1936).

NATURE OF CASE: Action on appeal to collect on a promise.

FACT SUMMARY: Webb (P) saved the now deceased J. McGowin from grave bodily injury or death by placing himself in grave danger and subsequently suffering grave bodily harm. J. McGowin, in return, promised Webb (P) compensation. McGowin's executors (D) now refuse to pay the promised compensation.

> ## ⚖ RULE OF LAW
> A moral obligation is a sufficient consideration to support a subsequent promise to pay where the promisor has received a material benefit.

FACTS: Webb (P), while in the scope of his duties for the W.T. Smith Lumber Co., was clearing the floor, which required him to drop a 75-lb. pine block from the upper floor of the mill to the ground. Just as Webb (P) was releasing the block, he noticed J. McGowin below and directly under where the block would have fallen. In order to divert the fall of the block, Webb (P) fell with it, breaking an arm and leg and ripping his heel off. The fall left Webb (P) badly crippled and incapable of either mental or physical labor. In return for Webb's (P) act, J. McGowin promised to pay Webb (P) $15 every two weeks for the rest of Webb's (P) life. J. McGowin paid the promised payments until his death eight years later. Shortly after J. McGowin's death, the payments were stopped and Webb (P) brought an action against N. McGowin (D) and J.F. McGowin (D) as executors of J. McGowin's estate for payments due him. The executors (D) of the estate were successful in obtaining a nonsuit against Webb (P) in the lower court. Webb (P) appealed.

ISSUE: Was the moral obligation to compensate as promised sufficient consideration?

HOLDING AND DECISION: (Bricken, J.) Yes. It is well settled that a moral obligation is a sufficient consideration to support a subsequent promise to pay where the promisor has received a material benefit, although there was no original duty or liability resting on the promisor. Reversed and remanded.

CONCURRENCE: (Samford, J.) The strict letter of the rule as stated by the judges would perhaps bar the plaintiff from recovery. As Chief Justice Marshall stated in *Hoffman v. Porter*, 2 Brock. 156, however, " . . . [the] law

ought [not] to be separated from justice, where it is most doubtful."

▶ ANALYSIS

In most cases where the moral obligation is asserted, the court feels that the promise ought not be enforced; instead of going into the uncertain field of morality, the court chooses to rely upon the rule that moral obligation is not a sufficient consideration. On the other hand, in cases where the promise is one which would have been kept by most citizens, and the court feels that enforcement is just, a few courts will enforce the promise using the *Webb v. McGowin* rule. In general, the *Webb v. McGowin* rule is the minority rule and the *Mills v. Wyman* rule is the majority rule.

■═■

Quicknotes

MATERIAL BENEFIT An advantage gained by entering into a contract that is essential to the performance of the agreement and without which the contract would not have been entered into.

MORAL OBLIGATION A duty that is not enforceable at law, but is consistent with ethical notions of justice.

■═■

CHAPTER 4

The Statute of Frauds

Quick Reference Rules of Law

Crabtree v. Elizabeth Arden Sales Corp.

Sales manager (P) v. Cosmetics company (D)

N.Y. Ct. App., 305 N.Y. 48, 110 N.E.2d 551 (1953).

NATURE OF CASE: Appeal from affirmance of judgment for plaintiff in action for damages for breach of an employment contract.

FACT SUMMARY: Crabtree (P) was hired by Arden (D) to be the latter's sales manager. No formal contract was signed but separate writings pieced together showed Crabtree to have been hired for a two-year term with pay raises after the first and second six months. When he did not receive his second pay raise, Crabtree (P) sued for damages for breach.

> **RULE OF LAW**
> Separate writings, connected as to subject matter and occasion, may be pieced together to find an enforceable contract under the Statute of Frauds.

FACTS: In Sept. 1947, Crabtree (P) began negotiating with Arden (D) for the position of the latter's sales manager. Being unfamiliar with the cosmetics business and giving up a well-paying, secure job, Crabtree (P) insisted upon an agreement for a definite term. He asked for three years at $25,000 per year. But Arden (D) offered two years, with $20,000 per year the first six months, $25,000 per year the second six months, and $30,000 per year the second year. This was written down by Arden's (D) personal secretary with the notation "2 years to make good." A few days later, Crabtree (P) telephoned Mr. Johns, Arden's (D) executive vice-president, his acceptance. Crabtree (P) received a "welcome" wire from Miss Arden (D). When he reported for work, a "payroll change" card was made up and initialed by Mr. Johns showing the above pay arrangement with a salary increase noted "as per contractual agreement." Crabtree (P) received his first pay raise as scheduled, but not his second one. Miss Arden (D) allegedly refused to approve the second increase, denying Crabtree (P) had been hired for any specific period.

ISSUE: May separate writings, connected as to subject matter and occasion, be pieced together to find an enforceable contract under the Statute of Frauds?

HOLDING AND DECISION: (Fuld, J.) Yes. Separate writings, connected as to subject matter and occasion, may be pieced together to find an enforceable contract under the Statute of Frauds. First, as it is alleged that the contract is for a period of two years, there must be written evidence of its terms to be enforceable as the two-year performance places it within the Statute of Frauds. The payroll cards, one initialed by Arden's (D) executive vice-president and the other by its comptroller, unquestionably constituted a memorandum under the statute. It is enough

that they were signed with the intent to authenticate the information contained therein and that such information does evidence the terms of the contract. The cards had all essential terms except for duration. But as the memorandum can be pieced together from more than one document, all that is required between the papers is a connection established simply by reference to the same subject matter or transaction. Parol evidence is permissible in order to establish the connection. As the note prepared by Arden's (D) personal secretary shows, it was made in Miss Arden's (D) presence as well as that of Johns and of Crabtree (P), the dangers of parol evidence are at a minimum. All of the terms must be set out in writing and cannot be shown by parol. That memo, the paper signed by Johns, and the paper signed by the comptroller all refer on their face to the Crabtree (P) transaction. The comptroller's paper shows that it was prepared for the purpose of a "salary increase per contractual arrangements with Miss Arden" (D). That is, a reference to more comprehensive evidence and parol evidence can so explain. "2 years to make good" probably had no other purpose than to denote the duration of the arrangement and parol evidence may explain its meaning. Affirmed.

◤ ANALYSIS

When there is more than one writing and all are signed by the party to be charged, and it is clear by their contents that they relate to the same transaction, there is little problem. When not all the documents are signed, difficulties obviously crop up. It becomes difficult to say the memorandum has been authenticated to the party to be charged. When the unsigned document is physically attached to the signed writing, the Statute of Frauds is satisfied. And, as illustrated by this case, this is true when the signed document by its terms expressly refers to the unsigned document. The cases conflict where the papers are not attached or fail to refer to the other. The minority holds that that is a failure to show sufficient authentication. The better view is that if the signed document does not expressly refer to the unsigned, it is sufficient if internal evidence refers to the same subject matter or transaction. If so, extrinsic evidence is admissible to help show the connection between the documents.

━■━

Continued on next page.

Quicknotes

PAROL EVIDENCE RULE Doctrine precluding parties to an agreement from introducing evidence of prior or contemporaneous agreements in order to repudiate or alter the terms of a written contract.

STATUTE OF FRAUDS A statute that requires specified types of contracts to be in writing in order to be binding.

■▬■

Beaver v. Brumlow

Seller of land (P) v. Buyer of land (D)

N.M. Ct. App., 148 N.M. 172, 231 P.3d 628 (2010).

NATURE OF CASE: Appeal from judgment for defendants/counterclaim plaintiffs in action for ejectment.

FACT SUMMARY: The Beavers (P), who orally agreed to sell land to the Brumlows (D), but then reneged on the agreement, contended that the statute of frauds barred specific performance of the agreement because the Brumlows' (D) part performance was not "unequivocally referable" to the verbal agreement, and the verbal agreement was not certain as to the purchase price and time of performance.

🏛 RULE OF LAW
Specific performance of an oral contract for the sale of land is not barred by the statute of frauds where the terms of the contract other than the purchase price have been proved, there has been part performance by both parties to the agreement, the part performance refers unequivocally to the sale of land through possession and the making of improvements, and a remedy at law would be inadequate.

FACTS: The Beavers (P) agreed verbally to sell property to the Brumlows (D) on which the Brumlows (D) would site a house. Mr. Brumlow worked for the Beavers (P) at the time the agreement was made. In reliance on the Beavers' (P) promise, and with the Beavers' (P) permission, the Brumlows (D) cashed out their retirement plans and bought and installed a mobile home on the property and then added permanent improvements to it. The cost to the Brumlows (D) of purchasing the house and making improvements was around $85,000. The Beavers (P) supported the Brumlows' (D) efforts and helped them obtain necessary permits and applications. Throughout this time, the Brumlows (D) requested that the Beavers (P) formalize the parties' agreement, but the Beavers (P) never did, although they promised to and consulted an attorney about drafting the necessary documents. The parties also never agreed on a price or a date of closing. The Beavers (P) let the Brumlows (D) quietly enjoy possession of the land for several years. Then, all that changed. Mr. Brumlow (D) terminated his employment with the Beavers (P), as he was going to work for their competitor. Hurt and angry, the Beavers (P) decided not to sell the agreed upon tract of land to the Brumlows (D). Instead, they attempted to restructure the agreement as a "lease" by having the Brumlows (D) sign an agreement under which the Brumlows (D) would pay the Beavers (P) $400 per month, though the agreement used no language of a lease, so that the Brumlows (D) believed the agreement was for payment for the land. When the Brumlows (D)

began writing "Land Payment" on the checks, the Beavers (P) stopped cashing the checks and alleged that the "agreement" was for rental. The Brumlows (D) attempted to amicably resolve the dispute by offering to pay cash in the amount of the fair market value for the property and to have the property surveyed at their expense. The Beavers (P) refused, and then filed an ejectment action, alleging that the Brumlows (D) were in violation of their "rental" agreement. The Brumlows (D) denied the existence of a rental agreement and affirmatively alleged that their occupancy was pursuant to an agreement to purchase the property. The Brumlows (D) also filed counterclaims that included claims for breach of contract, fraud, and prima facie tort. The Beavers (P) pleaded the statute of frauds as a defense, arguing that the Brumlows' (D) part performance was not "unequivocally referable" to the verbal agreement, and the verbal agreement was not certain as to the purchase price and time of performance. The trial court held that the parties had entered into an agreement for the sale of land, and that by reneging on that agreement, the Beavers (P) injured the Brumlows (D), so that they committed a prima facie tort, which they knew would harm the Brumlows (D). The court rejected the statute of frauds defense on the grounds that part performance of the contract by both parties was sufficient to remove the contract from the statute of frauds. The court gave the Brumlows (D) a choice between money damages for the tort and specific performance of the contract, with the purchase price to be determined by an independent appraisal of the fair market value of the property, payable in cash within 30 days; the Brumlows (D) chose specific performance. The state's intermediate appellate court granted review.

ISSUE: Is specific performance of an oral contract for the sale of land barred by the statute of frauds where the terms of the contract other than the purchase price have been proved, there has been part performance by both parties to the agreement, the part performance refers unequivocally to the sale of land through possession and the making of improvements, and a remedy at law would be inadequate?

HOLDING AND DECISION: (Vigil, J.) No. Specific performance of an oral contract for the sale of land is not barred by the statute of frauds where the terms of the contract other than the purchase price have been proved, there has been part performance by both parties to the agreement, the part performance refers unequivocally to the sale of land through possession and the making of

Continued on next page.

improvements, and a remedy at law would be inadequate. The statute of frauds generally bars actions on contracts for the sale of land or interests in land where there has been no written agreement for the sale, signed by the party to be charged or the party's representative. However, a judicially created exception to this rule known as the doctrine of part performance—effected to overcome the harshness and injustice that might result from a literal and mechanical application of the rule—provides that where an oral contract not enforceable under the statute of frauds has been performed to such extent as to make it inequitable to deny effect thereto, equity may consider the contract as removed from operation of the statute of frauds and decree specific performance. Here, it is uncontested that the agreement was made, or even that the parties partially performed. The key objection by the Beavers (P) to application of the part performance doctrine is that the character of the Brumlows' (D) performance was not sufficiently indicative of an oral agreement to sell land to qualify as partial performance. To satisfy the part performance doctrine, part performance must be referable to the contract. In other words, it must be shown that there was no other reason for the performance than performance under the contract. Here, the Beavers (P) argue that the Brumlows' (D) conduct was consistent with those taken by a person who needs a place to live and who is given an opportunity to reside on another person's property. The Beavers (P) argue that if there is an alternative explanation for the actions taken in reliance of the oral contract, those actions are not "unequivocally referable" to the contract, and application of the part performance doctrine is improper. This argument is rejected. First, the "unequivocally referable" concept does not mean that outside of the contract, there can be no other plausible explanation for the part performance. Instead, it means that an outsider, knowing all of the circumstances of a case except for the claimed oral agreement, would naturally and reasonably conclude that a contract existed regarding the land, of the same general nature as that alleged by the claimant. In other words, the performance must lead an outsider to "naturally and reasonably" conclude that the contract alleged actually exists. Two indicators of such performance are taking possession of the property, and making valuable, permanent, and substantial improvements to the property. Here, the Brumlows (D) did both. In sum, the Brumlows' (D) reliance on the agreement and their part performance were sufficient to take the oral agreement outside of the statute of frauds. The Brumlows (D) also argue that the trial court impermissibly imposed on them a purchase price to which they had never agreed when the court ordered that the purchase price would be established by an appraisal and that the terms of the payment would be in cash payable within 30 days. Precedent provides that a claim for specific performance of a contract involving land will not fail for failure to specify a price where the contract is otherwise complete, and there has been part performance of the contract by a transfer of possession. In such situations, equity may imply a reasonable price to avoid inequity. Here, the contract was otherwise complete, and the Brumlows (D) relied on it to their detriment by taking possession and making improvements. Therefore, the trial court, in the exercise of its equitable powers, did not err in ordering that the purchase price be determined by an independent appraisal at fair market value. Significantly, the Beavers (P) do not challenge the fairness of the purchase price established by the trial court. Similarly, where a closing date has not been agreed to, equity may supply a reasonable time for performance. Finally, because it is well settled that land is unique and is assumed to have special value not replaceable in money, the Brumlows (D) did not have an adequate remedy at law. Affirmed.

▶ ANALYSIS

As did the court in this case, the majority of courts, in deciding whether a promisee's performance is "unequivocally referable" to the contract, look for two key factors: (1) whether the party seeking enforcement has obtained possession of the property, and (2) whether that party has made valuable improvements to the property. If these two factors are present, the majority of courts will apply the part performance exception. For these courts, mere payment of money usually is not enough. The Restatement (Second) of Contracts does not use the "unequivocally referable" standard, but, instead, focuses on whether the party seeking enforcement has, in reliance on the contract, so changed his position that only specific performance can avoid injustice.

Quicknotes

BREACH OF CONTRACT Unlawful failure by a party to perform its obligations pursuant to contract.

COUNTERCLAIM An independent cause of action brought by a defendant to a lawsuit in order to oppose or deduct from the plaintiff's claim.

EJECTMENT An action to oust someone in unlawful possession of real property and to restore possession to the party lawfully entitled to it.

FAIR MARKET VALUE The price of particular property or goods that a buyer would offer and a seller would accept in the open market following full disclosure.

FRAUD A false representation of facts with the intent that another will rely on the misrepresentation to his detriment.

PART PERFORMANCE Partial performance of a contract, promise or obligation.

PRIMA FACIE CASE An action where the plaintiff introduces sufficient evidence to submit the issue to the judge or jury for determination.

Continued on next page.

REMEDY AT LAW Compensation for violation of a right or injuries sustained that is available in a court of law, as opposed to a court of equity.

SPECIFIC PERFORMANCE An equitable remedy whereby the court requires the parties to perform their obligations pursuant to a contract.

STATUTE OF FRAUDS A statute that requires specified types of contracts to be in writing in order to be binding.

TORT DAMAGES Monetary compensation awarded by the court to a party injured as the result of the tortious act of another.

■══■

Alaska Democratic Party v. Rice

Employer (D) v. Former employee (P)

Alaska Sup. Ct., 934 P.2d 1313 (1997).

NATURE OF CASE: Appeal from damages award for plaintiff in suit based on misrepresentation and promissory estoppel.

FACT SUMMARY: When Rice (P) was promised a job that never materialized, she sued on a theory of promissory estoppel.

🏛 RULE OF LAW

A promise which the promisor should reasonably expect to induce action or forbearance on the part of the promisee or a third person and which does induce the action or forbearance is enforceable notwithstanding the Statute of Frauds if injustice can be avoided only by enforcement of the promise.

FACTS: The chair-elect of the Alaska Democratic Party (Party) (D) orally offered a job to Rice (P) as executive director of the Party (D) for two years. The resulting obligation fell into the Statute of Frauds because it could not be performed within one year. After quitting another job and moving to Alaska, Rice (P) was told she did not have the job. When Rice (P) sued on the alleged oral contract, the jury awarded her damages. The Party (D) appealed.

ISSUE: Is a promise which the promisor should reasonably expect to induce action or forbearance on the part of the promisee or a third person and which does induce the action or forbearance enforceable notwithstanding the Statute of Frauds if injustice can be avoided only by enforcement of the promise?

HOLDING AND DECISION: (Rabinowitz, J.) Yes. A promise which the promisor should reasonably expect to induce action or forbearance on the part of the promisee or a third person and which does induce the action or forbearance is enforceable notwithstanding the Statute of Frauds if injustice can be avoided only by enforcement of the promise. Section 139 (2) of the Restatement (Second) of Contracts enumerates factors to consider in making the determination of whether injustice can be avoided only by enforcement of the promise. A plaintiff's burden in overriding the Statute is to establish the promisor's existence by clear and convincing evidence. This court joins those states which endorse the Restatement approach in employment disputes such as this one. The Statute of Frauds represents a traditional contract principle that is largely formalistic and does not generally concern substantive rights. The need to satisfy the clear and convincing proof standard to establish the making and the terms of the promise ensures that promissory estoppel

will not render the Statute of Frauds superfluous in the employment context. The court adopts section 139 as the law of this jurisdiction. Affirmed.

▶ ANALYSIS

The first Restatement also contemplated the possibility that an estoppel could operate to override the Statute of Frauds' requirement of a written document. An estoppel might preclude a defendant's assertion of the Statute of Frauds as a barrier to enforcement only if detrimental reliance could be shown. Reliance could be based on a misrepresentation of fact or on a promise to make a memorandum if the statute would otherwise operate to defraud.

Quicknotes

CLEAR AND CONVINCING An evidentiary standard requiring a demonstration that the fact sought to be proven is reasonably certain.

PROMISSORY ESTOPPEL A promise that is enforceable if the promisor should reasonably expect that it will induce action or forbearance on the part of the promisee, and does in fact cause such action or forbearance, and it is the only means of avoiding injustice.

STATUTE OF FRAUDS A statute that requires specified types of contracts to be in writing in order to be binding.

Buffaloe v. Hart

Buyer (P) v. Seller (D)

N.C. Ct. App., 114 N.C. App. 52, 441 S.E.2d 172 (1994).

NATURE OF CASE: Appeal from denial of defendants' motions for directed verdict and judgment notwithstanding the verdict in an action for breach of a contract for the sale of goods.

FACT SUMMARY: Buffaloe (P) alleged that an oral contract he had with the Harts (D) to purchase their barns was valid because it fell under the partial performance exception to the Statute of Frauds.

RULE OF LAW

A contract is taken out of the Statute of Frauds if there is sufficient evidence of part performance; that is, if the seller delivered the goods and the buyer accepted them.

FACTS: Buffaloe (P) sought damages for breach of a contract he allegedly had for the purchase of tobacco barns. The Harts (D) denied the existence of the contract and contended that the alleged contract, made orally and with a handshake, was unenforceable because it violated the Statute of Frauds. Specifically they argued that a check that Buffaloe (P) had presented to them in attempting to fulfill his part of the contract did not have their endorsement and therefore did not satisfy the state's statute of frauds. That statute requires that for a check to constitute a writing sufficient to support a contract, it must be "signed by the party or his authorized agent against whom enforcement is sought." The jury found there was a valid contract and awarded Buffaloe (P) damages. The Harts (D) filed a motion for judgment notwithstanding the verdict, which was denied. The Harts (D) appealed and the state's intermediate appellate court granted review.

ISSUE: Is a contract taken out of the Statute of Frauds if there is sufficient evidence of part performance, that is, if the seller delivered the goods and the buyer accepted them?

HOLDING AND DECISION: (Greene, J.) Yes. A contract is taken out of the statute of frauds if there is sufficient evidence of part performance; that is, if the seller delivered the goods and the buyer accepted them. To qualify under the partial performance exception, acceptance must be voluntary and unconditional and may be inferred from the buyer's conduct in taking physical possession of the goods or some part of them. Part payment may be made by money or check, accepted by the seller. In this case, the evidence established that Buffaloe (P) told several people about purchasing the barns, reimbursed the Harts (D) for insurance on the barns, paid for improvements, took possession, enlisted the aid of an auctioneer and the paper to sell the barns, and received deposits from three buyers on the barns. Buffaloe (P) also delivered a check for $5,000 to the Harts (D) and the check was not returned until several days later. These acts represented substantial relevant evidence that a reasonable mind might accept as adequate to support the conclusions reached by the jury. The trial court did not err in denying the Harts' (D) motion for directed verdict or motion for judgment notwithstanding the verdict. Affirmed.

▶ ANALYSIS

The court in this case first considered whether the buyer's check represented a memorandum sufficient to satisfy the Statute. But since the sellers never signed the check, it could not be enforced against them. Under the partial performance exception, a buyer is required to deliver something that is accepted by the seller as such performance. In this case, the $5,000 check served this purpose.

Quicknotes

BREACH OF CONTRACT Unlawful failure by a party to perform its obligations pursuant to contract.

MEMORANDUM A brief written note outlining the terms of a transaction or an agreement.

STATUTE OF FRAUDS A statute that requires specified types of contracts to be in writing in order to be binding.

CHAPTER 5

Principles of Interpretation and the Parol Evidence Rule

Quick Reference Rules of Law

Joyner v. Adams

Property owner (P) v. Substituted lessee (D)

N.C. Ct. App., 87 N.C. App. 570, 361 S.E.2d 902 (1987).

NATURE OF CASE: Appeal of award of damages for breach of contract.

FACT SUMMARY: Joyner (P) contended that the rent escalation clause of a lease was triggered by Adams's (D) failure to properly develop the property.

RULE OF LAW
The determination of whether a party to a contract had knowledge of the other party's interpretation is essential to properly enforce a disputed provision of an agreement.

FACTS: Joyner (P), owner of property known as Waters Edge Office Park, contracted with Brown Investment Company to lease and develop the property in 1972. Three years later, the lease was amended to substitute Adams (D) as the lessee. The lease amendment, drafted by Adams (D), also suspended the annual rent increases provided for in the lease. Instead, Adams (D) agreed to pay Joyner (P) a fixed rate until 1980, contingent on Adams's (D) developing the property by that time. Adams (D) developed most of the property accordingly, except for one lot on which sewer and water lines were constructed but no buildings were erected. Joyner (P) asserted that this failure to properly develop the property made Adams (D) liable for the suspended rent increases pursuant to the lease amendment. Adams (D) disputed this interpretation, claiming that the contract did not require that buildings be constructed. Joyner (P) filed suit, and the trial court awarded $93,695.75 in damages. Adams (D) appealed, and review was granted.

ISSUE: Is a determination of whether a party to a contract had knowledge of the other party's interpretation essential to properly enforce a disputed provision of an agreement?

HOLDING AND DECISION: (Eagles, J.) Yes. The determination of whether a party to a contract had knowledge of the other party's interpretation is essential to properly enforce a disputed provision of an agreement. The contract should be enforced pursuant to the meaning of the innocent party, i.e., the party who did not have knowledge of the other's interpretation. The trial court failed to determine whether Adams (D) had knowledge that Joyner (P) understood the development provision to include building construction. Conversely, it is also necessary to ascertain whether Joyner (P) had knowledge that Adams (D) thought at the time of the contract that development meant only preparation for building. The trial court mistakenly based its decision solely on the fact that Adams (D)

had drafted the agreement. Affirmed in part, reversed and remanded in part.

ANALYSIS

The decision is in accord with the view of the Restatement (Second) of Contracts §§ 20 and 201(2). On remand, the court determined that Adams (D) had knowledge that Joyner (P) interpreted the contract to mean that buildings had to be erected by 1980. Therefore, the award of damages to Joyner (P) was reinstated. The decision of the trial court, which was reversed here, was based upon the principle of contra proferentem, which holds that contractual ambiguity should be resolved against the party who drafted the agreement. Generally, this principle is employed where the parties have unequal bargaining positions but is not expressly limited to those situations.

Quicknotes

AMBIGUITY Language that is capable of more than one interpretation.

MUTUAL MISTAKE A mistake by both parties to a contract, who are in agreement as to what the contract terms should be, but the agreement as written fails to reflect that common intent; such contracts are voidable or subject to reformation.

UNILATERAL MISTAKE Occurs when only one party to an agreement makes a mistake and is generally not a basis for relief by rescission or reformation.

Frigaliment Importing Co. v. B.N.S. International Sales Corp.

Chicken purchaser (P) v. Seller (D)

190 F. Supp. 116 (S.D.N.Y. 1960).

NATURE OF CASE: Action for breach of warranty of a contract for the sale of goods.

FACT SUMMARY: Frigaliment Importing Co. (Frigaliment) (P) ordered a large quantity of "chicken" from B.N.S. International Sales Corp. (B.N.S.) (D), intending to buy young chicken suitable for broiling and frying, but B.N.S. (D) believed, in considering the weights ordered at the prices fixed by the parties, that the order could be filled with older chicken, suitable for stewing only, and termed "fowl" by Frigaliment (P).

🏛 RULE OF LAW
The party who seeks to interpret the terms of the contract in a sense narrower than their everyday use bears the burden of persuasion to so show, and if that party fails to support its burden, it faces dismissal of its complaint.

FACTS: Frigaliment Importing Co. (Frigaliment) (P), a Swiss corporation, and B.N.S. International Sales Corp. (B.N.S.) (D), a New York corporation, made two almost identical contracts for the sale of chicken by the latter to the former as follows: U.S. fresh frozen chicken, Grade A, government inspected, eviscerated, all wrapped and boxed suitably for export, 75,000 lbs. 2½–3 lbs. at $33.00 per 100 lbs. and 25,000 lbs. 1½–2 lbs. at $36.50 per 100 lbs. The second contract was the same except for 25,000 lbs. less of the heavier chicken and a price of $37.00 per 100 lbs. for the lighter birds. B.N.S. (D), which was new to the poultry business, believed any kind of chicken could be used to fill the order including stewing chickens. Most of the order for heavier birds was filled with stewers because that was the only way B.N.S. (D) could make a profit on the contract.

ISSUE: Does the party who seeks to interpret the terms of the contract in a sense narrower than their everyday use bear the burden of persuasion to so show, and if that party fails to support its burden, does it face dismissal of its complaint?

HOLDING AND DECISION: (Friendly, J.) Yes. The party who seeks to interpret the terms of the contract in a sense narrower than their everyday use bears the burden of persuasion to so show, and if that party fails to support its burden, it faces dismissal of its complaint. Frigaliment (P) failed to support its burden. While cables leading up to negotiations were predominantly in German, the use of the English word "chicken" as meaning "young chicken" rather than the German word "Huhn" meaning broilers and stewers lost its force when B.N.S. (D) asked if any kind of chickens were wanted to which an affirmative answer meaning "huhn" was given. B.N.S. (D), being new to the chicken trade, the other party must show the other's acceptance of the trade use of a term. Frigaliment (P) failed to offer such proof. There was conflicting evidence anyway as to the trade use of the word "chicken." B.N.S.'s (D) price of $33.00 per 100 lbs. for the larger birds was $2.00 to $4.00 less than for broilers. Frigaliment (P) could not say that the price appeared reasonable because it was closer to the $35.00 broiler price than the $30.00 stewer price. B.N.S. (D) could be expected not to sell at a loss. While the evidence is generally conflicting, overall it appeared that B.N.S. (D) believed it could comply by supplying stewing chicken. This did conform with one dictionary meaning, with the definition in the department of animal regulations to which at least there was a contractual reference, and with some trade usage. This evidence must be relied upon as the contract language itself could not settle the question here. Dismissed.

▶ ANALYSIS

In determining the intent of the parties the court will turn first to the language of the contract to see whether the meaning of the ambiguous term can be raised. If this is unsuccessful, the court must look to other evidence. Under Restatement (First), § 235, certain guidelines aid in determining meaning. First, the ordinary meaning of language throughout the country is given to words unless circumstances show that a different meaning is applicable. Also, all circumstances surrounding the transaction may be taken into consideration. Also, if after consideration of all factors, it is still uncertain what meaning should be given, a reasonable, lawful, and effective meaning to all manifestations of intention is preferred to an interpretation which leaves a part of such unreasonable, unlawful, or ineffective. Restatement (First) § 236(a). Even so, the principal apparent purpose of the parties should be given greater weight in determining the meaning to be given.

Quicknotes

AMBIGUITY Language that is capable of more than one interpretation.

COURSE OF DEALING Previous conduct between two parties to a contract which may be relied upon to interpret their actions.

C & J Fertilizer, Inc. v. Allied Mutual Insurance Co.

Insured company (P) v. Insurer (D)

Iowa. Sup. Ct., 227 N.W.2d 169 (1975).

NATURE OF CASE: Appeal from judgment for defendant on action to recover for burglary loss.

FACT SUMMARY: C & J Fertilizer, Inc. (P) had an insurance policy with Allied Mutual Insurance Co. (Allied) (D) covering it for burglary loss. A burglary occurred, but Allied (D) refused to pay because there were no visible marks or physical damage to the building exterior at the place of entry, as required under the policy.

🏛 RULE OF LAW
Insurance policies contain an implied warranty of fitness for their intended purpose, and the reasonable expectations of the policyholder will be honored, with unconscionable clauses disallowed.

FACTS: C & J Fertilizer, Inc. (C & J) (P) had an insurance policy with Allied Mutual Insurance Co. (Allied) (D) covering burglary loss at its fertilizer plant. A burglary occurred, but Allied (D) refused to pay on the grounds that there were no visible marks or physical damage on the building exterior at the place of entry of the burglar. This requirement was included in the insurance policy under its definition of burglary. Its purpose was to prevent fraud and payments on "inside jobs." An interior door had been damaged when the burglar entered a separate room and stole chemicals. The lower court held for Allied (D), stating that the definition of burglary under the policy was unambiguous and not met in this case. C & J (P) relied on the theories of reasonable expectation, implied warranty of fitness for intended purpose, and unconscionability of the burglary definition. The trial court found that there had been no discussion of policy provisions between the parties at the time the policy was secured, and there was no evidence that C & J (P) knew the policy definition of burglary.

ISSUE: Do insurance policies contain an implied warranty of fitness for their intended purpose, and will the reasonable expectations of the policyholder be honored, with unconscionable clauses dishonored?

HOLDING AND DECISION: (Reynoldson, J.) Yes. Insurance policies contain an implied warranty of fitness for their intended purpose, and the reasonable expectations of the policyholder will be honored, with unconscionable clauses disallowed. Insurance policies, such as the one here, are mass-produced, standardized adhesion policies. The policyholder should not be bound to unknown terms which are beyond the range of reasonable expectation. Here, nothing led C & J (P) to reasonably anticipate that it would have no coverage unless the exterior of the premises was marked or damaged. Further, Allied (D) breached an implied warranty that the policy would be reasonably fit for its intended purpose. There is no reason why this doctrine should not apply to insurance policies as well as the sale of tangible goods, as it now does. Finally, C & J (P) should prevail because the liability-avoiding provision in the definition of burglary is, in these circumstances, unconscionable, based on the standardized nature of the contract, the unequal bargaining positions, and the unreasonably favorable terms of the definition to Allied (D). Reversed and remanded.

DISSENT: (LeGrand, J.) The definition of burglary as contained in the policy was unambiguous, and its purpose was to omit coverage for "inside jobs." Contracts that clearly state their meaning should not be disturbed simply because the meaning is disliked.

▶ ANALYSIS

There is a definite trend in recent cases to disallow unconscionable terms in adhesion contracts, especially insurance contracts. The courts will either deny enforcement of the contract as a whole or as to the unconscionable terms only. The term "unconscionable" is derived from the Uniform Commercial Code, § 2-302, and refers to terms in a contract that are so manifestly unfair as to be oppressive.

■■▬■

Quicknotes

ADHESION CONTRACT A contract that is not negotiated by the parties and is usually prepared by the dominant party on a "take it or leave it" basis.

BOILERPLATE Standard language commonly appearing in documents having a definite meaning in the same context without variation.

UNCONSCIONABILITY Rule of law whereby a court may excuse performance of a contract, or of a particular contract term, if it determines that such term(s) are unduly oppressive or unfair to one party to the contract.

■■▬■

Thompson v. Libby

Seller of logs (P) v. Purchaser (D)

Minn. Sup. Ct., 34 Minn. 374, 26 N.W. 1 (1885).

NATURE OF CASE: Appeal from denial of motion for new trial in action for breach of contract.

FACT SUMMARY: Thompson (P) brought an action to enforce a written contract for the sale of logs. Libby (D) defended on an oral warranty.

🏛 RULE OF LAW
Where a contract is complete on its face, parol testimony is inadmissible to vary its terms, such as warranties of quality.

FACTS: Thompson (P) and Libby (D) entered into a contract for the sale of logs. The contract contained all necessary terms. Libby (D) later refused to pay for the logs. Thompson (P) brought a suit for the contract price and Libby (D) defended on the basis of a parol contemporary warranty which was allegedly breached by Thompson (P). At trial, the court allowed the introduction of evidence concerning the warranty of quality orally given at the time of sale. It found for Libby (D) on this basis. The state's highest court granted review.

ISSUE: Where a contract is complete on its face, is parol testimony admissible to vary its terms, such as warranties of quality?

HOLDING AND DECISION: (Mitchell, J.) No. Where a contract is complete on its face, parol testimony is inadmissible to vary its terms, such as warranties of quality. In the case of a sale of personal property a warranty of quality is considered a part of the contract and not a collateral contract. The contract contains all necessary terms and is complete on its face. The parol evidence rule provides that contemporaneous parol evidence may not be admitted to contradict or vary the terms of a written contract which is complete on its face. Since a warranty is considered a contract term, it must be included in the contract. Parol evidence cannot be admitted to show that the contract is not a complete statement of the parties' agreement. The judge must determine whether the contract, based on its terms, represents the complete embodiment of the agreement. Since the contract here is complete on its face, the trial court was incorrect in allowing the parol evidence of the warranty to be admitted. Reversed.

▌ ANALYSIS

Parol evidence of subsequent agreements may always be admitted. The parties are free to alter or modify the contract terms at any time. Separate collateral contracts may also be introduced. These do not alter or vary the terms of the written contract. However, it is necessary to show that the matter is collateral and would not normally have been included in the principal contract.

■=■

Quicknotes

BREACH OF CONTRACT Unlawful failure by a party to perform its obligations pursuant to contract.

PAROL EVIDENCE RULE Doctrine precluding parties to an agreement from introducing evidence of prior or contemporaneous agreements in order to repudiate or alter the terms of a written contract.

■=■

Taylor v. State Farm Mutual Automobile Insurance Co.

Insured (P) v. Insurance company (D)

Ariz. Sup. Ct., 175 Ariz. 148, 854 P.2d 1134 (1993) (en banc).

NATURE OF CASE: Review of a decision reversing a jury verdict in plaintiff's favor in a bad faith insurance claim action.

FACT SUMMARY: Taylor (P) alleged that the court of appeals erroneously held that his insurance bad faith claim was barred by a release he signed in 1981.

🏛 RULE OF LAW
A judge must first consider the offered evidence and, if he or she finds that the contract language is "reasonably susceptible" to the interpretation asserted by its proponent, admit the evidence to determine the meaning intended by the parties.

FACTS: Taylor (P) was insured by State Farm Mutual Automobile Insurance Co. (State Farm) (D) when he was involved in an automobile accident with two other vehicles. The other parties obtained combined verdicts against Taylor (P) for approximately $2.5 million in excess of his insurance policy limits. The court of appeals affirmed those judgments. Taylor (P) sued State Farm (D) for bad faith, seeking damages for the excess judgment, and claiming that State Farm (D) improperly failed to settle within policy limits. State Farm (D) moved for summary judgment, asserting that Taylor (P) had relinquished his bad faith claim when he signed a release drafted by his attorney in exchange for State Farm's (D) payment of $15,000 in uninsured motorist benefits. The judge denied the motion, finding that the release was ambiguous and therefore parol evidence was admissible at trial to aid in interpreting the release. The jury returned a verdict in favor of Taylor (P) for compensatory damages of $2.1 million plus attorney's fees. The court of appeals reversed, holding that the release agreement was not ambiguous and should have been strictly enforced. Taylor (P) appealed.

ISSUE: Must a judge first consider the offered evidence and, if he or she finds that the contract language is "reasonably susceptible" to the interpretation asserted by its proponent, admit the evidence to determine the meaning intended by the parties?

HOLDING AND DECISION: (Feldman, C.J.) Yes. A judge must first consider the offered evidence and, if he or she finds that the contract language is "reasonably susceptible" to the interpretation asserted by its proponent, the evidence is admissible to determine the meaning intended by the parties. Taylor (P) argued that the bad faith claim sounded in tort and was therefore neither covered nor intended to be covered by the language releasing "all contractual" claims. Because the legal character of bad faith was and is not universally established, the release reasonably could be interpreted as Taylor (P) asserts. The

trial court, therefore, did not err in concluding that the text of the release did not necessarily cover claims for bad faith. The potential size of the bad faith claim, the fact that the parties used limiting language in the release, and the recent authority characterizing the claim as a tort all support Taylor's (P) contention that the release language was not intended to release his bad faith claim. Since interpretation was needed because the extrinsic evidence established controversy over what occurred and what inferences to draw from the events, the matter was properly submitted to the jury. The jury's resolution of the release issue in Taylor's (P) favor is left undisturbed. The decision of the court of appeals is vacated and the matter remanded for resolution of the remaining issues.

CONCURRENCE: (Corcoran, J.) Wavering and over-lapping lines of interpretation, rather than bright straight borders prevail in this area of contract interpretation. The problem with an amorphous rule is that ultimately it means that only this court must decide every contract dispute subject to its analysis.

▌ *ANALYSIS*

The court in this case compared two views of the parol evidence rule. The "plain meaning" view of Farnsworth holds that if a writing appears to be plain and unambiguous on its face, its meaning must be determined from the four corners of the instrument. The Corbin view, which has been embraced by Arizona courts, holds that a court may consider surrounding circumstances and all of the proffered evidence to determine its relevance to the parties' intent, and then apply the parol evidence rule to exclude only the evidence that contradicts or varies the meaning of the agreement.

Quicknotes

EXTRINSIC EVIDENCE Evidence that is not contained within the text of a document or contract but which is derived from the parties' statements or the circumstances under which the agreement was made.

FOUR CORNERS The express terms of a written document.

PAROL EVIDENCE RULE Doctrine precluding parties to an agreement from introducing evidence of prior or contemporaneous agreements in order to repudiate or alter the terms of a written contract.

Sherrodd, Inc. v. Morrison-Knudsen Co.

Construction subcontractor (P) v. General contractor (D)

Mont. Sup. Ct., 249 Mont. 282, 815 P.2d 1135 (1991).

NATURE OF CASE: Appeal from summary judgment for defendants in a suit for quantum meruit plus tort damages.

FACT SUMMARY: Sherrodd, Inc. (P), a construction subcontractor, alleged that the price provisions in the written construction contract should be set aside because of Morrison-Knudsen Co.'s (D) subcontractor's alleged fraud and breach of the covenant of good faith and fair dealing.

🏛 RULE OF LAW
A written contract may be altered only by a subsequent contract in writing or by an executed oral agreement.

FACTS: Sherrodd, Inc. (P), a family-owned construction company, subcontracted with the general contractors, Morrison-Knudsen Co. (D), to do certain earth-moving work involved in the construction of new family housing. Sherrodd (P) contended that a representative of Morrison-Knudsen (D) told him there were 25,000 cubic yards of excavation to be performed on the job and that he based his bid on reliance on that representation. Morrison-Knudsen (D) denied that its representative made such a statement to Sherrodd (P). Sherrodd's (P) bid was accepted and he began work before a written contract was signed. While performing the work, Sherrodd (P) discovered that the quantity of work far exceeded 25,000 cubic yards. The written contract Sherrodd (P) later signed did not specify the quantity in cubic yards, and Sherrodd (P) later sued to set aside the price provisions in the contract and to recover in quantum meruit for the work performed. Sherrodd (P) also alleged both actual and constructive fraud and breach of the covenant of good faith and fair dealing. Morrison-Knudsen (D) moved for summary judgment, which was granted based on the parol evidence rule regarding modification of written contracts. Sherrodd (P) appealed.

ISSUE: May a written contract be altered only by a subsequent contract in writing or by an executed oral agreement?

HOLDING AND DECISION: (Turnage, C.J.) Yes. A written contract may be altered only by a subsequent contract in writing or by an executed oral agreement. Because the written agreement supersedes all previous oral agreements, the parol evidence rule prohibits admission of any evidence of the alleged fraudulent statement of Morrison-Knudsen's (D) representative. The compensation of Sherrodd (P) is governed exclusively by the written contract and his claims are barred under the parol evidence

rule. The parol evidence rule is the public policy of this state and it is clearly established by statute and court precedent. Affirmed.

DISSENT: (Trieweiler, J.) The result of the majority's decision will be a grave injustice insofar as no party with superior bargaining power will ever be held liable for fraudulent conduct relating to an oral contract where it has obtained a signature on a written agreement from the party with inferior bargaining power. Taking Sherrodd's (P) assertions as true, he has adequately pled that Morrison-Knudsen's (D) agent engaged in fraud. An important exception to the parol evidence rule provides that evidence to explain fraud is not to be excluded, and the legislature has provided that parol evidence can be offered to establish that a contract was induced by fraud. There is no exception in the statute where the fraudulent oral agreement contradicts the written agreement.

▶ ANALYSIS

The court in this case applied a rule from an old case which the dissent claimed led to a great injustice. In *Continental Oil v. Bell*, 95 Mont. 123 (1933), the court had held that parol evidence of fraud was not admissible when the oral promise directly contradicted a provision of the written contract. The dissent claimed that only fraudulent parties who are in a superior bargaining position stand to benefit from this rule, which totally defeated the purpose of the fraud exception. The dissent also contended that the majority's reliance on the case was misplaced because the case contradicted the current statute governing the issue.

■=∎

Quicknotes

FRAUD A false representation of facts with the intent that another will rely on the misrepresentation to his detriment.

PAROL EVIDENCE RULE Doctrine precluding parties to an agreement from introducing evidence of prior or contemporaneous agreements in order to repudiate or alter the terms of a written contract.

■=∎

Nanakuli Paving & Rock Co. v. Shell Oil Co.

Concrete purchaser (P) v. Seller (D)

664 F.2d 772 (9th Cir. 1981).

NATURE OF CASE: Appeal from judgment n.o.v. denying damages for breach of contract.

FACT SUMMARY: Shell Oil Co. (D) contended it had not breached a supply contract as its course of conduct established the unwritten terms of the agreement.

🏛 RULE OF LAW
Trade usage and past course of dealings between contracting parties may establish terms not specifically enumerated in the contract, so long as no conflict is created with the written terms.

FACTS: Nanakuli Paving & Rock Co. (Nanakuli) (P) entered into a contract to purchase its requirements of concrete from Shell (D). The contract was in effect for several years and renewed several times. Nanakuli (P) sued over a one-year contract, contending Shell Oil Co. (Shell) (D) had failed to protect it from price increases. It argued that although such protection was not enumerated in the contract, it was part of the trade usage in concrete and thus implied in the contract. Further, Shell (D) had previously performed this service. Shell (D) argued the contract did not call for such, and its past conduct did not constitute a practice of protection. Rather it was a temporary waiver of the contract price. The trial court granted Shell (D) judgment n.o.v., and Nanakuli (P) appealed.

ISSUE: May trade custom and usage and past course of dealings establish contract terms?

HOLDING AND DECISION: (Hoffman, J.) Yes. Trade usage and past course of dealings between contracting parties may establish terms not specifically enumerated in the contract, so long as no conflict is created with the written terms. There was substantial evidence that the jury could rely upon in finding a consistent course of conduct including price protection. As a result, the entry of judgment n.o.v. was improper. Reversed and remanded.

CONCURRENCE: (Kennedy, J.) Here, the case involves specific pricing practices, not an allegation of unfair dealing generally. Therefore, the court's opinion should not be interpreted to permit juries to read into contracts price protection terms that are derived from a concept of good faith unless the parties know from custom and usage, or are otherwise on notice, that such good faith is expected. Here, the evidence of custom and usage regarding price protection in the asphaltic paving trade was not contradicted, so the jury could find that the parties knew or should have known of the practice at the time of making the contract. This principle applies to either theory

of the case, namely, interpretation of the contract based on how the contract was performed or finding that good faith required the seller to hold the price.

▶ ANALYSIS

The Parol Evidence Rule precludes extraneous evidence of contract terms unless such terms are ambiguous. The price protection term was so prevalent in the concrete trade that it was reasonable to find that the parties impliedly incorporated it into the contract. This was supported by Shell's (D) past history of price protection.

■■■

Quicknotes

COURSE OF DEALING Previous conduct between two parties to a contract which may be relied upon to interpret their actions.

JUDGMENT N.O.V. A judgment entered by the trial judge reversing a jury verdict if the jury's determination has no basis in law or fact.

REQUIREMENTS CONTRACT An agreement pursuant to which one party agrees to purchase all his required goods or services from the other party exclusively for a specified time period.

TRADE USAGE A course of dealing or practice commonly used in a particular trade.

■■■

CHAPTER 6

Implied Terms, the Obligation of Good Faith, and Warranties

Quick Reference Rules of Law

Wood v. Lucy, Lady Duff-Gordon

Marketer and licensor of designs (P) v. Designer (D)

N.Y. Ct. App., 222 N.Y. 88, 118 N.E. 214 (1917).

NATURE OF CASE: Appeal from reversal of an order denying defendant's motion for judgment on the pleadings in action for damages for breach of a contract for an exclusive right.

FACT SUMMARY: Wood (P), in a complicated agreement, received the exclusive right for one year, renewable on a year-to-year basis if not terminated by 90 days' notice, to endorse designs with Lucy's (D) name and to market all her fashion designs for which she (D) would receive one-half the profits derived. Lucy (D) broke the contract by placing her endorsement on designs without Wood's (P) knowledge.

🏛 RULE OF LAW
If a promise may be implied from a writing even though it is imperfectly expressed, there is a valid contract.

FACTS: Lucy (D), a famous-name fashion designer, contracted with Wood (P) that for her granting to him an exclusive right to endorse designs with her name and to market and license all of her designs, they were to split the profits derived by Wood (P) in half. The exclusive right was for a period of one year, renewable on a year-to-year basis, and terminable upon 90 days' notice. Lucy (D) placed her endorsement on fabrics, dresses, and millinery without Wood's (P) knowledge and in violation of the contract. Lucy (D) claimed that the agreement lacked the elements of a contract as Wood (P) allegedly was not bound to do anything.

ISSUE: If a promise may be implied from a writing even though it is imperfectly expressed, is there a valid contract?

HOLDING AND DECISION: (Cardozo, J.) Yes. If a promise may be implied from a writing even though it is imperfectly expressed, there is a valid contract. While the contract did not precisely state that Wood (P) had promised to use reasonable efforts to place Lucy's (D) endorsement and market her designs, such a promise can be implied. The implication arises from the circumstances. Lucy (D) gave an exclusive privilege and the acceptance of the exclusive agency was an acceptance of its duties. Lucy's (D) sole compensation was to be one-half the profits resulting from Wood's (P) efforts. Unless he gave his efforts, she could never receive anything. Without an implied promise, the transaction could not have had such business efficacy as they must have intended it to have. Wood's (P) promise to make monthly accounting and to acquire patents and copyrights as necessary showed the intention of the parties that the promise has value by showing that Wood (P) had some duties. The promise to pay Lucy (D) half the profits and make monthly accounting was a promise to use reasonable efforts to bring profits and revenues into existence. Reversed.

▶ ANALYSIS

A bilateral contract can be express, implied in fact, or a little of each. The finding of an implied promise for the purpose of finding sufficient consideration to support an express promise is an important technique of the courts in order to uphold agreements which seem to be illusory and to avoid problems of mutuality of obligation. This case is the leading case on the subject. It is codified in Uniform Commercial Code (U.C.C.) § 2-306(2), where an agreement for exclusive dealing in goods imposes, unless otherwise agreed, an obligation to use best efforts by both parties.

■■■

Quicknotes

BILATERAL CONTRACT An agreement pursuant to which each party promises to undertake an obligation, or to forbear from acting, at some time in the future.

U.C.C. § 2-306 Permits the seller to refuse to deliver unreasonable amounts demanded by a customer under a requirements contract.

■■■

Leibel v. Raynor Manufacturing Co.

Area distributor (P) v. Product manufacturer (D)

Ky. Ct. App., 571 S.W.2d 640 (1978).

NATURE OF CASE: Appeal of summary denial of damages for breach of contract.

FACT SUMMARY: Raynor Manufacturing Co. (D), without notice, abrogated an exclusive distribution agreement with Leibel (P).

🏛 RULE OF LAW
Reasonable notification is required in order to terminate an ongoing oral agreement creating a manufacturer-distributor relationship.

FACTS: Raynor Manufacturing Co. (D) orally contracted with Leibel (P) for Leibel (P) to become an area-exclusive distributor of Raynor's (D) products. Raynor (D) subsequently became dissatisfied with Leibel (P) and sent Leibel (P) a notice of termination. Leibel (P) sued, contending that reasonable notice was not given prior to termination. The trial court granted summary judgment for Raynor (D) as to the breach of contract cause of action, and Leibel (P) appealed.

ISSUE: Is reasonable notification required in order to terminate an ongoing oral agreement creating a manufacturer-distributor relationship?

HOLDING AND DECISION: (Howerton, J.) Yes. Reasonable notification is required in order to terminate an ongoing oral agreement creating a manufacturer-distributor relationship. The threshold question is whether the Uniform Commercial Code (U.C.C.) applies. By its terms, Article 2 applies to transactions involving goods or merchandise. It is quite apparent that a contract between a manufacturer and a distributor involves goods or merchandise, and therefore Article 2 should apply. Section 2-309 provides that where successive performances over an indefinite period of time are involved, reasonable notification of termination is required. An exception is made where invocation of this rule would be unconscionable. However, in a situation such as that presented here, the distributor undoubtedly incurs expenses in reliance upon continuing the relationship. It is certainly not unconscionable to require reasonable notification. For this reason, a triable issue of fact exists regarding whether the termination was given with reasonable notice. Reversed and remanded.

▶ ANALYSIS

"Reasonable time" is not defined in § 2-309. This is not surprising, as the issue will always turn on the facts of the case. Reasonable notice is to some extent coextensive with the standard of good faith and fair dealing.

■══■

Quicknotes

GOOD FAITH An honest intention to abstain from any unconscientious advantage of another.

IMPLIED WARRANTY An implied promise made by one party to a contract that the other party may rely on a fact, relieving that party from the obligation of determining whether the fact is true and indemnifying the other party from liability if that fact is shown to be false.

U.C.C. § 2-309 Provides that reasonable notification of termination be given if successive performances have come to be expected over an indefinite time period.

■══■

Seidenberg v. Summit Bank

Seller of business (P) v. Purchaser of business (D)

N.J. Super. Ct., App. Div., 348 N.J. Super. 243, 791 A.2d 1068 (2002).

NATURE OF CASE: Appeal from dismissal, for failure to state a claim, of an action for a breach of the implied covenant of good faith and fair dealing.

FACT SUMMARY: Seidenberg and Raymond (collectively, "Seidenberg") (P) claimed that Summit Bank (D) breached the implied covenant of good faith and fair dealing that arose from a contract between the parties by engaging in a bad-faith course of conduct that thwarted Seidenberg's (P) reasonable expectations, relating to compensation, under the contract.

RULE OF LAW

(1) A claim of breach of the implied covenant of good faith and fair dealing is not precluded because the parties possessed equal bargaining power, because the plaintiff was not financially vulnerable during the contract's formation, and because the plaintiff negotiated the contract with the assistance of highly competent counsel.

(2) When a plaintiff asserts a claim of breach of the implied covenant of good faith and fair dealing, the parol evidence rule does not impact the plaintiff's ability to substantiate claims of reasonable expectations arising from the contract or that the defendant failed to perform its contractual obligations in good faith.

(3) A claim of breach of the implied covenant of good faith and fair dealing may not be dismissed where the complaint alleges facts that if proven true show that the defendant exercised a right to terminate in bad faith or used its discretionary rights to thwart the contract's purpose.

(4) Allegations of bad faith and ill motives are sufficient to survive dismissal where it is asserted that the plaintiff suffered from defendant's actions that were "wanton and willful and without privilege or right."

FACTS: Seidenberg and Raymond (collectively, "Seidenberg") (P) owned brokerage firms, which they sold to Summit Bank (Summit) (D). As part of the transaction, Seidenberg (P) retained his position as executive of the brokerage firms and also was to be placed in charge of the daily operations of any other employee benefits insurance business that might be acquired by Summit (D). Seidenberg's (P) employment agreements with Summit (D) acknowledged the parties' joint obligation to work together with respect to the future performance of the brokerage firms, as Seidenberg's (P) compensation was tied to the growth and success of the firms and this line of business at Summit (D). After Seidenberg (P) was terminated, he brought suit claiming, inter alia, that Summit (D) had breached the implied covenant of good faith and fair dealing by failing to support, and even by actively thwarting, the growth of the firms and business. Seidenberg (P) alleged that Summit's (D) conduct demonstrated that Summit (D) never had any intention of performing its side of the bargain, and that Summit (D), from the start, was not committed to developing the business with Seidenberg (P), but rather simply wanted to acquire the business and seek out its own broker to run it or grow it. Summit (D) moved to dismiss this claim, and the trial granted Summit's (D) motion, finding that Seidenberg (P) was seeking to prove the existence (and obtain enforcement) of an oral agreement allegedly made beyond the four corners of the written transaction agreements in violation of the parol evidence rule, and that the respective parties had equal bargaining power. The state's intermediate appellate court granted review.

ISSUE:
(1) Is a claim of breach of the implied covenant of good faith and fair dealing precluded because the parties possessed equal bargaining power, because the plaintiff was not financially vulnerable during the contract's formation, and because the plaintiff negotiated the contract with the assistance of highly competent counsel?

(2) When a plaintiff asserts a claim of breach of the implied covenant of good faith and fair dealing, does the parol evidence rule impact the plaintiff's ability to substantiate claims of reasonable expectations arising from the contract or that the defendant failed to perform its contractual obligations in good faith?

(3) May a claim of breach of the implied covenant of good faith and fair dealing be dismissed where the complaint alleges facts that if proven true show that the defendant exercised a right to terminate in bad faith or used its discretionary rights to thwart the contract's purpose?

(4) Are allegations of bad faith and ill motives sufficient to survive dismissal where it is asserted that the plaintiff suffered from defendant's actions that were "wanton and willful and without privilege or right"?

HOLDING AND DECISION: (Fisher, J.)
(1) No. A claim of breach of the implied covenant of good faith and fair dealing is not precluded because the parties possessed equal bargaining power, because the

Continued on next page.

plaintiff was not financially vulnerable during the contract's formation, and because the plaintiff negotiated the contract with the assistance of highly competent counsel. The bargaining power of the parties is not the only factor determinative of whether there has been a breach of the implied covenant. Here merely because the parties were all sophisticated, financially strong, and represented by competent counsel does not preclude a finding that the implied covenant was breached. Although these factors are significant, and must be weighed accordingly by a fact finder, they are not exclusively determinative of the issue.

(2) No. When a plaintiff asserts a claim of breach of the implied covenant of good faith and fair dealing, the parol evidence rule does not impact the plaintiff's ability to substantiate claims of reasonable expectations arising from the contract or that the defendant failed to perform its contractual obligations in good faith. The parol evidence rule does not even come into play until it is first determined what the true agreement of the parties is. Accordingly, the rule cannot inhibit the application of the implied covenant of good faith and fair dealing because that covenant is contained in all contracts as a matter of law. Because the key premise of the implied covenant is the enhanced status of the parties' reasonable expectations, a vigorous application of the parol evidence rule would extremely limit the opportunity to pursue such a claim. The implied covenant is applied in three situations: (a) where terms and conditions which have not been expressly set forth in the written contract need to be added to give effect to the parties' expectations; (b) where there has been the bad faith performance of an agreement even when the defendant has not breached any express term; and (c) where a party's exercise of discretion expressly granted by a contract's terms is in derogation of the parties' expectations. Here, the second and third situations are implicated, and the parol evidence rule potentially could come into play regarding either one, but it should not. The parol evidence rule is not impacted in a case such as this because the obligation to act with good faith and fair dealing is, by its very nature, "implied." The prohibition on parol evidence to alter or vary a written contract relates only to the creation of the contract. Seidenberg (P) does not seek to contradict or alter any express term in a written contract, but rather questions Summit's (D) bona fides in both its performance and termination of the contract. Therefore, there is no concern that the particular manner in which Seidenberg (P) would have the implied covenant applied would run afoul of the parol evidence rule. To determine whether there was good faith performance, the court must consider the expectations of the parties and the purposes for which the contract was made. It would be difficult, if not impossible, to make that determination without considering evidence outside the written contract. Therefore, in determining whether a breach of the

covenant has occurred, a court must allow for parol evidence and a ruling that the need for parol evidence is fatal to the complaint is erroneous.

(3) No. A claim of breach of the implied covenant of good faith and fair dealing may not be dismissed where the complaint alleges facts that if proven true show that the defendant exercised a right to terminate in bad faith or used its discretionary rights to thwart the contract's purpose. As discussed above (in Issue #2) these are two of the three facets of the implied covenant. The trial court's job is to determine whether a cause of action consistent with any of these categories has been sufficiently alleged. Here, the allegation by Seidenberg (P) that Summit (D) terminated in bad faith, despite having the express right to do so, and Seidenberg's (P) expectation of continued employment, sufficiently pleads a claim under the second facet. Allegations that Summit (D) failed to take action in discretionary areas sufficiently alleges a claim under the third facet.

(4) Yes. Allegations of bad faith and ill motives are sufficient to survive dismissal where it is asserted that the plaintiff suffered from defendant's actions that were "wanton and willful and without privilege or right." A party exercising its discretion right under a contract acts in bad faith if that party exercises its discretionary authority arbitrarily, unreasonably, or capriciously, with the objective of preventing the other party from receiving its reasonably expected fruits under the contract. Whether a defendant has acted in bad faith requires inquiry into the defendant's state of mind and the context in which the claim arose, and is, therefore, a fact-specific inquiry. Ultimately, the question of whether there was bad faith resides in the eye of the trier of fact, and, therefore, the issue cannot be resolved until the parties are at least given a full and fair opportunity for further investigation and discovery. Here, by claiming that he was injured by Summit's (D) actions that were "wanton and willful and without privilege or right," Seidenberg (P) has sufficiently pled bad faith for the issue to go to trial. Reversed and remanded.

▶ ANALYSIS

It is important to keep in mind that the implied covenant of good faith and fair dealing is never used to override or alter an express contract term. Instead, the implied obligation of good faith can be viewed as a device for protecting the bargain that the parties themselves have made against later attempts by one side to undermine it.

■■■

Quicknotes

BREACH The violation of an obligation imposed pursuant to contract or law, by acting or failing to act.

Continued on next page.

IMPLIED COVENANT OF GOOD FAITH AND FAIR DEALING An implied warranty that the parties will deal honestly in the satisfaction of their obligations and without an intent to defraud.

PAROL EVIDENCE RULE Doctrine precluding parties to an agreement from introducing evidence of prior or contemporaneous agreements in order to repudiate or alter the terms of a written contract.

■▬■

Morin Building Products Co. v. Baystone Construction, Inc.

Siding installer (P) v. Construction firm (D)

717 F.2d 413 (7th Cir. 1983).

NATURE OF CASE: Appeal of award of damages for breach of contract.

FACT SUMMARY: General Motors Corp. refused, for aesthetic reasons, to approve aluminum siding installed by Morin Building Products (P), which was subsequently not paid.

> ## 🏛 RULE OF LAW
> Acceptance of performance in a contract whose purpose is primarily functional will be based on an objective standard.

FACTS: As part of a construction project for General Motors Corp., Baystone Construction, Inc. (Baystone) (D) subcontracted with Morin Building Products (Morin) (P) to install aluminum siding. General Motors retained final approval rights. General Motors' agent rejected the siding due to a minor aesthetic flaw. The purpose of the siding was strictly functional. Baystone (D) had another subcontractor redo the job, and refused to pay Morin (P), which sued for breach. The trial court held that the standard of acceptability of Morin's (P) performance was objective, and the jury held it objectively adequate. Baystone (D) appealed.

ISSUE: Will acceptance of performance in a contract whose purpose is primarily functional be based on an objective standard?

HOLDING AND DECISION: (Posner, J.) Yes. Acceptance of performance in a contract whose purpose is primarily functional will be based on an objective standard. The majority rule is that where the contract in question involves performance of commercial quality, an objective, reasonable person standard will be used in determining whether performance was adequate. It is unreasonable to expect a party to such a contract to permit his financial outcome to depend on whim. Therefore, in the absence of explicit language to the contrary, only if performance is inadequate objectively will performance be considered inadequate. Affirmed.

> ## ▶ ANALYSIS
>
> Generally speaking, a party will not be held to an objective standard when assessing the adequacy of performance when the nature of the contract is aesthetic. Even then, the law usually does not grant unfettered discretion. A good faith requirement will generally be read into the contract.

Quicknotes

BREACH OF CONTRACT Unlawful failure by a party to perform its obligations pursuant to contract.

CONDITION Requirement; potential future occurrence upon which the existence of a legal obligation is dependent.

Locke v. Warner Bros., Inc.

Actress/director (P) v. Studio (D)

Cal. Ct. App., 57 Cal. App. 4th 354, 66 Cal. Rptr. 2d 921 (1997), *rev. denied*, (Nov. 19, 1997).

NATURE OF CASE: Appeal from summary judgment for defendant in action for breach of contract.

FACT SUMMARY: Locke (P) claimed that Warner Bros., Inc. (D) denied her the benefit of her bargain, breached her contract, fraudulently entered into the agreement with her, and discriminated against her on the basis of sex when it refused to develop any projects she presented.

🏛 RULE OF LAW
Where a contract confers on one party a discretionary power affecting the rights of the other, a duty is imposed to exercise that discretion in good faith and in accordance with fair dealing.

FACTS: Locke (P), an actress and former girlfriend of Clint Eastwood, entered into an agreement with Warner Bros., Inc. (Warner) (D) in exchange for dropping her case against Eastwood. The agreement included provisions that Locke (P) would receive $250,000 from Warner (D) for three years for a non-exclusive first look deal for any picture she was thinking of developing, and a $750,000 "pay or play" directing deal. Locke contended that the development deal was a sham and that Warner (D) never intended to make any films with her, and filed suit alleging various causes of action. When Warner's (D) motion for summary judgment on all claims was granted, Locke (P) appealed.

ISSUE: Where a contract confers on one party a discretionary power affecting the rights of the other, is a duty imposed to exercise that discretion in good faith and in accordance with fair dealing?

HOLDING AND DECISION: (Klein, J.) Yes. Where a contract confers on one party a discretionary power affecting the rights of the other, a duty is imposed to exercise that discretion in good faith and in accordance with fair dealing. The trial court's ruling missed the mark by failing to distinguish between Warner's (D) right to make a subjective creative decision, which is not reviewable for reasonableness, and the requirement that the dissatisfaction be bona fide or genuine. In every contract there is an implied covenant that neither party shall do anything which will have the effect of destroying or injuring the right of the other party to receive the fruits of the contract. If Warner (D) acted in bad faith by categorically rejecting Locke's (P) work and refusing to work with her, irrespective of the merits of her proposals, such conduct is not beyond the reach of the law. Whether Warner (D) violated the implied covenant and breached the contract

by categorically refusing to work with Locke (P) is a question for the trier of fact. The judgment is reversed with respect to the claims alleging breach of covenant and fraudulent promise. The court in this case affirmed the dismissal of the other two claims raised by Locke (P) in her complaint. Since Locke (P) did not timely assert any error in the trial court's disposition of her two causes of action alleging sex discrimination, any error was waived. The issue of fraudulent intent was, according to this court, one for the trier of fact to decide, and otherwise affirmed.

■━■

Quicknotes

BENEFIT OF THE BARGAIN Calculation of assessing damages in actions for breach of contract measured as the difference between the actual value and the purported value of the goods being bought.

FRAUD A false representation of facts with the intent that another will rely on the misrepresentation to his detriment.

■━■

Donahue v. Federal Express Corp.

Employee (P) v. Employer (D)

Pa. Super. Ct., 753 A.2d 238 (2000).

NATURE OF CASE: Employee's appeal from the trial court's granting of a demurrer to his complaint in a suit against his employer for wrongful discharge.

FACT SUMMARY: Brion Donahue (P) worked for Federal Express Corp. (FedEx) (D) as an at-will employee from November 1979 until he was discharged in January 1997, working his way up to Commercial MX Service Administrator. At the time he left FedEx, Marshall was his immediate supervisor. During his time with FedEx, Donahue (P) often questioned company policies and practices. Appellant appealed his termination, and FedEx management upheld the termination. Donahue then filed this employment case alleging various causes of action, including wrongful termination and that FedEx breached an implied duty of good faith and fair dealing.

⚖ RULE OF LAW
An employee cannot, as a matter of law, maintain an action for the breach of an implied duty of good faith and fair dealing insofar as the underlying claim is for the termination of an at-will employment relationship.

FACTS: Brion Donahue (P) was an employee of Federal Express Corporation (FedEx) (D) for 18 years, during which time he questioned numerous company practices that he claimed to be improper. He was accused of making a racial remark in front of another FedEx (D) employee, and was accused of making derogatory remarks about his immediate supervisor to vendors and others. Upon his discharge from FedEx (D), Donahue (P) brought suit against them for wrongful termination. The trial court granted FedEx's (D) demurrer to the complaint on the grounds that an employee cannot, as a matter of Pennsylvania law, maintain an action for the breach of an implied duty of good faith and fair dealing insofar as the underlying claim was for the termination of at-will relationship. Donahue (P) appealed.

ISSUE: Can an employee maintain an action for the breach of an implied duty of good faith and fair dealing insofar as the underlying claim is for the termination of an at-will employment relationship?

HOLDING AND DECISION: (Lally-Green, J.) No. An employee cannot, as a matter of law, maintain an action for the breach of an implied duty of good faith and fair dealing insofar as the underlying claim is for the termination of an at-will employment relationship. Here, Donahue (P), an at-will employee, failed to establish that his employer FedEx's (D) guaranteed fair treatment

procedure for employee grievances imposed any contractual duties on FedEx (D), hence he could not maintain a cause of action for the breach of any implied duty of good faith and fair dealing arising out of his claim that he was not treated fairly under the employer's fair treatment procedure. FedEx's (D) fair treatment procedure stated that the policies set forth provided guidelines, but it did not create any contractual rights regarding employee termination or otherwise. Although in an appropriate case, courts may announce that a particular practice violates public policy, for purposes of a public policy exception to an at-will employment even in the absence of legislative pronouncement to that effect, a court's power to announce public policy is limited since public policy is to be ascertained by reference to the laws and legal precedents and not from general considerations of supposed public interest. No Pennsylvania appellate court has held that an implied duty of good faith and fair dealing applies to the termination of a pure at-will employment relationship. Accordingly, Donahue (P) cannot as a matter of law maintain an action for the breach of an implied duty of good faith and fair dealing insofar as the underlying claim is for the termination of the at-will employment relationship. Affirmed.

▶ ANALYSIS

The *Donahue* court noted that a general allegation of superior work performance is insufficient to establish additional consideration so as to overcome the presumption of an at-will employment; performing well on the job does not generally confer a substantial benefit on an employer beyond that which an employee is paid to do, and performing well on the job does not generally constitute a detriment beyond that which is incurred by all manner of salaried professionals. Nevertheless, additional consideration may exist, said the court, when an employee affords the employer "a substantial benefit other than the services which the employee is hired to perform, or when the employee undergoes a substantial hardship other than the services which he is hired to perform." For example, the court noted that a sufficient additional consideration had been found where an employee, in response to an employer's persistent recruitment efforts, gave up a stable position in another state, sold his house, and relocated to a new city with his pregnant wife, only to be fired after sixteen days on the job. *Cashdollar v. Mercy Hosp. of Pittsburgh*, 406 Pa. Super. 606, 595 A.2d 70, 72–73 (1991).

▬▬▬

Continued on next page.

Quicknotes

AT-WILL EMPLOYMENT The rule that an employment relationship is subject to termination at any time, or for any cause, by an employee or an employer in the absence of a specific agreement otherwise.

FAIR DEALING An implied warranty that the parties will deal honestly in the satisfaction of their obligations and without an intent to defraud.

GOOD FAITH An honest intention to abstain from any unconscientious advantage of another.

WRONGFUL TERMINATION Unlawful termination of an individual's employment.

■━■

Bayliner Marine Corp. v. Crow

Boat manufacturer (D) v. Boat purchaser (P)

Va. Sup. Ct., 257 Va. 121, 509 S.E.2d 499 (1999).

NATURE OF CASE: Boat manufacturer's appeal from a judgment against it in a breach of warranty suit.

FACT SUMMARY: In the summer of 1989, John Crow (P) was invited by a sales representative for Tidewater Yacht Agency, Inc. (Tidewater) to ride on a new model sport fishing boat manufactured by Bayliner Marine Corp. (Bayliner) (D). Crow (P) was most interested in the speed of the boat, and after being given copies of "prop matrixes" and other promotion material, Crow (P) entered into a written contract for the purchase of the 3486 Trophy Convertible in which he had ridden. He took delivery in September 1989, and in 1992, filed suit for breached express warranties, implied warranties of merchantability, and fitness for a particular purpose (alleging lack of attainment of maximum speed).

> ## 🏛 RULE OF LAW
> In assessing the merchantability of goods, Uniform Commercial Code (U.C.C.) § 2-314(2)(a),(c) requirement that goods must be such as would "pass without objection in the trade" concerns whether a significant segment of the buying public would object to buying the goods, while the requirement that goods "are fit for the ordinary purposes for which such goods are used" concerns whether the goods are reasonably capable of performing their ordinary functions.

FACTS: John Crow (P) sought to purchase a fishing boat. When he asked the manufacturer, Bayliner (D), about the maximum speed, Bayliner's representative explained that he had no personal experience with the boat. Therefore, the representative consulted two documents described as "prop matrixes," which were included by Bayliner (D) in its dealer's manual. The representative gave Crow (P) copies of the "prop matrixes" which listed the boat models offered by Bayliner (D) and stated the recommended propeller sizes, gear ratios, and engine sizes for each model. The "prop matrixes" also listed the maximum speed for each model. The 3486 Trophy Convertible (the boat ultimately purchased) was listed as having a maximum speed of 30 miles per hour when equipped with a size "20 × 20" or "20 × 19" propeller. The boat Crow (P) purchased did not have either size propeller but, instead, had a size "20 × 17" propeller. At the bottom of one of the "prop matrixes" was the following disclaimer: "This data is intended for comparative purposes only, and is available without reference to weather conditions or other variables. All testing was done at or near sea level, with full fuel and water tanks, and approximately 600 lb. passenger and gear weight."

Crow (P) purchased the boat. During the next 12 to 14 months, Crow (P) made numerous repairs and adjustments to the boat in an attempt to increase its speed capability. Despite these efforts, the boat consistently achieved a maximum speed of only 17 miles per hour, except for one brief period. Crow (P) sued the manufacturer Bayliner (D), arguing it had breached express warranties and implied warranties of merchantability and fitness for a particular purpose. Judgment was rendered for Crow (P), and Bayliner (D) appealed.

ISSUE: In assessing the merchantability of goods, does the U.C.C. § 2-314(2)(a),(c) requirement that goods must be such as would "pass without objection in the trade" concern whether a significant segment of the buying public would object to buying the goods, while the requirement that goods, "are fit for the ordinary purposes for which such goods are used" concern whether the goods are reasonably capable of performing their ordinary functions?

HOLDING AND DECISION: (Keenan, J.) Yes. U.C.C. § 2-314 provides that in all contracts for the sale of goods by a merchant, a warranty is implied that the goods will be merchantable. Under U.C.C. § 2-314(2)(a),(c) to be merchantable, the goods must be such as would "pass without objection in the trade" and as "are fit for the ordinary purposes for which such goods are used." The first phrase concerns whether a "significant segment of the buying public" would object to buying the goods, while the second phrase concerns whether the goods are "reasonably capable of performing their ordinary functions." In order to prove that a product is not merchantable, the complaining party must first establish the standard of merchantability in the trade. Here, Bayliner (D) correctly noted that the record contained no evidence of the standard of merchantability in the offshore fishing boat trade. Nor did the record contain any evidence supporting a conclusion that a significant portion of the boat-buying public would object to purchasing an offshore fishing boat with the speed capability of the 3486 Trophy Convertible (the boat at issue). Crow (P), nevertheless, relied on his own testimony that the boat's speed was inadequate for his intended use, and another witness's opinion testimony that the boat took "a long time" to reach certain fishing grounds in the Gulf Stream off the coast of Virginia. However, this evidence failed to address the standard of merchantability in the trade or whether Crow's (P) boat failed to meet that standard. Thus, Crow (P) failed to prove that the boat would not "pass without objection in the trade" as required by the U.C.C. As to whether the record

Continued on next page.

supported a conclusion that Crow's (P) boat was not fit for its ordinary purpose as an offshore sport fishing boat, the evidence was uncontroverted that Crow (P) used the boat for offshore fishing, at least during the first few years after purchasing it, and that the boat's engines were used for 850 hours. While Crow (P) stated that many of those hours were incurred during various repair or modification attempts and that the boat was of little value to him, this testimony did not support a conclusion that a boat with this speed capability is generally unacceptable as an offshore fishing boat. Finally, the statement in the sales brochure that the model of boat bought by Crow (P) "delivers the kind of performance you need to get to the prime offshore fishing grounds" merely expressed Bayliner's (D) opinion concerning the quality of the boat's performance and did not create an express warranty that the boat was capable of attaining a speed of 30 miles per hour. Reversed.

▶ *ANALYSIS*

In *Bayliner*, Crow (P) contended that the "particular purpose" for which the boat was intended was use as an offshore fishing boat capable of traveling at a maximum speed of 30 miles per hour. However, to establish an implied warranty of fitness for a particular purpose, the buyer must prove as a threshold matter that he made known to the seller the particular purpose for which the goods were required. In this regard, the *Bayliner* court noted that the record did not support a conclusion that Crow (P) had informed the manufacturer or the seller of this precise requirement. Although Crow (P) had informed them that he intended to use the boat for offshore fishing and discussed the boat's speed in this context, these facts did not establish that the seller actually knew on the date of sale that a boat incapable of travelling at 30 miles per hour was unacceptable to Crow (P). Accordingly, the *Bayliner* court concluded that the evidence failed to support the trial court's ruling that Bayliner (D) had breached an implied warranty of fitness for a particular purpose.

■═■

Quicknotes

EXPRESS WARRANTY An express promise made by one party to a contract that the other party may rely on a fact, relieving that party from the obligation of determining whether the fact is true and indemnifying the other party from liability if that fact is shown to be false.

■═■

Caceci v. Di Canio Construction Corp.

Home buyers (P) v. Builder-seller (D)

N.Y. Ct. App., 72 N.Y.2d 521, 526 N.E.2d 266 (1988).

NATURE OF CASE: Appeal from judgment for plaintiff for breach of an implied warranty with respect to latent defects.

FACT SUMMARY: The Cacecis (P) sued Di Canio Construction Corp. (D), the builder of their new home, when the floor began to crack and the slab foundation had to be replaced after several years.

🏛 RULE OF LAW
The "Housing Merchant" warranty imposes by legal implication a contractual liability on a homebuilder for skillful performance and quality of a newly constructed home.

FACTS: The Cacecis (P) contracted with Di Canio Construction Corp. (Di Canio) (D) for a parcel of land on which a one-family ranch home was to be constructed. Di Canio (D) guaranteed the plumbing, heating, and electrical work, roof and basement walls for one year from title closing. When the kitchen floor started dipping four years later, Di Canio (D) unsuccessfully attempted to repair the cracks and dips in the floor. The Cacecis (P) sued for breached duties under negligence and implied warranty theories, and the trial court awarded damages for the reasonable cost of correcting Di Canio's (D) slipshod performance. The Appellate Division affirmed solely on the implied warranty theory, holding that there was an implied term in the express contract between the builder-vendor and purchasers that the house be constructed in a skillful manner free from material defects. Di Canio (D) appealed.

ISSUE: Does the "Housing Merchant" warranty impose by legal implication a contractual liability on a homebuilder for skillful performance and quality of a newly constructed home?

HOLDING AND DECISION: (Bellacosa, J.) Yes. The "Housing Merchant" warranty imposes by legal implication a contractual liability on a homebuilder for skillful performance and quality of a newly constructed home. The doctrine that the buyer must beware (caveat emptor) may not be invoked by Di Canio (D), a builder-seller, against the Cacecis (P), the purchasers. Homes contracted for sale prior to construction involve an agreement between two parties who generally do not bargain as equals. Inspection of the premises is impossible, especially with respect to latent defects. Thus, the purchaser has no meaningful choice but to rely on the builder-vendor to deliver what was bargained for—a house reasonably fit for the purpose for which it was intended. The affirmed award of damages after a nonjury trial must be upheld. Affirmed.

▶ ANALYSIS

The court in this case described the evolution of the implied warranty of merchantability. By analogy, the home building industry has also qualified the doctrine of caveat emptor. This case provided the court with its first opportunity to address the departure from the rule of caveat emptor in such circumstances, and to recognize an implied warranty of skillful construction.

■═■

Quicknotes

CAVEAT EMPTOR Let the buyer beware; doctrine that a buyer purchases something at his own risk.

IMPLIED WARRANTY OF MERCHANTABILITY An implied promise made by a merchant in a contract for the sale of goods that such goods are suitable for the purpose for which they are purchased.

■═■

CHAPTER 7

Incapacity, Bargaining Misconduct, Unconscionability, and Public Policy

Quick Reference Rules of Law

Dodson v. Shrader

Auto purchaser (P) v. Sellers of truck (D)

Tenn. Sup. Ct., 824 S.W.2d 545 (1992).

NATURE OF CASE: Appeal from award of rescission of contract.

FACT SUMMARY: Dodson (P) bought a car when he was 16 and, after it "blew up," wanted the purchase contract rescinded and refused to pay for depreciation to the truck while it had been in his hands.

🏛 RULE OF LAW
Even if a minor's contract is rescinded, the merchant may keep an amount equal to the decrease in value of the items returned rather than refund the full purchase price.

FACTS: Dodson (P), aged 16, bought a pick-up truck from the Shraders (D) for $4,900. Although the truck developed a burnt valve nine months later, Dodson (P) drove it anyway until it "blew up." Parking the inoperable truck in his parents' yard, he contacted the Shraders (D) and demanded that his contract be rescinded and his money returned. The Shraders (D) refused. Dodson (P) filed suit requesting rescission of his contract. When the general sessions court dismissed the case, Dodson (P) appealed. While his appeal was pending, he tendered the truck again. The Shraders (D) refused to take the truck unless Dodson (P) would pay for all the depreciation which had occurred while it had been in his hands. He refused. The circuit court held a new trial and granted rescission, ordering refund of the full purchase price. The Shraders (D) appealed on the ground that they were entitled to keep an amount for depreciation.

ISSUE: After rescission of a minor's contract, may a merchant keep an amount equal to the decrease in value of the items returned rather than refund the full purchase price?

HOLDING AND DECISION: (O'Brien, J.) Yes. If a minor's contract has been rescinded, a merchant may still keep an amount equal to the decrease in value of the items returned. The rule permitting the contracts of minors to be rescinded exists to protect them from unscrupulous persons who would take advantage of their inexperience. However, a merchant who deals with a minor in good faith also should receive some protection. Therefore, if there has been no undue influence or fraud exercised on the part of the merchant, he may keep a reasonable compensation for the use and depreciation of and the willful or negligent damage to the item returned. This rule will prevent minors from taking advantage of merchants should they purchase an item, use it up, and then demand

rescission. Reversed and remanded to determine the amount of depreciation.

▌ANALYSIS

Generally, a minor's contracts are considered voidable, not void. This means the merchant cannot claim the contract is void, or, stated another way, the minor can elect to keep a contract if he so desires. Note that this rule has an exception: a minor's contracts for necessities such as food, clothing, and shelter are not voidable. Also, once the minor reaches majority, he must request rescission of an offensive contract within a reasonable amount of time, or he will be considered to have affirmed the contract as an adult. See, e.g., *Bobby Floars Toyota Inc. v. Smith*, 269 S.E.2d 320 (N.C. Ct. App. 1980) (no rescission of contract where minor kept car for 10 months after attaining majority).

■═■

Quicknotes

RESCISSION The canceling of an agreement and the return of the parties to their positions prior to the formation of the contract.

UNDUE INFLUENCE Improper influence that deprives the individual of freedom of choice or substitutes another's choice for the person's own choice.

VOIDABLE CONTRACT A valid contract which may be legally voided at the option of one of the parties.

■═■

Hauer v. Union State Bank of Wautoma

Customer (P) v. Bank (D)

Wis. Ct. App., 192 Wis. 2d 576, 532 N.W.2d 456 (1995).

NATURE OF CASE: Appeal from a judgment in favor of plaintiff voiding a bank loan.

FACT SUMMARY: Hauer (P) alleged that she was actually mentally incompetent at the time she entered into an agreement to provide collateral for a loan from Union State Bank (D), and that the Bank (D) failed to act in good faith in granting the loan.

🏛 RULE OF LAW
A contracting party exposes itself to a voidable contract where it is put on notice or given a reason to suspect the other party's incompetence such as would indicate to a reasonably prudent person that inquiry should be made of the party's mental condition.

FACTS: Hauer had suffered a brain injury in a motorcycle accident and was subsequently adjudicated to be incompetent, resulting in a guardian being appointed by the court. The next year, Hauer's (P) guardianship was terminated based upon a letter from her treating physician. Hauer (P) had a mutual fund worth approximately $80,000, which she agreed could be used as collateral for a friend's loan from the Bank (D). When the loan matured, Hauer (P) filed suit, alleging that the Bank (D) knew or should have known she lacked the mental capacity to understand the loan, and the Bank (D) had breached its duty of good faith and fair dealing, as well as its fiduciary duty to Hauer (P). The jury found that Hauer (P) was mentally incompetent at the time of the loan and that the Bank (D) failed to act in good faith in granting the loan. The loan was voided and the Bank (D) was required to return Hauer's (P) collateral. The Bank (D) appealed.

ISSUE: Does a contracting party expose itself to a voidable contract where it is put on notice or given a reason to suspect the other party's incompetence such as would indicate to a reasonably prudent person that inquiry should be made of the party's mental condition?

HOLDING AND DECISION: (Snyder, J.) Yes. A contracting party exposes itself to a voidable contract where it is put on notice or given a reason to suspect the other party's incompetence such as would indicate to a reasonably prudent person that inquiry should be made of the party's mental condition. Competency must be determined on the date the instrument was executed. Although there is evidence which the jury could have relied on to find that Hauer (P) was competent, the court must accept the inference that favors the jury's verdict when the evidence permits more than one inference. The infancy doctrine, which permits a minor to disaffirm a contract even when the minor cannot return the property, does not apply to cases of mental incompetence. However, there were red flags alerting the Bank (D) and that would have prompted a reasonable banker to move more slowly and more carefully in the transaction. The evidence and reasonable inferences that can be drawn therefrom support the jury's conclusion that the Bank (D) failed to act in good faith. Affirmed.

▶ ANALYSIS

The court in this case referred to state law which reads the duty of good faith into every contract. The unadjudicated mental incompetence of one of the parties is not a sufficient reason for setting aside an executed contract if the parties cannot be restored to their original positions, if the contract was made in good faith, for a fair consideration, and without knowledge of the incompetence. Although there was no duty to investigate, the Bank (D) took a risk here since it knew of facts supporting the claim of inability to contract.

■=■

Quicknotes

INFANCY Minority; refers to the state of not yet achieving the age of legal majority.

INFERENCE A deduction from established facts.

MENTAL INCAPACITY Lack of capacity or ability to function intellectually.

■=■

Totem Marine Tug & Barge, Inc. v. Alyeska Pipeline Service Co.

Construction materials transporter (P) v. Construction company (D)

Alaska Sup. Ct., 584 P.2d 15 (1978).

NATURE OF CASE: Appeal from denial of damages for breach of contract.

FACT SUMMARY: Totem (P) claimed that Alyeska (D) had used economic duress to get Totem (P) to sign a binding release of all claims it had against Alyeska (D) after Alyeska (D) terminated a contract with Totem (P).

🏛 RULE OF LAW
A contract can be voided if it was entered into as the result of economic duress.

FACTS: Totem (P) had contracted to transport pipeline construction materials from Houston, Texas, to a designated port in southern Alaska for Alyeska (D). According to Totem (P), Alyeska's (D) failure to proceed in accordance with the terms and specifications in the contract caused considerable delays and occasioned the hiring of a second tug to handle the extra tonnage in materials that were waiting to be loaded when Totem (P) arrived in Houston. Alyeska (D) eventually terminated the contract without reason. When Totem (P) submitted invoices and began pressing for payment, it was in a serious cash-flow crisis and faced the possibility of bankruptcy. This, it maintained, led it to accept Alyeska's (D) offer of $97,500 in cash for settlement of all claims by Totem (P). Later, Totem (P), claiming economic duress, sought to recover in a contract action. A summary judgment was granted in favor of Alyeska (D).

ISSUE: Is economic duress a ground for avoiding a contract?

HOLDING AND DECISION: (Burke, J.) Yes. Avoidance of a contract on the grounds that it was entered into as a result of economic duress is recognized by this and many other courts. According to Professor Williston, the party alleging economic duress must show that he has been the victim of a wrongful or unlawful act or threat and that such act or threat deprived him of his unfettered will. Thus, Totem (P) would have to show that wrongful acts or threats by Alyeska (D) intentionally caused Totem (P) to involuntarily enter into the settlement agreement. This would mean showing that Totem (P) had no reasonable alternative to agreeing to Alyeska's (D) settlement terms. Certainly, the facts of this case are such as would lend themselves to such proof. It is up to Totem (P) to prove its allegations, but the facts indicate that a summary judgment was improper. Reversed and remanded for trial in accordance with the legal principles set forth herein.

▶ ANALYSIS

Section 492 of the Restatement of Contracts focused on the exercise of "free will and judgment" in defining duress, while the revised Restatement looks to the victim's having "no reasonable alternative." At early common law, avoidance of a contract on the ground of duress was available only it a party could show that it was entered into for fear of loss of life or limb, mayhem, or imprisonment.

■━■

Quicknotes

DURESS Unlawful threats or other coercive behavior by one person that causes another to commit acts that he would not otherwise do.

ECONOMIC DURESS A defense to an action that a party was unlawfully coerced into the performance of an action by another due to fear of imminent economic loss and was not acting in accordance with his own free volition in performing the action.

■━■

Odorizzi v. Bloomfield School District

Teacher (P) v. School district (D)

Cal. Dist. Ct. App., 246 Cal. App. 2d 123, 54 Cal. Rptr. 533 (1966).

NATURE OF CASE: Appeal from judgment dismissing action to rescind resignation based on undue influence.

FACT SUMMARY: Odorizzi (P) was arrested on homosexual charges. Immediately after his release the School District (D) convinced him to resign.

🏛 RULE OF LAW
When a party's will has been overborne, so that in effect his actions are not his own, a charge of undue influence may be sustained.

FACTS: Odorizzi (P) was arrested for criminal homosexual activities. At the time he was under contract as a teacher for the School District (D). Immediately after he was released on bail, the School District (D) convinced him to resign. Odorizzi (P) was subsequently acquitted of the charges, but was refused reemployment by the District (D). He brought suit to rescind his resignation. He charged duress, menace, fraud, and undue influence. He claimed that the superintendent of the District (D) and the principal of his school came to his apartment immediately after his release. He had not slept in nearly 40 hours and was under severe emotional and physical stress. He was told that if he did not immediately resign the District (D) would be forced to suspend him and then dismiss him. This would occasion embarrassing and humiliating publicity. However, if he resigned, the matter would be kept quiet and his chance for future jobs would not be impaired. The trial court found nothing wrong with these actions, no confidential relationship existed, and the District (D) would have been forced by law to suspend Odorizzi (P).

ISSUE: When a party's will has been overborne, so that in effect his actions are not his own, may a charge of undue influence be sustained?

HOLDING AND DECISION: (Fleming, J.) Yes. When a party's will has been overborne, so that in effect his actions are not his own, a charge of undue influence may be sustained. While none of Odorizzi's (P) allegations has any basis, he has made out a prima facie case of undue influence. In essence the charge involves the use of excessive pressures to persuade one vulnerable to such pressures to decide a matter contra to one's own judgment. Extreme weakness or susceptibility is an important factor in establishing undue influence. It is normally found in cases of extreme youth or age or sickness. While it normally involves fiduciary or other confidential relationships, they are not necessary to the action. Here, extreme pressures were leveled against Odorizzi (P). He had just gone through an arrest, booking, and interrogation procedure for a crime which, if well publicized, would subject him to public humiliation. He was threatened with such publicity if he did not immediately resign. He was approached at his apartment immediately after his release. He was not given the opportunity to think the matter over or to consult outside advice. He was told that in any event he would be suspended and dismissed. These factors present a jury issue. If Odorizzi (P) can establish that he wouldn't have resigned but for these pressures and the jury finds that they were unreasonable and overbore his will, Odorizzi (P) could rescind his resignation. Judgment reversed for a new trial.

▶ ANALYSIS

Many types of contracts may be rescinded for undue influence. Mortmaine statutes are in effect in some states. These hold that bequests made to churches shortly before death and after a visit by religious leaders are void and unenforceable. Wills may be declared invalid where they were procured through undue influence. Contracts to sell land for far less than its value and transfers made in fear of civil or criminal prosecution are other examples.

■━■

Quicknotes

BEQUEST A transfer of property that is accomplished by means of a testamentary instrument.

RESCISSION The canceling of an agreement and the return of the parties to their positions prior to the formation of the contract.

UNDUE INFLUENCE Improper influence that deprives the individual freedom of choice or substitutes another's choice for the person's own choice.

■━■

Syester v. Banta

Dance lesson purchaser (P) v. Dance studio owner (D)

Iowa Sup. Ct., 257 Iowa 613, 133 N.W.2d 666 (1965).

NATURE OF CASE: Action in damages for fraud and misrepresentation.

FACT SUMMARY: Syester (P) signed up for 4,057 hours of dancing lessons at a price of $29,174.

🏛 RULE OF LAW
Equity may, if fair to do so, relieve a party from the consequences of a release executed through a mistaken belief of fact and law.

FACTS: Syester (P) was talked into signing up for 4,057 hours of dancing lessons at a price of $29,174. Syester (P), an incredibly gullible 68-year-old widow, was continually flattered and cajoled into signing up for more and more lessons through a planned campaign of the school's staff. Syester (P) finally learned the truth about the operation and brought suit against the studio's owner Banta (D) to recover the payments. Various tricks and other devices were used to persuade Syester (P) to drop the suit and to get her to distrust her attorney. Syester (P) executed a full release for $6,090, apparently without consulting her attorney. The suit was dropped. A second release with an unsigned note for $4,000 was executed subsequently. No payments were ever made on it. Syester (P) then brought suit alleging fraud and misrepresentation in the sale of lessons and in the obtaining of the two releases.

ISSUE: Will equity relieve a party from the consequences of a release executed through a mistaken belief of fact and law?

HOLDING AND DECISION: (Snell, J.) Yes. Where the other party's conduct has been egregious, equity may relieve a party of the consequences of a release signed under a mistaken belief of law and facts. There was sufficient evidence from which a jury could find overreaching influence, unconscionability, misrepresentation, and fraud throughout the course of dealings between Banta (D) and Syester (P). Under such circumstances a jury may relieve a party of unread or misunderstood contracts or releases. The original release for $6,090 was wholly inadequate and the second one was unenforceable since it was never signed by Banta (D). The judgment for Syester (P) is affirmed.

▌ ANALYSIS

Syester is a very modern approach to equitable relief from mistakes. Most courts have, in the past, held that, absent fraud, a party will not be relieved from the consequences of a unilateral mistake. In *Syester* it was unnecessary for the court to reach the ultimate question of fraud, but it probably would have found that it was present under the unique set of facts herein.

■═▪

Quicknotes

FRAUD A false representation of facts with the intent that another will rely on the misrepresentation to his detriment.

MISTAKE OF FACT An unintentional mistake in knowing or recalling a fact without the will to deceive.

MISTAKE OF LAW An error involving a misunderstanding or incorrect application of law.

■═▪

Hill v. Jones

Home purchaser (P) v. Seller (D)

Ariz. Ct. App., 151 Ariz. 81, 725 P.2d 1115, *review denied* (1986).

NATURE OF CASE: Appeal from summary dismissal of action for rescission of real estate purchase contract.

FACT SUMMARY: Before buying Jones's (D) home, Hill (P) asked whether it had been infested with termites, and Jones (D) denied that there had been previous infestations, despite firsthand knowledge of them.

🏛 RULE OF LAW
Where the seller of a home knows of facts materially affecting the value of the property which are not readily observable and are not known to the buyer, the seller is under a duty to disclose them.

FACTS: During escrow for the purchase of Jones's (D) home, Hill (P) expressed concern about a "ripple" in a parquet floor. Jones (D) claimed that the problem was due to flooding from a broken water heater, when in fact it demonstrated a termite infestation. Hill (P) asked that a termite inspection report be placed in escrow. An exterminator inspected Jones's (D) home but failed to find instances of prior infestation due to strategic placement of boxes and plants. When the results of the termite report were revealed to Hill (P) by his realtor, Hill (P) closed escrow with Jones (D). After moving in, Hill (P) found termites and discovered that the previous seller of the home had paid for termite guarantees and semiannual inspections when he sold the house to Jones (D). Despite previous infestations which had been treated during Jones's (D) ownership and occupancy of the house, Jones (D) had said nothing about termites to either Hill (P) or the exterminator. Hill (P) sued to rescind the purchase contract on grounds of intentional nondisclosure of the termite damage. The trial court dismissed the action on summary judgment for failure to state a claim, and Hill (P) appealed.

ISSUE: Where the seller of a home knows of facts materially affecting the value of the property which are not readily observable and are not known to the buyer, is the seller under a duty to disclose them?

HOLDING AND DECISION: (Meyerson, J.) Yes. Where the seller of a home knows of facts materially affecting the value of the property which are not readily observable and are not known to the buyer, the seller is under a duty to disclose them to the buyer. Such a disclosure is necessary to correct mistakes of the purchaser as to a basic assumption on which he is making the contract and to protect him from misplaced trust in the vendor. The existence of termite damage in a residential dwelling is the type of material fact which gives rise to the duty to disclose because it is a matter to which a reasonable person would attach importance in deciding whether or not to purchase such a dwelling. Here, Jones (D) failed to reveal the home's prior history of termite infestation, despite knowledge of such infestation and previous attempts to treat it. Allegations to this effect raise triable issues of material fact which must be determined by the trier of fact. Whether Hill (P) was put on reasonable notice of the termite problem despite Jones's (D) nondisclosure or whether he exercised reasonable diligence in informing himself about the termite problem should also be left to the trier of fact. Reversed and remanded.

▶ ANALYSIS

This case is somewhat exceptional in that the court recognized a duty of disclosure between parties in an ordinary arm's-length, commercial transaction. More typically, courts will recognize a "duty to speak up" only in the presence of a confidential or fiduciary relationship. See, for example, *Vai v. Bank of America Trust & Savings Association*, 15 Cal. Rptr. 71, 364 P.2d 247 (1961) (community property settlement set aside on grounds that husband had failed to disclose value of property involved to his wife). Beyond the existence of a confidential or fiduciary relationship, courts traditionally have imposed a duty of disclosure between businessmen only when necessary to correct a previous misstatement or mistaken impression.

▬▭▬

Quicknotes

DUTY TO DISCLOSE The duty owed by a fiduciary to reveal those facts that have a material effect on the interests of the party that must be informed.

MATERIAL FACT A fact without the existence of which a contract would not have been entered.

MISREPRESENTATION A statement or conduct by one party to another that constitutes a false representation of fact.

▬▭▬

Park 100 Investors, Inc. v. Kartes

Lessor (P) v. Lessee (D)

Ind. Ct. App., 650 N.E.2d 347 (1995).

NATURE OF CASE: Appeal from judgment for defendant in an action to collect under a personal guarantee provision in a lease.

FACT SUMMARY: Park 100 (P) sought to collect unpaid rent from the Karteses (D) under a provision of the lease which was induced through fraudulent means.

🏛 RULE OF LAW
A contract of guaranty cannot be enforced by the guarantee, where the guarantor has been induced to enter into the contract by fraudulent misrepresentations or concealment on the part of the guarantee.

FACTS: The Karteses (D) negotiated with Park 100 (P) to lease space for their growing business in 1984. A lease agreement was signed which did not include any provisions for a personal guaranty of the lease and a personal guaranty was never mentioned. A representative of Park 100 (P) later had the Karteses (D) also sign a "lease agreement," but did not tell them that what they were signing was actually a personal guaranty of lease. The Karteses (D) called their attorney, who confirmed that he had examined and approved the lease agreement, and then signed. When the Karteses (D) later found out about the personal guaranty, they immediately disavowed the guaranty and refused to affirm that part of the tenant agreement. Park 100 (P) later brought suit to collect the unpaid rent from the Karteses (D) under the personal guaranty. The trial court found that Park 100 (P) obtained the signatures of the Karteses (D) on the personal guaranty of lease through fraudulent means, that the Karteses (D) had acted with ordinary care and diligence, and that they were not liable for any unpaid rent. Park 100 (P) appealed.

ISSUE: Can a contract of guaranty be enforced by the guarantee, where the guarantor has been induced to enter into the contract by fraudulent misrepresentations or concealment on the part of the guarantee?

HOLDING AND DECISION: (Barteau, J.) No. A contract of guaranty cannot be enforced by the guarantee, where the guarantor has been induced to enter into the contract by fraudulent misrepresentations or concealment on the part of the guarantee. Where one employs misrepresentation to induce a party's obligation under a contract, one cannot bind the party to the terms of the agreement. Whether fraud is present in a case is rooted in the surrounding facts and circumstances and is for the trial court to determine. The evidence supports the trial court's

conclusion here; the findings support the judgment and are not clearly erroneous. Affirmed.

▶ ANALYSIS

The court in this case found that Park 100 (P) used fraudulent means to procure the Karteses' (D) signature. The elements of fraud are: a material misrepresentation of past or existing fact by the party to be charged, which was false, was made with knowledge or in reckless ignorance of the falsity, was relied upon by the complaining party, and proximately caused the complaining party injury. Park 100 (P) claimed that the third element of reliance was not proven, but the court found that the Karteses (D) had exercised ordinary care and diligence because they acted with reasonable prudence in calling their attorney before signing.

Quicknotes

FRAUD A false representation of facts with the intent that another will rely on the misrepresentation to his detriment.

GUARANTOR A party who agrees to be liable for the debt or default of another.

Williams v. Walker-Thomas Furniture Co.

Furniture buyer (D) v. Furniture company (P)

350 F.2d 445 (D.C. Cir. 1965).

NATURE OF CASE: Appeal from affirmance of judgment for furniture company in its suit to replevy goods for breach of contract.

FACT SUMMARY: Walker-Thomas (P) sold to Williams (D) furniture burdened by a cross-collateral clause and, subsequent to Williams's (D) default, sought to replevy all goods previously purchased by Williams (D).

🏛 RULE OF LAW
The courts have the power to refuse enforcement of contracts found to be unconscionable.

FACTS: Walker-Thomas (P) sold furniture to Williams (D) under a printed form contract containing a cross-collateral clause the effect of which was to keep a balance due on every item purchased until the balance due on all items, whenever purchased, was liquidated. As a result, Walker-Thomas (P) retained—by the terms of the contract—the right to repossess all items previously purchased in the event of any default. At the time Williams (D) made her last purchase, she had a balance of $164 still owing from her prior purchases, although she had already paid $1,400 toward clearing her account. Subsequently, Williams (D) defaulted on payment and now Walker-Thomas (P) sought to replevy all goods previously sold to Williams (D). The trial court held for Walker-Thomas (P) and an intermediate appellate court affirmed. Because the case was in the District of Columbia, the federal district court granted review.

ISSUE: Do the courts have the power to refuse enforcement of contracts found to be unconscionable?

HOLDING AND DECISION: (Wright, J.) Yes. The courts have the power to refuse enforcement of contracts found to be unconscionable. "Where the element of unconscionability is present at the time a contract is made, the contract should not be enforced. Unconscionability has generally been recognized to include an absence of meaningful choice on the part of one of the parties together with contract terms which are unreasonably favorable to the other party." Meaningfulness of choice is to be determined in light of all the circumstances—for example, gross disparity of bargaining power. Remanded to determine whether the contract was unconscionable.

DISSENT: (Danaher, J.) The judicial approach to issues raised by this case should be a cautious one that gives parties great leeway in making their own contracts. Any remedy to protect the public from exploitive contracts more appropriately resides with the legislature (in this case, Congress) since numerous public policy issues are implicated. Otherwise, the risk of decisions like the one handed down by the majority is that they will undo otherwise legitimate, nonexploitive installment credit contracts into which the parties thereto have knowingly entered.

▶ ANALYSIS

The majority opinion, written by Wright, relies heavily on U.C.C. § 2-302 to suppose its position. But the meaning and effect of § 2-302 has been hotly debated. Comment 1 to that provision defines "unconscionable ability" in terms of itself and says its principle is to prevent "oppression and unfair surprise," not to disturb the "allocation of risks because of superior bargaining power." Note that any court which declares a contract "substantively" unconscionable is dealing in the dangerous and tenuous business of substituting its own valuation of contract goods for that of the parties involved. This kind of paternalism should be approached with caution.

■=■

Quicknotes

UNCONSCIONABILITY Rule of law whereby a court may excuse performance of a contract, or of a particular contract term, if it determines that such term(s) are unduly oppressive or unfair to one party to the contract.

U.C.C. § 2-302 Provides that courts exercise their discretion to limit specific contract provisions that have unconscionable results.

■=■

Higgins v. Superior Court of Los Angeles County

Television show participant (P) v. Trial court (D)

Cal. Ct. App., 140 Cal. App. 4th 1238; 45 Cal. Rptr. 3d 293 (2006).

NATURE OF CASE: Petition for writ of mandate challenging a trial court's ruling.

FACT SUMMARY: The Higginses (P) contended that arbitration provisions of a written agreement and release compelling arbitration of claims arising from the production and broadcast of a television program were unconscionable.

🏛 RULE OF LAW
An arbitration clause in a written agreement may not be enforced if only the clause, as opposed to the entire agreement, is being challenged and the clause is unconscionable.

FACTS: Five siblings (the "Higginses") (P), ranging in age from 14 to 21, whose parents were deceased, were living with the Leomitis. The Higginses (P) and the Leomitis were approached by the producers of the television program *Extreme Makeover: Home Edition (Extreme Makeover)* about making a show based on the loss of the Higginses' (P) parents and that they were now living with the Leomitis. Eventually, the Higginses (P) and the Leomitis were chosen to participate in the program in which the Leomitis' home would be completely renovated. The producers sent to the Higginses (P) and the Leomitis a contract that contained 24 single-spaced pages and 72 numbered paragraphs. Attached to it were several pages of exhibits, including an authorization for release of medical information, an emergency medical release, and, as exhibit C, a one-page document entitled "Release." The first page of the agreement warned potential signors not to sign unless they had read the agreement. Close to the end of the agreement, a paragraph stated that the signor had read the agreement and reviewed it with legal counsel or voluntarily declined such an opportunity. None of the last 12 numbered paragraphs contained a heading or title. Among these was paragraph 69, which required that all disputes or controversies arising under the agreement would be resolved by binding arbitration. There was nothing in the agreement that brought the reader's attention to this paragraph. The one-page release also contained a similar arbitration provision. No discussion took place between the Higginses (P) and the television producers or anyone else affiliated with the show, and the Higginses (P) did not participate in a meeting at the Leomitis' home where the agreement was presented. After this meeting, the Leomitis emerged with a packet of documents, which they handed to the Higginses (P), and Mrs. Leomiti instructed them to "flip through the pages and sign and initial the document where it contained a signature line or box," which they did without fully

understanding what they were signing. Afterward, a representative from the show began to reconstruct the Leomitis' home, and the program featuring the Higginses (P) and the Leomitis was broadcast. After the show was broadcast, the Leomitis forced the Higginses (P) to leave. The Higginses (P) informed the producers of what had happened and requested help, but none was forthcoming. The show was rebroadcast. The Higginses (P) brought suit against various parties associated with the show (the "television defendants") (D), and also against the Leomitis. One of the claims was breach of contract. The television defendants (D) petitioned to compel arbitration. The Higginses (P) opposed on the ground that the arbitration provision was unconscionable. The trial court granted the petition, and the Higginses (P) filed a petition for writ of mandate challenging the trial court's ruling. The state's intermediate court of appeals granted review.

ISSUE: May an arbitration clause in a written agreement be enforced if only the clause, as opposed to the entire agreement, is being challenged and the clause is unconscionable?

HOLDING AND DECISION: (Rubin, J.) No. An arbitration clause in a written agreement may not be enforced if only the clause, as opposed to the entire agreement, is being challenged and the clause is unconscionable. Although the Federal Arbitration Act (FAA) governs the enforceability of arbitration clauses in contracts involving interstate commerce, state law treats arbitration agreements just like any other contracts. If an arbitration agreement is unconscionable, it will not be enforced. A starting point of analyzing whether a contract is unconscionable is to determine whether it is a contract of adhesion—a standardized contract that is imposed and drafted by the party of superior bargaining strength and relegates to the other party "only the opportunity to adhere to the contract or reject it." If the contract is one of adhesion, the next step is to determine whether it is unconscionable. Unconscionability has both a procedural and a substantive element. The procedural element focuses on "oppression" or "surprise" due to unequal bargaining power. The substantive element focuses on "overly harsh" or "one-sided" results. Both elements must be present, but not necessarily in the same degree, for a court to refuse enforcement of the contract. The FAA does not permit a court to entertain a claim that an arbitration provision is unenforceable if the claim is in reality a subterfuge for challenging the entire agreement. Thus, here, it must first be determined whether the

Continued on next page.

Higginses (P) are challenging just the arbitration provisions or the agreement and release in toto, and if it is found that they are truly just challenging only the arbitration provisions, then it must be determined whether those provisions are unconscionable. Here, the Hinginses' (P) opposition to arbitration was that the arbitration clause in particular, not the entire agreement or release, was unconscionable, and devoted considerable attention to paragraph 69. The clause was not set out or made distinguishable in any manner and was not identified with a caption other than being one of several paragraphs grouped together in a section titled "miscellaneous." This addresses procedural unconscionability. As to substantive unconscionability, the Higginses (P) argued that the provision was one-sided, only requiring the Higginses (P) to submit to arbitration, not the television defendants (D). Also rejected is the trial court's reasoning that arbitration should be compelled because the Higginses (P) had a chance to read the contract before signing it. There is no rule that if a party reads an agreement he or she is barred from claiming it is unconscionable. Because only the arbitration clauses were being challenged, and not the agreement and release in toto, the next question is whether those clauses were unconscionable. First, the agreement here was adhesive. It was a standardized contract drafted by the television defendants (D), who had more bargaining power than the Higginses (P). Finally, based on the fact that the Higginses (P) were not present at the meeting between the Leomitis and the television defendants (D), and that the documents had to be signed as a condition to their participation in the program, the agreement was presented to the Higginses (P) on a take-it-or-leave-it basis by the party with the superior bargaining position who was not willing to engage in negotiations. Second, the arbitration provisions in the agreement and release were procedurally unconscionable. This conclusion is supported by the fact that the arbitration clause appeared in one paragraph near the end of a lengthy, single-spaced document; that the Higginses (P) were known to the television defendants (D) to be young and unsophisticated and had recently lost their parents; the clause was neither highlighted in any way nor set off by bold letters, large fonts, capitalization, or any other textual means; and no box appeared next to the arbitration clause for the Higginses (P) to initial, unlike some of the other paragraphs. Although the top of the first page advised the reader to read the entire agreement before signing it and the second-to-last paragraph stated that the person signing acknowledged doing so, this language does not defeat the otherwise strong showing of procedural unconscionability. Third, the arbitration provisions were substantively unconscionable because the provision was one-sided, requiring only the Higginses (P) to submit their claims to arbitration, but not requiring the same of the television defendants (D). Under the agreement, the television defendants (D) could compel arbitration without fearing that doing so would preclude them from seeking injunctive or other equitable relief in court. Also, only the Higginses (P) were precluded

from seeking appellate review of the arbitrator's decision or of a provision requiring arbitration in accordance with the rules of the American Arbitration Association, which provide that arbitration costs are to be borne equally by the parties. For these reasons, the arbitration provisions were unconscionable and, therefore, unenforceable. The petition for writ of mandate is granted.

▶ *ANALYSIS*

A number of decisions have held that the fact that a contract is adhesive is enough of itself to render a contract procedurally unconscionable. Other decisions, however, have held that something more must be shown before an adhesion contract can be found to be procedurally unconscionable. Such a showing could be that there was a lack of market alternatives.

Quicknotes

ARBITRATION AGREEMENT A mutual understanding entered into by parties wishing to submit to the decision making authority of a neutral third party, selected by the parties and charged with rendering a decision.

UNCONSCIONABILITY Rule of law whereby a court may excuse performance of a contract, or of a particular contract term, if it determines that such terms are unduly oppressive or unfair to one party to the contract as a result of disparity in bargaining power during the formation of the contract.

WRIT OF MANDATE The written order of a court directing a particular action.

In re Checking Account Overdraft Litigation

[Parties not identified.]

694 F. Supp. 2d 1302 (S.D. Fla. 2010).

NATURE OF CASE: Motion for dismissal or judgment on the pleadings in multi-district litigation with claims for breach of contract and of the covenant of good faith, unconscionability, conversion, unjust enrichment, and violation of consumer protection laws.

FACT SUMMARY: Checking account customers (P) contended that federally chartered banks (Banks) (D) charged excessive overdraft fees for charges to their accounts on debit card transactions, primarily by entering charges debiting the customers' (P) accounts from the "largest to the smallest," thus maximizing the overdraft fee revenue for the Banks (D). The Banks (D) moved to dismiss on several grounds, including federal preemption; the customers' (P) contracts with the Banks (D) permitted the Banks' (D) conduct; and that unconscionability may be asserted only as a defense, not as an affirmative claim for injury.

RULE OF LAW

(1) State law claims against federally chartered banks are not federally preempted where the claims are not regulatory in nature and only incidentally affect the exercise of the banks' deposit taking powers.

(2) A claim for breach of the covenant of good faith and fair dealing can be maintained where the claim does not seek to alter the express terms of a contract but instead seeks to have the express terms carried out in good faith, and where the question of whether the terms are being carried out in good faith is one of fact.

(3) A court in the exercise of its equitable powers may entertain an affirmative claim of unconscionability of contract and fashion a remedy for such a claim.

(4) An affirmative claim of unconscionability will not be dismissed where plaintiffs have sufficiently pled that a contract is both procedurally and substantively unconscionable.

FACTS: Checking account customers (P) of federally chartered banks (Banks) (D) from different states brought similar actions against individual Banks (D) alleging that the Banks (D) charged excessive overdraft fees for charges to their accounts on debit card transactions, primarily by entering charges debiting the customers' (P) accounts from the "largest to the smallest," thus maximizing the overdraft fee revenue for the Banks (D). The litigation was consolidated in federal district court as multi-district litigation. The customers (P) alleged that the Banks (D) provided

them with debit cards for using funds from their accounts by engaging in "debit" or "point of sale" (POS) transactions, or by withdrawing money from their accounts at automated teller machines (ATMs). Regardless of whether a debit card is used to execute POS transactions or to withdraw cash from ATM machines, the transaction is processed electronically, and the Banks (D) are notified instantaneously when the card is physically passed (swiped) through a receiving machine. When a customer (P) swipes a debit card, the bank is able to determine immediately whether there are sufficient funds in the customer's (P) account to cover the attempted POS or ATM transaction. The Banks (D) have the option to accept or decline the transaction at that time, and they have the technological capability to decline debit card transactions (which they do if a pending transaction would exceed a predetermined overdraft limit for an account), or to notify customers (P) that the particular transaction will result in an overdraft. Rather than routinely declining debit card transactions or warning their customers (P) that completing the transaction would result in an overdraft fee, the Banks (D) allegedly adopted and implemented automatic, fee-based overdraft programs, processing debit card transactions and then charging their customers (P) overdraft fees. The customers (P) also alleged that the Banks (D) did not give them the option to decline to complete the debit transactions or provide other forms of payment. In addition, the Banks (D) failed to adequately disclose to their customers (P) that they could opt out of this overdraft policy, thereby avoiding all overdrafts and overdraft fees. The customers (P) further alleged that the Banks (D) used advanced software to automate their overdraft systems to maximize the number of overdrafts and, thus, the amount of overdraft fees charged per customer (P). The most common way this was done was by reordering debit transactions on a single day, or over multiple days, from largest to smallest amount, regardless of the actual chronological sequence in which the customer (P) engaged in these transactions. Almost without exception, reordering debit transactions from highest to lowest results in more overdrafts than if the transactions were processed chronologically. The customers (P) alleged that by holding charges rather than posting them immediately, the Banks (D) were able to amass a number of charges on an account, and also prevented customers (P) from determining accurate account balances. The customers (P) further charged that even when the Banks (D) had knowledge of outstanding transactions that already created a negative balance in

Continued on next page.

a customer's (P) account, they approved, rather than de-clined, subsequent debit card purchases and other electronic transactions. Further, the Banks (P) allegedly assessed overdraft fees at times when the actual funds in customer (P) accounts were sufficient to cover all debits that had been submitted for payment, by placing a "hold" on actual funds in customer (P) accounts. The customers (P) asserted that they were injured by these practices by having to pay excessive overdraft fees that deprived them of funds and caused significant and ascertainable monetary losses and damages to them. The customers (P) asserted state law claims for breach of contract and breach of the covenant of good faith and fair dealing, unconscionability, conversion, unjust enrichment, and for violations of vari-ous states' consumer protection statutes. The Banks (D) moved for dismissal or judgment on the pleadings on several grounds, including federal preemption; the custo-mers' (P) contracts with the Banks (D) permitted the Banks' (D) conduct; and that unconscionability may be asserted only as a defense, not as an affirmative claim for injury. The district court considered the motion.

ISSUE:

(1) Are state law claims against federally chartered banks federally preempted where the claims are not regulatory in nature and only incidentally affect the exercise of the banks' deposit taking powers?

(2) Can a claim for breach of the covenant of good faith and fair dealing be maintained where the claim does not seek to alter the express terms of a contract but instead seeks to have the express terms carried out in good faith, and where the question of whether the terms are being carried out in good faith is one of fact?

(3) May a court in the exercise of its equitable powers en-tertain an affirmative claim of unconscionability of contract and fashion a remedy for such a claim?

(4) Will an affirmative claim of unconscionability be dis-missed where plaintiffs have sufficiently pled that a contract is both procedurally and substantively unconscionable?

HOLDING AND DECISION: (King, J.)

(1) No. State law claims against federally chartered banks are not federally preempted where the claims are not regulatory in nature and only incidentally affect the exercise of the banks' deposit taking powers. The Banks (D) assert that the activities of national banks in conducting the "business of banking" are subject to exclusive federal regulation and any state law which attempts to regulate, limit, or condemn such activities is preempted. The customers (P) respond that they are not trying to prevent banks from engaging in the business of banking, they are merely asking the banks to do so in good faith. Specifically, the customers (P) claim they are not challenging the Bank's (D) right to charge overdraft fees, but are challenging the Banks' (D) practice of manipulating the overdraft fees to max-imize a benefit to them and to the great detriment of

their customers (P)—a practice that is not federally authorized—so that their claims are not preempted by federal law. At this point, the only inquiry is whether the state law claims, as alleged, more than incidentally affect the exercise of the banks' deposit taking power. It is clear that the claims do not, and, therefore, they are not preempted. The motion to dismiss on this ground is denied.

(2) Yes. A claim for breach of the covenant of good faith and fair dealing can be maintained where the claim does not seek to alter the express terms of a contract but instead seeks to have the express terms carried out in good faith, and where the question of whether the terms are being carried out in good faith is one of fact. The Banks (D) argue that the implied covenant of good faith and fair dealing cannot be used to vary express terms of a contract, such as those permitting the Banks (D) to order transactions in a manner of their choosing. The customers (P) counter, correctly, that they are not seeking to vary the language of the contract, but rather to have the express contractual terms carried out in good faith. They are not seeking to tell the Banks (D) how to order transactions, but simply that the ordering must be carried out as contemplated by the covenant of good faith and fair dealing. When one party is given discretion to act under a contract, such as the Banks (D) here, such discretion must be exercised in good faith. The Banks (D) also argue that that the practice of posting high-to-low is permitted by the Uniform Commercial Code (U.C.C.), which permits banks to post high-to-low with respect to checks, so that as a matter of law, their posting high-to-low with respect to debit cards must have been done in good faith. The customers (P) respond that decisions involving paper check transactions are inapposite, and they argue that there is a fundamental difference between check and electronic transactions, so that the U.C.C.'s endorsement of high-to-low posting for checks should not be extended to cover debit card transactions. At this point in the proceedings, however, the question of whether the Banks (D) are acting in good faith is a question of fact that should be deferred until discovery is taken and the facts before the court are further de-veloped. It is not appropriate to resolve this issue on a motion to dismiss. For these reasons, the Banks' (D) motion to dismiss the breach of contract claims is denied.

(3) Yes. A court in the exercise of its equitable powers may entertain an affirmative claim of unconscionability of contract and fashion a remedy for such a claim. The Banks (D) argue, correctly, that generally, unconscion-ability may be asserted only as a defense to enforce-ment of a contract. The customers (P) respond by asserting that a court can utilize its equitable powers

Continued on next page.

to issue a declaratory decree that contractual terms and practices are unconscionable. They further assert that, if the court finds the terms or practices to be unconscionable, the court has the power to award damages for the past enforcement of the terms. The customers (P) have the more persuasive argument. Here, if the overdraft fee provisions are found to be unconscionable, the court retains the authority and discretion to fashion appropriate equitable relief. Moreover, a declaration of unconscionability may affect the legal status of the contractual terms that the Banks (D) seek to enforce, which may, in turn, affect the analysis of the other causes of action brought by the customers (P). Finally, although it is true that ordinarily unconscionability is properly asserted as a defense to a contract rather than an affirmative cause of action, the particular circumstances of this case permit application of unconscionability affirmatively to avoid injustice. For these reasons, the motion to dismiss on these grounds is denied.

(4) No. An affirmative claim of unconscionability will not be dismissed where plaintiffs have sufficiently pled that a contract is both procedurally and substantively unconscionable. The Banks (D) claim the contract and their actions were not unconscionable. Unconscionability has two aspects: procedural and substantive. Procedural unconscionability relates to the manner in which a contract is made and involves consideration of issues such as the bargaining power of the parties and their ability to know and understand the disputed contract terms. Substantive unconscionability determines whether the contract terms are so outrageously unfair as to shock the judicial conscience. As to procedural unconscionability, here there was tremendous disparity in sophistication and bargaining power between the customers (P) and the Banks (D), and the contracts were contracts of adhesion, presented on a take-it-or-leave-it basis. The terms were contained in voluminous boilerplate language, and the customers (P) were not notified they had the option to decline the overdraft protection service. Thus, the customers (P) have sufficiently alleged procedural unconscionability. As to substantive unconscionability, no reasonable person would have agreed to allow the Banks (P) to post debits in a manner designed solely to maximize the number of overdraft fees, and the amount of overdraft fees was unconscionably excessive because the fees were not reasonably related to the costs or risks associated with providing overdraft protection. Moreover, the Banks' (D) reliance on the U.C.C. provisions permitting high-to-low posting for checks does not defeat a claim of unconscionability, because, as previously discussed, those provisions do not apply to debit card transactions. Thus, the customers (P) have also sufficiently alleged substantive unconscionability. For these reasons, the motion to dismiss is denied.

▌ *ANALYSIS*

To be clear, regarding the court's conclusions regarding unconscionability, the court in this case did not conclude that the challenged terms and practices were unconscionable, but merely found that the customers (P) had alleged sufficient facts to proceed with this claim. The doctrine of "unconscionability" is codified in U.C.C. § 2-302. Although this section applies strictly only to contracts for the sale of goods, its formulation of the unconscionability standard has been incorporated in the Restatement (Second) § 208 and has been regularly applied to all types of contracts. As this case illustrates, the doctrine has been used mostly defensively, and, on occasion, affirmatively, to avoid contracts or contract terms that represent grossly unfair bargains.

■═■

Quicknotes

BOILERPLATE Standard language commonly appearing in documents having a definite meaning in the same context without variation.

BREACH OF CONTRACT Unlawful failure by a party to perform its obligations pursuant to contract.

CONVERSION The act of depriving an owner of his property without permission or justification.

FAIR DEALING An implied warranty that the parties will deal honestly in the satisfaction of their obligations and without an intent to defraud.

GOOD FAITH An honest intention to abstain from taking advantage of another.

JUDGMENT ON THE PLEADINGS Motion for judgment after the pleadings are closed.

MOTION TO DISMISS Motion to terminate an action based on the adequacy of the pleadings, improper service or venue, etc.

REMEDY Compensation for violation of a right or for injuries sustained.

UNCONSCIONABILITY A situation in which a contract, or a particular contract term, is unenforceable if the court determines that such terms are unduly oppressive or unfair to one party to the contract.

UNJUST ENRICHMENT Principle that one should not be unjustly enriched at the expense of another.

■═■

Valley Medical Specialists v. Farber

Medical practice (P) v. Employee (D)

Ariz. Sup. Ct., 194 Ariz. 363, 982 P.2d 1277 (1999).

NATURE OF CASE: Appeal by a medical practice from an adverse judgment in suit to enforce a restrictive covenant in its shareholder/employment agreement with a physician.

FACT SUMMARY: In 1985, Dr. Steven Farber (D), an internist and pulmonologist, joined Valley Medical Specialists (P). A few years later, Dr. Farber (D) became a shareholder and a minority officer and director, and entered into stock and employment agreements, which included restrictive covenants, with Valley Medical. In 1994, Dr. Farber (D) left Valley Medical Specialists (VMS) and began practicing in the area defined by the restricted covenant. VMS brought suit to enforce the restrictive covenant.

🏛 RULE OF LAW

In light of the public policy interest involved in restrictive covenants not to compete between physicians, each agreement will be strictly construed for reasonableness.

FACTS: In 1985, Valley Medical Specialists (VMS) (P), a professional corporation, hired Steven Farber, D.O. (D), an internist and pulmonologist who, among other things, treated AIDS and HIV-positive patients and performed brachytherapy, a procedure that radiates the inside of the lung in lung cancer patients. Brachytherapy can only be performed at certain hospitals that have the necessary equipment. A few years after joining VMS (P), Dr. Farber (D) became a shareholder and subsequently a minority officer and director. Subsequently, the three directors, including Dr. Farber (D), entered into new stock and employment agreements. The employment agreement contained a restrictive covenant, the scope of which was amended over time. In 1994, Dr. Farber (D) left VMS (P) and began practicing within the area defined by the restrictive covenant. VMS (P) filed a complaint against Dr. Farber (D) seeking, inter alia, to enjoin him from violating the restrictive covenant. The trial court denied the injunction, finding that the restrictive covenant violated public policy or, alternatively, was unenforceable because it was too broad. Specifically, the trial court found that: any covenant over six months would be unreasonable; the five-mile radius from each of the three VMS (P) offices was unreasonable because it covered a total of 235 square miles; and the restriction was unreasonable because it did not provide an exception for emergency medical aid and was not limited to pulmonology. The intermediate appellate court reversed. Dr. Farber (D) appealed.

ISSUE: In light of the public policy interest involved in restrictive covenants not to compete between physicians, will each agreement be strictly construed for reasonableness?

HOLDING AND DECISION: (Feldman, J.) Yes. In light of the public policy interest involved in restrictive covenants not to compete between physicians, each agreement will be strictly construed for reasonableness. A covenant not to compete is invalid unless it protects some legitimate interest beyond the employer's desire to protect itself from competition. Despite the freedom to contract, the law does not favor restrictive covenants, and this disfavor is particularly strong concerning such covenants among physicians because the practice of medicine affects the public to a much greater extent. Each case in which a restrictive covenant is challenged must be decided on its own unique facts. Here, the restrictive covenant in VMS's (P) shareholder/employment agreement with Dr. Farber (D), prohibiting him from providing any and all forms of "medical care," including pulmonology, emergency medicine, brachytherapy treatment, and HIV-positive and AIDS patient care, for three years within a five mile radius of any office maintained or utilized by VMS (P) was unreasonable and unenforceable since VMS's (P) protectable interests were minimal compared to patients' rights to see the doctor of their choice, which was entitled to a substantial protection. Courts will sometimes "blue pencil" restrictive covenants, eliminating grammatically severable, unreasonable provisions. Here, the lower appellate court's modifications to the instant restrictive covenant in VMS's (P) shareholder/employment agreement with Dr. Farber (D) went further than cutting grammatically severable portions, but essentially and impermissibly rewrote the agreement in an attempt to make it enforceable; the lower appellate court determined that the covenant, which contained a severability clause, could be modified to allow the physician to provide emergency services within the restricted area, and allowed VMS (P) to stipulate that the physician could perform brachytherapy and treat AIDS and HIV patients. However, where the severability of an agreement is not evident from the contract itself, the court cannot create a new agreement for the parties to uphold the contract. Reversed in favor of Dr. Farber (D) and remanded.

Continued on next page.

▶ *ANALYSIS*

In the *Valley Medical* decision, the court noted that although stopping short of banning restrictive covenants
between physicians, the American Medical Association
(AMA) "discourages" such covenants, finding they are
not in the public interest. The Council on Ethical and
Judicial Affairs discourages any agreement between physicians which restricts the right of a physician to practice
medicine for a specified period of time or in a specified
area upon termination of employment or a partnership or a
corporate agreement. Such restrictive agreements are not
in the public interest. In addition, the AMA recognizes that
free choice of doctors is the right of every patient, and free
competition among physicians is a prerequisite of optimal
care and ethical practice. In line with this viewpoint, the
Valley Medical court concluded that the doctor-patient
relationship is special and entitled to unique protection,
stating that it cannot be easily or accurately compared to
other relationships in the commercial context.

■≡■

Quicknotes

RESTRICTIVE COVENANT A promise contained in a deed to
limit the uses to which the property will be made.

■≡■

R.R. v. M.H. & Another

Father (P) v. Surrogate mother (D)

Mass. Sup. Jud. Ct., 426 Mass. 501, 689 N.E.2d 790 (1998).

NATURE OF CASE: Review of decision that a surrogacy parenting agreement was enforceable.

FACT SUMMARY: M.H. (D), a surrogate mother, changed her mind after signing a surrogacy agreement, and wanted to keep the child.

🏛 RULE OF LAW
By statute, no mother may effectively agree to surrender her child for adoption earlier than the fourth day after its birth.

FACTS: The New England Surrogate Parenting Advisors (NESPA) brought together R.R. (P) and his wife, who was infertile, with M.H. (D), who was married and had applied to NESPA to be a surrogate because she needed the money. They entered into a surrogacy agreement and M.H.'s (D) attempt at conception was successful. After accepting an initial payment of $500 from R.R. (P), M.H. (D) told her lawyer she had changed her mind, wanted to keep the child, and returned the next check uncashed. R.R. (P) then commenced this action seeking to establish his paternity, alleging breach of contract, and requesting a declaration of his rights under the surrogacy agreement. M.H. (D) moved to determine whether surrogacy contracts were enforceable in Massachusetts. The judge entered an order directing M.H. (D) to give the child to R.R. (P), the father, and granting him temporary physical custody of the child, based in part on her conclusion that the surrogacy agreement was enforceable. The judge reported the propriety of her order and set forth certain questions as to the enforceability of surrogacy agreements. M.H. (D) appealed. On its own motion, the Supreme Court of Massachusetts took jurisdiction of the appeal.

ISSUE: By statute, may a mother effectively agree to surrender her child for adoption earlier than the fourth day after its birth?

HOLDING AND DECISION: (Wilkins, C.J.) No. By statute, no mother may effectively agree to surrender her child for adoption earlier than the fourth day after its birth. The mother's purported consent to custody in the agreement is ineffective because no such consent should be recognized unless given on or after the fourth day following the child's birth. The statutory prohibition of payment for receiving a child through adoption suggests that, as a matter of policy, a mother's agreement to surrender custody in exchange for money should be given no effect in deciding the custody of a child. In any event, no private agreement concerning adoption or custody can be

conclusive because a judge, passing on custody of a child, must decide what is in the best interests of the child. A declaration shall be entered that the surrogacy agreement is not enforceable. Reversed and remanded.

▶ ANALYSIS

The court in this case reviewed statutes and decisions in other states on the same issue. A few states had enacted legislation requiring a judicially approved surrogacy agreement before conception. Some states simply deny the enforcement of any such agreements.

■■■

Quicknotes

SURROGACY AGREEMENT An agreement pursuant to which a woman agrees to be artificially inseminated with the semen of the husband of another woman in order to give birth to a child, after which she is to surrender all of her parental rights to the father and his wife.

■■■

Mistake, Changed Circumstances, and Contractual Modifications

Quick Reference Rules of Law

Lenawee County Board of Health v. Messerly

Country board (P) v. Property owners (D)

Mich. Sup. Ct., 417 Mich. 17, 331 N.W.2d 203 (1982).

NATURE OF CASE: Appeal from reversal of judgment against counterclaimant-defendants seeking rescission of contract.

FACT SUMMARY: When the Lenawee County Board of Health (P) found a defective sewage system shortly after the Pickleses purchased rental property from Mr. and Mrs. Messerly (D) and sought a permanent injunction proscribing human habitation, the Pickleses sought rescission of their contract on the grounds of mutual mistake.

🏛 RULE OF LAW
A mutual mistake of fact does not require rescission of a contract where the party seeking rescission has assumed the risk of loss.

FACTS: When Mr. Bloom owned the property on which there was a three-unit apartment building, he installed a septic tank without a permit and in violation of the applicable health code. This was not known to the Messerlys (D) when they subsequently bought it, nor to Barnes when he purchased it on a land contract from the Messerlys (D). After Barnes defaulted on the land contract, an arrangement was made whereby the land was quit-claimed back to the Messerlys (D), and they sold it on a new land contract to the Pickleses. About six days later, the Pickleses discovered raw sewage seeping out of the ground. The Lenawee County Board of Health (P) condemned the property and sought an injunction against human habitation until it was brought into compliance with the sanitation code. In resulting cross-actions, the Pickleses sought rescission of the contract on grounds of mutual mistake. Focusing on the "as is" clause in their land contract, the trial court denied rescission and awarded the Messerlys (D) a judgment against the Pickleses on the land contract. The court of appeals reversed, and the state's highest court granted review.

ISSUE: Does a mutual mistake of fact require rescission of a contract where the party seeking rescission has assumed the risk of loss?

HOLDING AND DECISION: (Ryan, J.) No. A mutual mistake of fact does not require rescission of a contract where the party seeking rescission has assumed the risk of loss. A mutual mistake that is the prerequisite for rescission is one that relates to a basic assumption of the parties upon which the contract was made and which materially affects the agreed performance of the parties. However, rescission need not be granted in every case where there is such a mistake. It cannot be ordered to relieve a party who has assumed the risk of loss in connection with the mistake. Furthermore, where both parties are innocent, as in this case, the court exercises its equitable powers to determine which blameless party should assume the loss. Here, the "as is" clause suggests it should be the Pickleses. Reversed.

▶ ANALYSIS

According to 1 Restatement Contracts (Second) § 124, a party bears the risk of mistake if it is allocated to him by agreement of the parties, or he is aware at the time of contracting of his limited knowledge of the facts to which the mistake relates but treats his limited knowledge as sufficient, or the court allocates it to him because "it is reasonable in the circumstances to do so."

■══▪

Quicknotes

MUTUAL MISTAKE A mistake by both parties to a contract, who are in agreement as to what the contract terms should be, but the agreement as written fails to reflect that common intent; such contracts are voidable or subject to reformation.

RESCISSION The canceling of an agreement and the return of the parties to their positions prior to the formation of the contract.

■══▪

Wil-Fred's, Inc. v. Metropolitan Sanitary District

Contractor (P) v. Regulatory Agency (D)

Ill. App. Ct., 57 Ill. App. 3d 16, 372 N.E.2d 946 (1978).

NATURE OF CASE: Appeal of rescission of contract.

FACT SUMMARY: Contractor Wil-Fred's, Inc. (P) withdrew a bid when its subcontractor proved unable to meet a subcontract commitment.

🏛 RULE OF LAW
A contractor may obtain rescission of a contract formed by a bid which was mistakenly priced too low.

FACTS: The Metropolitan Sanitary District of Chicago (D) submitted an invitation for contractors to bid on a project involving rehabilitation on a water reclamation plant. The invitation contained a clause whereby each bidder had to deposit $100,000, which would be forfeited if the bid was accepted but the bidder failed to perform. Wil-Fred's (P) submitted a bid of $882,000, over $235,000 lower than the next bid. Upon discovering that its bid was so low, Wil-Fred's (P) contacted its excavation subcontractor, Cigalo Excavating, Inc., which discovered it had materially erred in its excavation subcontract bid. Two days after it submitted its bid, Wil-Fred's (P) notified Metropolitan (D) it was withdrawing its bid and requested that its deposit be returned. Metropolitan (D) refused, accepted the bid, and retained the $100,000. Wil-Fred's (P) brought an action for rescission. After a trial at which Wil-Fred's (P) principals testified about the previous reliability of both Wil-Fred's (P) and Cigalo, the court granted rescission. Metropolitan (D) appealed.

ISSUE: May a contractor obtain rescission of a contract formed by a bid which was mistakenly priced too low?

HOLDING AND DECISION: (Perlin, J.) Yes. A contractor may obtain rescission of a contract formed by a bid which was mistakenly priced too low. A unilateral mistake may afford ground for rescission where there is a material mistake and such mistake is so palpable that the party not in error will be put on notice of its existence. Also, the party in error must have exercised reasonable care, the mistake must be so grave that enforcement would be unconscionable, and the party not in error must not be too severely prejudiced by rescission. Here, the trial court found that the mistake was material. As it relates to cost, this is not surprising. The vast difference between Wil-Fred's (P) and the next lowest bidder should have put Metropolitan (D) on notice of some sort of mistake. It appears that Wil-Fred's (P) used reasonable care, as Cigalo had been dependable in the past. The trial court found that forfeiture of $100,000 would severely injure Wil-Fred's (P), and there is no evidence of clear error in this conclusion. Finally, since Wil-Fred's (P) served notice of its intention to withdraw its bid two days after the bid's submission, no prejudice to Metropolitan (D) can be shown. Affirmed.

▶ ANALYSIS

Probably the most well-known case in this area is *Drennan v. Star Paving Co.*, 51 Cal. 2d 408, 333 P.2d 757 (1958). This action involved a general contractor suing a subcontractor who refused to perform work upon which it had bid and whose bid the general contractor had incorporated into its bid. In *Drennan*, the party making the mistake lost. The main difference between *Drennan* and the present action would appear to be that in *Drennan* detrimental reliance was shown.

■═■

Quicknotes

DETRIMENTAL RELIANCE Action by one party, resulting in loss, that is based on the conduct or promises of another.

UNILATERAL MISTAKE Occurs when only one party to an agreement makes a mistake and is generally not a basis for relief by rescission or reformation.

■═■

Karl Wendt Farm Equipment Co. v. International Harvester Co.

Franchise (P) v. Farm equipment manufacturer (D)

931 F.2d 1112 (6th Cir. 1991).

NATURE OF CASE: Cross-appeals from judgment excusing performance of contract and a directed verdict upholding the validity of the contract.

FACT SUMMARY: International Harvester Co. (D) sold its unprofitable farm equipment division to a company which did not continue to do business with all of its franchisees.

🏛 RULE OF LAW
A party's performance is not excused where the occurrence of a foreseeable event such as a market downturn renders a contract unprofitable.

FACTS: During an economic downturn, International Harvester Co. (IH) (D) sold its unprofitable farm equipment division to a competitor. The competitor had many franchises in areas also served by IH (D) franchises. Karl Wendt Farm Equipment Co. (Wendt) (P) was the IH (D) franchisee in such an area, and when the competitor decided not to do business with him, he had no supplier. Wendt (P) sued IH (D) for breach of contract. IH (D) claimed that its performance under the franchise agreement was excused due to impracticability of performance caused by the recession, or, that the contract should be cancelled due to frustration of purpose since IH (D) was unable to make any profit on it. The jury found in favor of IH (D) on the impracticability of performance argument, while the judge ordered a directed verdict in favor of Wendt (P) as to frustration of purpose. IH (D) appealed the directed verdict, while Wendt (P) appealed the jury verdict on the grounds that the judge should not have permitted the jury to consider the defense of impracticability on these facts.

ISSUE: Will a party's performance be excused where the occurrence of a foreseeable event such as a market downturn renders the contract unprofitable?

HOLDING AND DECISION: (Jones, J.) No. A party's performance will not be excused where the occurrence of a foreseeable event such as a market downturn renders the contract unprofitable. The Restatement (Second) Contracts states that where performance has been made impracticable due to "the occurrence of an event the nonoccurrence of which was a basic assumption on which the contract was made" or where the principal purpose of a contract is frustrated by such an event, performance may be excused. However, Restatement (Second) Contracts § 261, Official Comments b and d, show that the discontinuance of existing market conditions are not an event of this kind. IH (D) cannot simply divest itself of its ability to perform and then cancel its contracts without

obligation. Reversed as to impracticability of performance; affirmed, as to frustration of purpose and remanded.

DISSENT: (Ryan, J.) Whether performance of a contract is impracticable is a question of fact, not of law. The trier of fact, in this case the jury, should decide whether or not the economic climate was so severe as to excuse performance.

▶ ANALYSIS

This case illustrates the majority rule: most courts won't cancel a contract for impracticability or frustration of purpose because market conditions have changed. Market changes are the normal risks of a contract which the parties are assumed to have considered and distributed among themselves when they made the contract. Courts hesitate to rewrite the agreement of the parties to redistribute risks or losses. An example of circumstances where relief was granted under frustration of purpose is *Molnar v. Molnar*, where a parent was permitted to discontinue payments of child support after the child died. 110 Mich App. 622, 313 N.W.2d 171 (1981).

Quicknotes

FRUSTRATION OF PURPOSE A doctrine relieving the parties to a contract from liability for nonperformance of their duties thereunder when the purpose of the agreement ceases to exist due to circumstances not subject to either party's control.

IMPRACTICABILITY A doctrine relieving the parties to a contract from liability for nonperformance of their duties thereunder, if the subject matter of the contract ceases to exist.

Mel Frank Tool & Supply, Inc. v. Di-Chem Co.

Landlord (P) v. Tenant (D)

Iowa Sup. Ct., 580 N.W.2d 802 (1998).

NATURE OF CASE: Tenant's appeal from a judgment in favor of the landlord for the breach of a lease.

FACT SUMMARY: Di-Chem Co. (D) signed a three-year lease to begin June 1, 1994, with Mel Frank Tool & Supply, Inc. (Mel Frank) (P) for a storage and distribution facility. Di-Chem (D) claimed it was going to be selling chemicals, but the use of the premises was limited to "storage and distribution." In July 1995, city officials inspected the premises and informed Di-Chem (D) that they had found Code violations (enacted after Di-Chem took occupancy) that had to be eliminated. Di-Chem (D) vacated the premises in October 1995, and Mel Frank (P) sued for breach of lease and damage to the property.

🏛 RULE OF LAW

A tenant is not relieved from the obligation to pay rent due to a subsequent governmental regulation which prohibits the tenant from legally using the premises for its originally intended purpose if there is a serviceable use still available consistent with the use provision in the lease, and the fact that the use of the premises is less valuable or less profitable or even unprofitable does not necessarily mean the tenant's use has been substantially frustrated.

FACTS: Di-Chem Co. (D), a chemical distributor, negotiated with Mel Frank Tool & Supply, Inc. (Mel Frank) (P) to lease a storage and distribution facility. Mel Frank's (P) real estate agent handled the negotiations. Mel Frank (P) asked Di-Chem (D) what it was going to be selling and was told chemicals. The lease limited Di-Chem's (D) use of the premises to "storage and distribution." Some of the chemicals Di-Chem distributes are considered "hazardous material." There was no testimony that Mel Frank (P) was aware of this at the time the three-year lease to commence June 1, 1994, was executed. In July 1995, city authorities informed Di-Chem (D) that it could no longer use its leased premises to store its hazardous chemicals because of a recently enacted ordinance, whereupon Di-Chem (D) vacated the premises, and Mel Frank (P) sued for breach of the lease. The trial court awarded judgment to Mel Frank (P), and Di-Chem (D) appealed, contending that the trial court should have found that the city's actions constituted extraordinary circumstances rendering the performance of the lease impossible.

ISSUE: Is a tenant relieved from the obligation to pay rent due to a subsequent governmental regulation which prohibits the tenant from legally using the premises for its originally intended purpose if there is a serviceable use still available consistent with the use provision in the lease even if the use of the premises is less valuable or less profitable or even unprofitable?

HOLDING AND DECISION: (Lavorato, J.) No. A tenant is not relieved from the obligation to pay rent due to a subsequent governmental regulation which prohibits the tenant from legally using the premises for its originally intended purpose if there is a serviceable use still available consistent with the use provision in the lease even if the use of the premises is less valuable or less profitable or even unprofitable. The fact of unprofitability of the lease does not necessarily mean that the tenant's use has been substantially frustrated as to relieve rent payment. The facts of this case fall within the parameters of § 265 of the Restatement (Second) of Contracts which provides that where, after a contract is made, a party's principal purpose is substantially frustrated without his fault by the occurrence of an event the nonoccurrence of which was a basic assumption on which the contract was made, his remaining duties to render performance are discharged unless the language or the circumstances indicate the contrary. The rule deals with the problem that arises when a change in circumstances makes one party's performance virtually worthless to the other, frustrating the purpose in making the contract. Here, not all of Di-Chem's (D) inventory consisted of hazardous material. Di-Chem (D) did not establish that its principal purpose for leasing the facility—storing and distributing chemicals—was substantially frustrated by the city's actions. Nor did Di-Chem (D) present evidence as to the nature of its inventory and what percentage of the inventory consisted of hazardous chemicals. Thus, there was no evidence from which the trial court could have found that the city's actions substantially frustrated Di-Chem's (D) principal purpose of storing and distributing chemicals. Put another way, there was insufficient evidence that the city's action deprived Di-Chem (D) of the beneficial enjoyment of the property for other uses, i.e., storing and distributing nonhazardous chemicals. Di-Chem failed to establish its affirmative defense of what it termed impossibility. Affirmed.

▶ ANALYSIS

The introduction to the Restatement (Second) of Contracts covers impossibility of performance, but with a different title: impracticability of performance and frustration of purpose. [Restatement (Second) of Contracts Ch. 11, at 309 (1981)] According to the Restatement, contract liability is

Continued on next page.

strict liability. The obligor is therefore liable in damages for the breach of a contract even if he or she is without fault and even if circumstances have made the contract more burdensome or less desirable than anticipated. An obligor who does not wish to undertake so extensive an obligation may contract for a lesser one by using one of a variety of common clauses. For example, they may reserve a right to cancel the contract. The extent of the obligation then depends on the application of the rules of interpretation. Furthermore, even though the obligor has not restricted his or her obligation by agreement, a court may still grant relief where an extraordinary circumstance may make performance so vitally different from what was reasonably to be expected as to alter the essential nature of that performance. In these circumstances, the court must determine whether justice requires a departure from the general rule that the obligor bear the risk that the contract may become more burdensome or less desirable. Whether extraordinary circumstances exist justifying discharge is a question of law for the court. In the *Mel Frank Tool* case, the court found that the tenant Di-Chem (D) failed to present sufficient evidence to establish such extraordinary circumstances.

■■■

Quicknotes

AFFIRMATIVE DEFENSE A manner of defending oneself against a claim not by denying the truth of the charge but by the introduction of some evidence challenging the plaintiff's right to bring the claim.

BREACH OF CONTRACT Unlawful failure by a party to perform its obligations pursuant to contract.

■■■

Alaska Packers' Association v. Domenico

Fishing company (D) v. Seaman (P)

117 F. 99 (9th Cir. 1902).

NATURE OF CASE: Appeal from judgment for plaintiffs in libel action for breach of contract.

FACT SUMMARY: Seamen (P), who had agreed to ship from San Francisco to Alaska at a fixed pay, refused to continue working once they reached Alaska, and demanded a new contract with more compensation.

🏛 RULE OF LAW
A promise to pay a man for doing that which he is already under contract to do is without consideration.

FACTS: A group of seamen (P) entered into a written contract with Alaska Packers' Association (D) to go from San Francisco to Alaska on the Packers' (D) ships, and to work as sailors and fishermen. Compensation was fixed at $60 for the season, and two cents for each salmon caught. Once they had reached port in Alaska, the seamen (P) refused to continue work and demanded that compensation be increased to $100. A superintendent for Packers' (D), unable to hire a new crew, drew up a new contract, substituted in the sum of $100, and signed it although he expressed doubt at the time that he had the authority to do so. The seamen (P) resumed work, but upon the ship's return to San Francisco, Packers' (D) refused to honor the new contract. The seamen (P) filed a libel action for breach of contract.

ISSUE: Is the performance of a preexisting legal duty guaranteed by contract sufficient consideration to support a promise?

HOLDING AND DECISION: (Ross, J.) No. The performance of a preexisting legal duty guaranteed by contract is not sufficient consideration to support a promise. No astute reasoning can change the plain fact that the party who refuses to perform, and thereby coerces a promise from the other party to pay him an increased compensation for doing that which he is legally bound to do, takes an unjustifiable advantage of the necessities of the other party. The parties in the present case have not voluntarily rescinded or modified their contract. The Packers' (D) second contract with the seamen (P) is unenforceable although the seamen (P) completed their performance in reliance on it. Reversed and remanded.

▶ ANALYSIS

A few cases have held that the promise to pay additional compensation is enforceable. Consideration is found in the promisee's giving up of his power to breach the first contract. In other words, by refusing to continue work, the promisee has invoked the option to pay money damages rather than to invest his labor in further performance. This view has been questioned on the ground that a promisee may have the power to breach a contract, but certainly not the legal right, and in any event, he should not be encouraged to do so.

■■■

Quicknotes

PREEXISTING DUTY A common law doctrine that renders unenforceable a promise to perform a duty, which the promisor is already legally obligated to perform, for lack of consideration.

■■■

Kelsey–Hayes Co. v. Galtaco Redlaw Castings Corp.

Buyer (P) v. Seller (D)

749 F. Supp. 794 (E.D. Mich. 1990).

NATURE OF CASE: Pending motions for summary judgment for defendant and for plaintiff to amend the complaint alleging breach of contract.

FACT SUMMARY: When Galtaco Redlaw Castings Corp. (D) experienced financial losses and threatened to shut down operations, Kelsey-Hayes Co. (P), which had signed a three-year requirements contract, was forced to agree to pay higher prices to keep operations going.

RULE OF LAW

A subsequent contract or modification is invalid and therefore does not supersede an earlier contract when the subsequent contract was entered into under duress.

FACTS: Galtaco Redlaw Castings Corp. (Galtaco) (D) supplied Kelsey-Hayes Co. (P) with castings that were incorporated into brake assemblies sold to automobile manufacturers, including Chrysler and Ford. Facing financial losses, Galtaco (D) decided to cease its production of castings, but offered its customers an agreement to keep its foundries operating for several months in exchange for a price increase of 30%. Since Kelsey-Hayes (P) could not find an alternate source of castings, it further agreed to another price hike of 30% when it signed a contract in 1989 for another year. Kelsey-Hayes (P) protested the breach of the original 1987 contract and later sued, alleging that the contract modifications were agreed to under duress because Galtaco (D) had threatened to breach its contract and go out of business, stopping production and delivery of castings, unless Kelsey-Hayes (P) agreed to significant price hikes. Galtaco (D) alleged that Kelsey-Hayes (P) could not sue for breach of the earlier contract because it had entered into a superseding contract, and moved for summary judgment.

ISSUE: Is a subsequent contract or modification invalid when the subsequent contract was entered into under duress?

HOLDING AND DECISION: (Cohn, J.) Yes. A subsequent contract or modification is invalid and therefore does not supersede an earlier contract when the subsequent contract was entered into under duress. There is sufficient evidence for a reasonable finder of fact to determine that Kelsey-Hayes (P) was under duress when it executed the 1989 agreements. A contract is voidable if a party's assent was induced through an improper threat by another party that leaves the victim no reasonable alternative. Economic duress can exist in the absence of an illegal threat. In addition, Kelsey-Hayes (P) presents a triable issue

of fact since it lacked a reasonable alternative, other than acquiescence to Galtaco's (D) demands for a contract modification. Galtaco's (D) motion for summary judgment is denied. Kelsey-Hayes's (P) motion to amend is granted.

ANALYSIS

The court in this case reviewed the history in Michigan of the doctrine of economic duress. Early decisions held that in order to make a claim of duress, a person must be subjected to the threat of an unlawful act in the nature of a tort or crime. The doctrine of duress has been greatly expanded since its common law origin, however, to include any wrongful threat.

Quicknotes

DURESS Unlawful threats or other coercive behavior by one person that causes another to commit acts that he would not otherwise do.

MODIFICATION A change to the terms of a contract without altering its general purpose.

Brookside Farms v. Mama Rizzo's, Inc.

Seller (P) v. Buyer (D)

873 F. Supp. 1029 (S.D. Texas 1995).

NATURE OF CASE: Pending motions for summary judgment.

FACT SUMMARY: Brookside Farms (P) alleged that Mama Rizzo's, Inc. (D) breached its contract to purchase fresh basil leaves.

🏛 RULE OF LAW
A contract which does not satisfy the Statute of Frauds, but which is valid in other respects, is enforceable with respect to goods for which payment has been made and accepted or which have been received and accepted.

FACTS: Brookside Farms (Brookside) (P) and Mama Rizzo's, Inc. (MRI) (D) had entered into a written requirements agreement whereby MRI (D) agreed to buy a minimum of 91,000 pounds of fresh basil leaves for one year. MRI (D) later requested that additional parts of the stems of the basil leaves be removed, a task not specifically required under the original contract, and Brookside (P) agreed, in exchange for a $0.50 per pound price increase. Because the contract contained a clause forbidding oral modification, MRI (D) agreed to make a notation of the price change on its copy of the contract. MRI (D) later discontinued its order, but then resumed its orders under the contract. Two more shipments were made and paid for at a higher price. When a check issued for payment by MRI (D) was dishonored by MRI's (D) bank, Brookside (P) sued for damages and breach of contract. MRI (D) countersued, alleging Brookside (P) breached the contract by raising prices in violation of the express language of the contract. Both parties moved for summary judgment.

ISSUE: Is a contract which does not satisfy the Statute of Frauds, but which is valid in other respects, enforceable with respect to goods for which payment has been made and accepted or which have been received and accepted?

HOLDING AND DECISION: (Kent, J.) Yes. A contract which does not satisfy the Statute of Frauds, but which is valid in other respects, is enforceable with respect to goods for which payment has been made and accepted or which have been received and accepted. Valid oral modification of the contract occurred on both estoppel and statutory grounds. It is undisputed that the parties agreed to alter the purchase price of the basil leaves. The actual later conduct of the parties involved the order, shipment, and acceptance of 24,430 pounds of basil leaves, 3,041 pounds of which were paid for by a bad check on MRI's (D) part. Receipt and acceptance either of goods or of the price constitutes an unambiguous overt admission by both parties that a contract actually exists. Brookside's (P) motion for partial summary judgment is granted on the claim that MRI (D) is liable to Brookside (P) for $20,526 in payment for the 3,041 pounds of basil leaves accepted but not paid for. Brookside (P) did not breach its contractual obligations, and MRI (D) is liable for a material breach of its obligation to buy a total of 91,000 pounds of basil. Plaintiff's motion for partial summary judgment is denied as to attorneys' fees and is granted as to claims that (1) MRI breached the executory portion of the parties' contract, (2) MRI is liable in the amount of $20,526.75 for the payment of the 3,041 pounds of basil accepted but not paid for, and (3) MRI is liable under the Perishable Agricultural and Commodities Act. Defendant's motion for summary judgment is denied on all counts for the same reasons, including the counterclaim that MRI is entitled to recover overpayments from Plaintiff for amounts it paid for basil. Defendant's counterclaim for overpayment is dismissed with prejudice. All relief not specifically granted herein is also denied. All parties must bear their own taxable costs incurred to date and may not file further pleadings in the matters set forth in this Order. For further relief to which the parties feel they are entitled, parties must turn to the Fifth Circuit.

▶ ANALYSIS

There was also a "no-oral-modifications" clause in the contract in this case. At common law, such clauses were held to be ineffective in restricting later modifications. Under the Uniform Commercial Code § 2-209(2), such a clause may be used to create a private statute of frauds between the parties.

Quicknotes

ESTOPPEL An equitable doctrine precluding a party from asserting a right to the detriment of another who justifiably relied on the conduct.

MODIFICATION A change to the terms of a contract without altering its general purpose.

STATUTE OF FRAUDS A statute that requires specified types of contracts to be in writing in order to be binding.

WAIVER CLAUSE A clause in a contract providing for the intentional or voluntary forfeiture of a recognized right.

Rights and Duties of Third Parties

Quick Reference Rules of Law

Vogan v. Hayes Appraisal Associates, Inc.

Borrowers (P) v. Appraiser (D)

Iowa Sup. Ct., 588 N.W.2d 420 (1999).

NATURE OF CASE: Appeal from adverse judgment by third-party contract beneficiaries.

FACT SUMMARY: Susan and Rollin Vogan (P) secured a mortgage from MidAmerica Savings Bank (MidAmerica) for $170,000 to build a house. The Vogans (P) hired builder Gary Markley of Char Enterprises, Inc. and MidAmerica contracted with Hayes Appraisal Associates, Inc. (Hayes Appraisal) (D) to do the initial appraisal and make periodic appraisals of the progress of the construction. MidAmerica was to release payments to the builder based upon the progress reports made by Hayes Appraisal (D). There were cost overruns and a second mortgage was necessary, including the addition of further funds. The Vogans (P) eventually brought suit against Hayes Appraisal (D) on a third-party beneficiary theory.

🏛 **RULE OF LAW**
Unless otherwise agreed between the promisor and promisee, a beneficiary of a promise is an intended beneficiary if recognition of a right to performance in the beneficiary is appropriate to effectuate the intention of the parties, and either the performance of the promise will satisfy an obligation of the promisee to pay money to the beneficiary, or the circumstances indicate that the promisee intends to give the beneficiary the benefit of the promised performance.

FACTS: Hayes Appraisal Associates, Inc. (Hayes Appraisal) (D) was hired by MidAmerica Savings Bank (MidAmerica) to monitor the progress of new home construction for the Vogans (P) who had obtained a construction loan from MidAmerica for $170,000. The contractor defaulted after all of the original construction loan proceeds and a subsequent portion of a second mortgage loan had been paid out by the bank. The Vogans (P) sued and recovered a judgment against Hayes Appraisal (D) on a third-party beneficiary theory based on its failure to properly monitor the progress of the construction, thus allowing funds to be improperly released by the lender to the defaulting contractor. The court of appeals reversed the judgment on the basis that erroneous progress reports by Hayes Appraisal (D) were not the cause of any loss to the Vogans (P). The Vogans (P) appealed.

ISSUE: Unless otherwise agreed between the promisor and promisee, is a beneficiary of a promise an intended beneficiary if recognition of a right to performance in the beneficiary is appropriate to effectuate the intention of the parties, and either the performance of the promise will satisfy an obligation of the promisee to pay money to the beneficiary, or the circumstances indicate that the promisee

intends to give the beneficiary the benefit of the promised performance?

HOLDING AND DECISION: (Carter, J.) Yes. Unless otherwise agreed between the promisor and promisee, a beneficiary of a promise is an intended beneficiary if recognition of a right to performance in the beneficiary is appropriate to effectuate the intention of the parties, and either the performance of the promise will satisfy an obligation of the promisee to pay money to the beneficiary, or the circumstances indicate that the promisee intends to give the beneficiary the benefit of the promised performance. The primary question in a third-party beneficiary case is whether the contract manifests an intent to benefit a third party. The intent need not be to benefit a third party directly. Here, the Vogans (P), who were the borrowers, were third-party beneficiaries of the contract between the construction lender and Hayes Appraisal (D), under which Hayes Appraisal (D) agreed to issue reports monitoring the general contractor's progress in the construction of the Vogans' (P) home where the appraiser's performance was to have been of pecuniary benefit to the Vogans (P), and the inspection reports issued by Hayes Appraisal (D) naming the Vogans (P) as home purchasers gave Hayes Appraisal (D) reason to know that the lender's purpose in contracting for periodic inspection reports was to provide protection for the money which the Vogans (P) had invested in the project. Accordingly, the jury could properly find that the faulty progress reports issued by Hayes Appraisal (D) to the construction lender, in which the appraiser overstated the extent of the contractor's progress, caused injury to the Vogans (P) where, when the initial construction loan funds were exhausted due to cost overruns, the Vogans (P) deposited their own funds into the construction account, and much of those funds were paid to the contractor based on Hayes Appraisal's (D) faulty reports, before the contractor defaulted. Vacate court of appeals judgment and affirm district court.

▶ **ANALYSIS**

As noted by the *Vogan* court, recovery by the Vogans (P) from Hayes Appraisal (D) of sums advanced to the contractor by the construction lender based upon Hayes Appraisal's (D) faulty progress reports, in which the appraiser overstated the extent of the contractor's progress, was not beyond the appraiser's contemplation at the time it entered into the contract to provide the Vogans (P) with such progress reports, thus recovery did not violate

Continued on next page.

the rule of *Hadley v. Baxendale*, 156 Eng. Rep. 145 (1854), even though, due to cost overruns, substantially more funds were advance to the contractor than the amount of the original construction loan.

■══■

Quicknotes

INTENDED BENEFICIARY A third party who is the recipient of the benefit of a transaction undertaken by another.

THIRD-PARTY BENEFICIARY Party who benefits from a promise made pursuant to a contract although he is not a party to the agreement.

■══■

Chen v. Chen

Mother (P) v. Father (D)

Penn. Sup. Ct., 893 A.2d 87 (2006).

NATURE OF CASE: Appeal from affirmance of ruling permitting intervention in a parent's support action asserting breach of contract, and from judgment for plaintiff in that action.

FACT SUMMARY: Richard Chen (Father) (D) contended that his daughter, Theresa (Daughter), should not be permitted to intervene in a support action brought by his former wife and the daughter's mother, Wheamei Chen (Mother) (P), because, he contended, Daughter was only an incidental beneficiary, not an intended beneficiary, of the property settlement agreement (Agreement) at issue.

🏛 RULE OF LAW
A child may not bring suit or intervene in an action to enforce support provisions of her parents' property settlement agreement where support payments are to be made to the custodial parent.

FACTS: When Richard Chen (Father) (D) and Wheamei Chen (Mother) (P) divorced, they entered into a property settlement agreement (Agreement). At the time, they had a son and a daughter, Theresa (Daughter). Mother (P) received custody over Daughter, who was one year old, and, as part of the Agreement, Father (D) was to pay $25.00 per week as child support of Daughter. Father (D) further agreed that upon obtaining regular employment or upon any increase in salary the $25.00 support award would be increased in accordance with the county's domestic relations guidelines. The Agreement was incorporated by reference but not merged into the divorce decree. Pursuant to the Agreement, Father (D) paid $25.00 per week to Mother (P) until Daughter's eighteenth birthday. However, he did not increase the payments as required for employment and salary increases. When Daughter turned 18, the county informed Mother (P) that support payments would cease. In response, Mother (P) filed a petition requesting enforcement of the property settlement agreement and a finding of contempt of court. Mother (P) sought to enforce the Agreement's provision for increases in child support and to collect total support/arrearages based upon Father's (D) salary increases over the almost 18 years the Agreement had been in effect. Shortly after turning 18, Daughter filed a petition to intervene as a party to Mother's (P) action, asserting that intervention was appropriate because she had a legally enforceable interest as a third party intended beneficiary under the Agreement. The trial court, applying case law that relied on Restatement (Second) of Contracts, § 302, concluded that Daughter should be permitted to intervene. The court found that § 302's liberal standard

of permitting intervention by a third party had been satisfied. Section 302 provides that a beneficiary is an intended beneficiary if recognition of a right to performance in the beneficiary will effectuate the intentions of the parties and the circumstances indicate that the promisee intended to give the beneficiary the benefit of the promised performance. Specifically, the court determined that the parties' to the Agreement clearly intended that the child support provision of the Agreement was to benefit Daughter throughout her minority. Daughter was permitted to intervene, whereupon Mother (P) withdrew as a party, leaving Daughter and Father (D) as party-opponents. Interpreting the Agreement as an independent contract, the trial court concluded that Father (D) had breached the contract and ordered him to pay around $59,000 in arrearages due under the Agreement. On appeal, the state's intermediate appellate court affirmed, finding that the trial court correctly permitted Daughter to intervene, and correctly determined that Father (D) had breached the support provisions of the Agreement. In doing so, the court rejected Father's (D) argument that Daughter had no direct right to the payments, but only to her parents' support. The state's highest court granted review.

ISSUE: May a child may bring suit or intervene in an action to enforce support provisions of her parents' property settlement agreement where support payments are to be made to the custodial parent?

HOLDING AND DECISION: (Baer, J.) No. A child may not bring suit or intervene in an action to enforce support provisions of her parents' property settlement agreement where support payments are to be made to the custodial parent. The issue is one of first impression in this jurisdiction, and is one purely of law. Father (D) contends that Daughter is not an intended beneficiary, but an incidental beneficiary. He argues that neither parent intended Daughter to receive the payments dollar for dollar, and that permitting children to intervene in their parents' support agreements will open the door to a child suing one or both of her parents by equating the right to be supported with the right to support payments. Under the state's procedural rules, a party has the right to intervene where the determination of the action "may affect any legally enforceable interest of such person whether or not such person may be bound by a judgment in the action." Daughter asserts that she has a "legally enforceable interest" as an intended beneficiary to her parents' separation agreement. To determine whether Daughter has a legally

Continued on next page.

enforceable interest, the Agreement is interpreted pursuant to contract principles because property settlement agreements incorporated but not merged into divorce decrees are considered independent contracts, interpreted according to the law of contracts. Under contract law principles, the intent of the parties is paramount. If the contract is unambiguous, the intent is determined from the contract itself. Here, the Agreement did not expressly name Daughter as an intended beneficiary. However, Daughter may still be considered an intended beneficiary if she satisfies the Restatement's two-part test. The first part of that test is a standing test, and the question here, under that first part, is whether recognition of a right in Daughter to seek performance of the provision to increase Father's (D) weekly payments upon employment or increases in salary in accordance with the support guidelines is "appropriate to effectuate the intentions of the parties." It is clear that the second part of the test is satisfied, since circumstances indicate that Mother (P) intended to give Daughter the benefit of the promised performance. The question raised by the first part of the test raises competing policy considerations. On the one hand, support of minor children is favored, and parents are obligated to render such support in the best interests of minor children. Courts may abandon contract principles to uphold the best interests of minor children. The best interests of a minor child are not implicated here, however, because Daughter is grown, so that contract principles must be adhered to. Also at issue is a parents' fundamental right to direct the care, custody, and control of their children. Support agreement or orders do not provide for direct payment of support payments to minor children, and parents are given discretion as to how to direct support funds. Parents have the final say regarding the family's budget. Accordingly, many courts are reluctant, absent unusual circumstances such as the death of a parent, to allow children to enforce their parents' agreements where the custodial parent was a signatory to the agreement and the designated recipient of the payments. This reluctance is often rooted in a desire to promote familial harmony and foster the parent-child relationship, neither of which are served when a child litigates support obligations against a parent. Such an approach is correct. Strong public policy favors denying a child standing to seek the specific dollars one parent owes the other for the child's generalized support pursuant to a separation agreement, absent special circumstances such as a direct designation that a benefit be paid to the child or the custodial parent's inability to enforce the agreement due to death or disability. Here, Mother (P) and Father (D) clearly intended to provide support for Daughter, but they did not intend for her to receive payments directly. Instead, the Agreement left Mother (P) to exercise her prerogative as a parent to direct the care, custody, and control of Daughter, and determine how to best use the support funds provided by Father (D). Accordingly, Daughter is not an intended beneficiary under § 302 and because recognition of Daughter's right to performance is not "appropriate to effectuate the intention of the parties." Reversed.

CONCURRENCE: (Cappy, C.J.) Insofar as the majority rests the case on contract law principles, its decision is correct. However, the majority should not have gone beyond the contract law issues presented, e.g., it should not have broadened the scope of the issue to include discussion of policy issues and other matters.

CONCURRENCE: (Castille, J.) The case should have been resolved on contract principle alone, and could easily have been resolved by limiting the inquiry to whether § 302's two-part test was met. The majority correctly determined that Daughter met part two of the test, and that the key issue was whether she satisfied part one. To resolve this issue, the majority needlessly addressed extraneous policy issues. The issue could have been resolved by merely looking at the Agreement's unambiguous language, which provided that Father (D) would make support payments to Mother (P) for Daughter's benefit, not for Daughter to be the direct recipient of the payments. Accordingly, Daughter was not an intended beneficiary under § 302.

CONCURRENCE: (Saylor, J.) As the Agreement was one for support, Daughter was an intended beneficiary during her minority. The resolution of the question of whether she should be permitted to intervene is a policy question that can be answered without resort to contract principles or the overlay of the two-part test of § 302. As a policy matter, minor children should not be accorded standing to initiate such legal actions absent express statutory authority.

▌ *ANALYSIS*

As this case intimates, courts generally permit children to enforce provisions of their parents' separation agreements that provide for benefits to flow directly to the children. In such cases, it is clear pursuant to the agreements' express provisions that the children are intended, rather than incidental, beneficiaries, and resolution of such cases can be accomplished through contract principles alone, without resorting to policy considerations as the majority did in this case.

■≡■

Quicknotes

BREACH OF CONTRACT Unlawful failure by a party to perform its obligations pursuant to contract.

CONTEMPT OF COURT Conduct that is intended to obstruct the court's effective administration of justice or to otherwise disrespect its authority.

DIVORCE DECREE A decree terminating a marriage.

Continued on next page.

INCIDENTAL BENEFICIARY A person for whom a trust is not specifically created and who has no right to assert an interest in the trust, yet derives incidental benefits therefrom.

INTENDED BENEFICIARY A third party who is the recipient of the benefit of a transaction undertaken by another.

INTERVENTION The method by which a party, not an initial party to the action, is admitted to the action in order to assert an interest in the subject matter of a lawsuit.

PROPERTY SETTLEMENT AGREEMENT An agreement entered into by spouses upon dissolution of the marriage that is either agreed to by the spouses and sanctioned by the court or based on the court's division of the marital estate following the divorce proceeding.

Herzog v. Irace

Assignee (P) v. Attorneys (D)

Me. Sup. Ct., 594 A.2d 1106 (1991).

NATURE OF CASE: Appeal of an award of damages for breach of assignment.

FACT SUMMARY: Although notified of Jones's assignment of a personal injury claim to Herzog (P), Jones's attorneys, Irace and Lowry (D) failed to pay the settlement to Herzog (P).

RULE OF LAW
An assignment is binding upon the obligor where there is an intent to relinquish the right to the assignee and the obligor is notified.

FACTS: Jones, who had been injured in a motorcycle accident, hired attorneys Irace and Lowry (D) to represent him in a personal injury action. Jones required surgery for his injuries which was performed by Herzog (P), a physician. Since Jones was unable to pay for this treatment, he signed a letter stating that he "request that payment be made directly . . . to John Herzog" of money received in settlement for his claim. Herzog (P) notified Irace and Lowry (D) of the assignment in 1988. The following year Jones received a $20,000 settlement for his claim. Jones instructed Irace and Lowry (D) to pay the money to him rather than to Herzog (P). Irace and Lowry (D) followed this instruction; Jones failed to pay Herzog (P) for the medical treatment. Herzog (P) brought a breach of assignment action against Irace and Lowry (D), and the trial court ruled in favor of Herzog (P). The superior court affirmed, and Irace and Lowry (D) appealed.

ISSUE: Is an assignment binding upon the obligor where the assignor has intended to relinquish the right and the obligor has been notified?

HOLDING AND DECISION: (Brody, J.) Yes. An assignment is binding upon an obligor when the assignor has intended to relinquish his rights and the obligor has been notified. The letter directing payment to be made directly to Herzog (P) clearly and unequivocally demonstrated Jones's intent to relinquish his control over any money received for his personal injury claim. Irace and Lowry (D) were duly notified of this assignment and therefore the settlement money should have been paid to Herzog (P). Although the assignment did interfere with the ethical obligations that Irace and Lowry (D) owed to Jones, the professional conduct rules do not prohibit the client's right to assign the proceeds of a lawsuit to a third party. Affirmed. The client's right prevails over any limitations on his lawyers. Affirmed.

ANALYSIS

Although assignment of contract rights is generally valid, some limitations on the right exist. Nearly every jurisdiction has a statute which restricts the assignment of wages. Furthermore, public policy considerations may protect assignors who attempt to assign future rights. Restatement (Second) § 317(2) does not allow assignment where the duty to the obligor would be materially changed.

Quicknotes

ASSIGNMENT A transaction in which a party conveys his or her entire interest in property to another.

OBLIGOR Promisor; party who has promised or is obligated to perform.

Sally Beauty Co. v. Nexxus Products Co.

Competitor (P) v. Beauty products company (D)

801 F.2d 1001 (7th Cir. 1986).

NATURE OF CASE: Appeal from summary judgment dismissing action for damages for breach of contract.

FACT SUMMARY: Nexxus Products Co. (Nexxus) (D) abrogated an exclusive distribution agreement when the distributor was purchased by Sally Beauty Co. (P), a direct competitor of Nexxus (D).

🏛 **RULE OF LAW**
A distribution agreement may be abrogated by the manufacturer if the distributor is purchased by a direct competitor of the manufacturer.

FACTS: Nexxus Products Co. (Nexxus) (D), a manufacturer of hair care products, contracted with Best Barber & Beauty Supply Co. (Best) for the latter to serve as exclusive distribution agent for Nexxus (D) products in most of the Texas market. Subsequent to this, Best was purchased by Sally Beauty Co. (Sally) (P), a wholly owned subsidiary of Alberto-Culver Co., a major manufacturer of hair care products and a direct competitor of Nexxus (D). Nexxus (D) soon thereafter abrogated the distribution agreement. Sally (P) sued for breach of contract. The district court entered summary judgment for Nexxus (D), dismissing the action on the grounds that the contact had been one for personal services and was therefore not assignable without Nexxus's (D) consent. The court of appeals granted review.

ISSUE: May a distribution agreement be abrogated by the manufacturer if the distributor is purchased by a direct competitor of the manufacturer?

HOLDING AND DECISION: (Cudahy, J.) Yes. A distribution agreement may be abrogated by the manufacturer if the distributor is purchased by a direct competitor of the manufacturer. [The court first held that because triable issues of fact existed, the district court erred in granting summary judgment on the basis of a personal service contract, although it did not find this to be reversible error. It then discussed the impact of the Uniform Commercial Code (U.C.C.).] An agreement for distribution of goods is not per se a contract for the sale of goods, but courts have generally held such agreements to be sufficiently similar that the U.C.C., which by its terms deals with "transactions in goods," should be applied. U.C.C. § 2-210(1) provides that a contractual right may be assigned except where the obligee has a substantial interest in having his original promisor perform or control the acts pertaining to the contract. Essentially, an obligee should not have to accept, via delegation, a bargain to which he did not agree. An exclusive distribution agreement, by its very nature, involves an implicit or explicit promise by the distributor to use its best efforts in executing the contract. Assignment of the contract to a competitor of the manufacturer of necessity raises the question of whether the distributor will use such efforts. This is sufficient under § 2-210(1) to allow a manufacturer to veto an assignment of an exclusive distribution contract, as Nexxus (D) did in this case. Affirmed.

DISSENT: (Posner, J.) It is improper for the court to conclude, as a matter of law, that Sally (P) will not use its best efforts in completing the contract. The court has decided the matter with no better foundation than judicial intuition about what businessmen might consider reasonable. Merely because Sally (P) is a subsidiary of a company that manufactures hair products—most of which are cheaper than Nexxus (D) products and aimed at a different market—does not mean, without further factual findings, that it will not use its best efforts to market Nexxus products. Precedent requires a factual inquiry into whether a change in business form is likely to impair performance of the contract, not a per se rule. This is especially true here, where the facts tend to indicate that Sally's (P) acquisition of Best would not especially hurt Nexxus (D), since Alberto-Culver does not have a monopoly on the market and Sally (P) carries brands that compete with those manufactured by Alberto-Culver. Instead of creating a per se rule, the majority should have a remanded for a factual inquiry "on whether the merger so altered the conditions of performance that Nexxus is entitled to declare the contract broken."

▌ *ANALYSIS*

The laws of most jurisdictions treat contracts for goods and services differently. Contracts for services are usually per se nonassignable without consent. Contracts for goods, subject to the U.C.C., are held to the standard quoted in the main opinion. As the present case illustrates, some contracts have elements of both goods and services, and the two can be sufficiently analogous to warrant application of U.C.C. principles in the services situation.

∎══∎

Quicknotes

ABROGATE Annul; cancel; void.

ASSIGNMENT A transaction in which a party conveys his or her entire interest in property to another.

Continued on next page.

U.C.C. § 2-210 A party may perform his duty through a delegate unless otherwise agreed or unless the other party has a substantial interest in having his original promisor perform or control the acts required by the contract.

■═■

Express Conditions, Material Breach, and Anticipatory Repudiation

Quick Reference Rules of Law

Oppenheimer & Co. v. Oppenheim, Appel, Dixon & Co.

Sublessor (P) v. Subtenant (D)

N.Y. Ct. App., 86 N.Y.2d 685, 660 N.E.2d 415 (1995).

NATURE OF CASE: Appeal from reinstatement of jury verdict for plaintiff in a breach of contract action.

FACT SUMMARY: When an express condition precedent was not satisfied, Oppenheim, Appel, Dixon & Co. (D) declared a sublease agreement void, and Oppenheimer & Co. (P) sued for breach of contract, claiming substantial performance.

🏛 RULE OF LAW
Substantial performance is not applicable to excuse the nonoccurrence of an express condition precedent.

FACTS: Oppenheimer & Co. (Oppenheimer) (P) moved to the World Financial Center in Manhattan and entered into a conditional letter agreement with Oppenheim, Appel, Dixon & Co. (Oppenheim, Appel) (D) to sublease Oppenheimer's former office space on the 33rd floor at One New York Plaza, since Oppenheim, Appel (D) already leased space on the 29th floor there. The letter agreement provided that the proposed sublease would be executed only upon the satisfaction of certain conditions. Oppenheimer (P) was to submit its plans and obtain the prime landlord's written consent to the proposed "tenant work," involving construction of a telephone communication linkage system between the 29th and 33rd floors. If the prime landlord's written consent was not received by the agreed date, both the agreement and the sublease were to be deemed null and void. Oppenheimer (P) timely satisfied the first condition, but never delivered the written consent on or before the modified deadline date. The written consent was eventually received by Oppenheim, Appel (D) 23 days after the deadline. The day after the deadline, Oppenheim, Appel (D) declared the agreement and sublease were invalid for failure to timely deliver the written consent. Oppenheimer (P) then commenced this action for breach of contract, asserting that Oppenheim, Appel (D) was estopped by virtue of its conduct from insisting on physical delivery of the written consent by the deadline, and that Oppenheimer (P) had substantially performed the conditions set forth in the letter agreement. The jury awarded Oppenheimer (P) damages, after finding that he had substantially performed the conditions set forth in the letter agreement. Oppenheim, Appel's (D) motion for judgment notwithstanding the verdict was granted by the court, which ruled as a matter of law that the doctrine of substantial performance had no application to this dispute, since the letter was free of any ambiguity. The Appellate Division reversed the judgment on law and facts, and reinstated the jury verdict because it found that the failure

to deliver the prime landlord's written consent was inconsequential. Oppenheim, Appel (D) appealed.

ISSUE: Is substantial performance applicable to excuse the nonoccurrence of an express condition precedent?

HOLDING AND DECISION: (Ciparick, J.) No. Substantial performance is not applicable to excuse the nonoccurrence of an express condition precedent. Inasmuch we are not dealing here with a situation where Oppenheimer (P) stands to suffer some forfeiture or undue hardship, we perceive no justification for engaging in a "materiality-of-the-nonoccurrence" analysis. To do so would frustrate the clearly expressed intention of the parties. Also, the issue of substantial performance is not one for the jury to resolve, but rather one for judges to determine. Reversed.

▶ *ANALYSIS*

The letter agreement in this case contained a further provision stating that the sublease would be invalid "unless and until" all conditions had been satisfied. The agreement further stated that failure of the conditioning event would cause the agreement to be of "no further force and effect." In such event, neither party would have any rights against or obligations to the other.

Quicknotes

BREACH OF CONTRACT Unlawful failure by a party to perform its obligations pursuant to contract.

CONDITION PRECEDENT The happening of an uncertain occurrence, which is necessary before a particular right or interest may be obtained or an action performed.

SUBSTANTIAL PERFORMANCE Performance of all the essential obligations pursuant to an agreement.

J. N. A. Realty Corp. v. Cross Bay Chelsea, Inc.

Lessor (P) v. Lessee (D)

N.Y. Ct. App., 42 N.Y.2d 392, 366 N.E.2d 1313 (1977).

NATURE OF CASE: Appeal of reversal of an unsuccessful ejectment action.

FACT SUMMARY: Cross Bay Chelsea (D) negligently failed to give lessor J. N. A. Realty Corp. (P) notice of intent to exercise a lease renewal option.

🏛 RULE OF LAW
Equity will protect a tenant who negligently fails to exercise a renewal option if failure to do so will result in a forfeiture.

FACTS: J. N. A. Realty Corp. (JNA) (P) executed a commercial lease to Cross Bay Chelsea's (Cross Bay's) (D) predecessor. When the predecessor assigned the lease to Cross Bay (D), the lease terms were amended to provide for a 24-year renewal option on six-month notice by Cross Bay (D). When the six-month mark approached, JNA (P) did not remind Cross Bay (D), which did not send notice, although it had real or constructive knowledge of its duty to do so. JNA (P) began negotiating with a prospective new tenant and demanded that Cross Bay (D), which had spent some $15,000 in improvements, vacate. When Cross Bay (D) failed to do so, JNA (P) filed an ejectment action. The trial court found in favor of Cross Bay (D), and the appellate term affirmed. The appellate division reversed. Cross Bay (D) appealed.

ISSUE: Will equity protect a tenant who negligently fails to exercise a renewal option if failure to do so will result in a forfeiture?

HOLDING AND DECISION: (Wachtler, J.) Yes. Equity will protect a tenant who negligently fails to exercise a renewal option if failure to do so will result in a forfeiture. While a party has no legal interest in a renewal period until the required notice is given, courts have recognized an equitable interest against forfeiture where a tenant has made improvements, and the failure to give notice was not willful, and the landlord is not harmed by equity's intervention. Here, Cross Bay (D) invested not only the cost of purchasing the lease, but put in $15,000 in improvements. Thus, a failure by equity to intervene will result in a forfeiture. However, as JNA (P) has been negotiating with a prospective tenant, JNA (P) may be harmed by intervention. This must be resolved at the trial level. Reversed and remanded.

DISSENT: (Breitel, C.J.) Tenant investment alone is not enough to justify intervention. This is an area which readily lends itself to manipulation and distortion, and a court should not be so ready to give relief. To do so injects great uncertainty into commercial transactions.

▶ ANALYSIS

The vast majority of jurisdictions will grant equitable relief when a party fails to exercise an option. However, the sorts of situations where such relief will be given vary greatly. More courts will grant relief to a tenant than to one holding a real estate purchase or stock option right, for instance.

■=■

Quicknotes

EJECTMENT An action to oust someone in possession of real property unlawfully and to restore possession to the party lawfully entitled to it.

INTERVENTION The method by which a party, not an initial party to the action, is admitted to the action in order to assert an interest in the subject matter of a lawsuit.

■=■

Jacob & Youngs, Inc. v. Kent

Home builder (P) v. Home buyer (D)

N.Y. Ct. App., 230 N.Y. 239, 129 N.E. 889 (1921).

NATURE OF CASE: Appeal from reversal of a directed verdict for defendant in action for damages for breach of a construction contract.

FACT SUMMARY: Jacobs & Youngs (P) was hired to build a $77,000 country home for Kent (D). When the dwelling was completed, it was discovered that through an oversight, pipe, not of Reading manufacture (though of comparable quality and price), which had been specified in the contract, was used. Kent (D) refused to make final payment of $3,483.46 upon learning of this.

🏛 RULE OF LAW
The measure of damages for breach of a construction contract where the breaching party has substantially performed with trivial deviation is the difference between the value of the construction as contracted for and the value of the construction as built, rather than complete forfeiture by the breaching party.

FACTS: Jacobs & Youngs (Jacobs) (P) built a country home for $77,000 for Kent (D) and sued for $3,483.46 which remained unpaid. Almost a year after completion, Kent (D) discovered that not all pipe in the home was of Reading manufacture as specified in the contract. Kent (D) ordered the plumbing replaced, but as it was encased in the walls, except in those spots where it must necessarily remain exposed, Jacobs (P) refused to replace the pipe, stating that the pipe used was of comparable price and quality. It appears that the omission was neither fraudulent nor willful and was due to oversight. Kent (D) refused to pay the balance of the construction cost still due.

ISSUE: Is the measure of damages for breach of a construction contract where the breaching party has substantially performed with trivial deviation the difference between the value of the construction as contracted for and the value of the construction as built, rather than complete forfeiture by the breaching party?

HOLDING AND DECISION: (Cardozo, J.) Yes. The measure of damages for breach of a construction contract where the breaching party has substantially performed with trivial deviation is the difference between the value of the construction as contracted for and the value of the construction as built, rather than complete forfeiture by the breaching party. Where the significance of the default or omission is grievously out of proportion to the oppression of the forfeiture, the breach is considered to be trivial and innocent. A change will not be tolerated if it is so dominant and pervasive so as to frustrate the purpose of the contract. The contractor cannot install anything he believes to be just as good. It is a matter of degree judged by the purpose to be served, the desire to be gratified, the excuse for deviation from the letter, and the cruelty of enforced adherence. Under the circumstances, the measure of damages should not be the cost of replacing the pipe which would be great. Instead, the difference in value between the dwelling as specified and the dwelling as constructed should be the measure even though it may be nominal or nothing. Usually, the owner is entitled to the cost of completion, but not where it is grossly unfair and out of proportion to the good to be obtained. This simply is a rule to promote justice when there is substantial performance with trivial deviation. Affirmed.

DISSENT: (McLaughlin, J.) Jacobs (P) failed to perform as specified. It makes no difference why Kent (D) wanted a particular kind of pipe. Failure to use the kind of pipe specified was either intentional or due to gross neglect which amounted to the same thing.

▶ ANALYSIS

Substantial performance cannot occur where the breach is intentional as it is the antithesis of material breach. The part unperformed must not destroy the purpose or value of the contract. Because here there is a dissatisfied landowner who stands to retain the defective structure built on his land, there arises the problem of unjust enrichment. Usually, it would appear that the owner would pocket the damages he collected rather than remedying the defect by tearing out the wrong pipe and replacing it with the specified pipe. The owner would have a home, substantially in compliance and a sum of money greatly in excess of the harm suffered by him. Note that under the doctrine of *de minimus non curat lex*, that is, that the law is not concerned with trifles, trivial defects, even if willful, will be ignored. The party who claims substantial performance has still breached the contract and is liable for damages, but in a lesser amount than for a willful breach.

■=■

Quicknotes

DE MINIMUS NON CURAT LEX Not of sufficient significance to invoke legal action.

SUBSTANTIAL PERFORMANCE Performance of all the essential obligations pursuant to an agreement.

■=■

Sackett v. Spindler

Shareholder (P) v. Publisher (D)

Cal. Ct. App., 248 Cal. App. 2d 220, 56 Cal. Rptr. 435 (1967).

NATURE OF CASE: Appeal from a trial court decision favoring a cross-complaint for breach of contract attached to a suit to recover money had and received.

FACT SUMMARY: Sackett's (P) continued delay in making the overdue final installment on the $85,000 purchase price for all 6,316 outstanding shares of S&S Newspaper was answered, after several extensions of time, by Spindler's (D) notice that there would be no sale. But a later offer by Spindler (D) to nonetheless accept a tender of the balance in cash or its equivalent (to which there was no reply) followed Sackett's (P) rejected request that he pay the balance over a period of time through a liquidating trust.

🏛 RULE OF LAW
A party can repudiate a contract where the other party thereto has committed a material—and therefore total—breach of the contract by continually failing to make required payments thereunder.

FACTS: Sackett (P) had a written contract with Spindler (D) to purchase from Spindler (D) all outstanding shares of S&S Newspapers for $85,000, to be paid in 3 installments. Sackett (P) made his initial installment of $6,000 on July 10, 1961 (when it was due); paid $19,800 on July 21 (to cover the $20,000 installment due on July 14); and gave a $59,200 check on August 10 (to cover the final $59,000 installment due on August 15). The agreement provided for 6% interest on any unpaid balance and delivery of the stock upon final payment under the contract. Therefore, when the $59,200 check bounced for insufficient funds on September 1, Spindler (D) reclaimed the shares of stock he had already put in escrow with Sackett's (P) attorneys. There followed a series of promises by Sackett (P) to pay at various times, a September 22 payment of $3,944.26 (to provide working capital), an October 4 telegram from Sackett (P) saying his divorce proceedings would no longer block payment, an October 5 letter from Spindler (D) notifying Sackett (P) that the sale would not take place because of the delay in final payment, and a final offer to accept payment of the balance in cash or its equivalent (which was in response to Sackett's (P) unacceptable offer to pay the sum over a period of time through a liquidating trust). During this time, the company needed working capital so Spindler (D): (1) mortgaged $4,000 of his personal property, (2) sold half of his stock for $10,000 in November, (3) changed operations, and (4) bought back for $10,000 those shares he had sold in November and sold all outstanding shares—about a year after the original agreement had been entered into—for

$22,000 (netting $20,680 after payment of brokerage commission). Thereafter, Sackett (P), sued Spindler (D) for money had and received, and Spindler (D) cross-complained for breach of contract. Spindler (D) was awarded $34,575.74 plus interest by the trial court. The state's intermediate appellate court granted review.

ISSUE: Can a party repudiate a contract where the other party thereto has committed a material—and therefore total—breach of the contract by continually failing to make required payments thereunder?

HOLDING AND DECISION: (Molinari, J.) Yes. A party can repudiate a contract where the other party thereto has committed a material—and therefore total—breach of the contract by continually failing to make required payments thereunder. Unlike a partial breach, a total breach (which is any material failure to perform as promised) renders proper a repudiation of the contract by the nonbreaching party. In this case, Spindler (D) was more than justified in terminating the contract on October 5. The following factors point to the material nature of the breach, which makes Spindler's (D) repudiation proper: (1) there was a high degree of uncertainty as to whether Sackett (P) intended to complete the contract and, if he did, when he would deign to do so; and (2) Sackett's (P) failure to perform could in no way be characterized as innocent, having been brought about by gross negligence or willful conduct. There was, therefore, no unlawful repudiation on which to base a release from the duties Sackett (P) had under the contract. Furthermore, Spindler's (D) repudiation, coming as it did before tender of final payment was made and Spindler's (D) performance was to thereby become due, was anticipatory in nature. So, his later offer to accept cash tender nullified that repudiation, as did Sackett's (P) own offer to pay through a trust (inasmuch as it evidenced a disregard for any repudiation and a desire to treat the contract as still being in full force). Finally, since the general rule requiring damages to be measured by the difference between contract and market prices can be modified to use other measures, such as sale price, when market price is unreliable or unavailable, the decision is affirmed as modified.

▶ ANALYSIS

Had Sackett's (P) actions not constituted a material breach but only a partial breach, Spindler's (D) October 5 letter might well have been interpreted to amount to a material

Continued on next page.

breach on his part. That would have given Sackett (P) the option of suing for damages or canceling the contract, suing to recover his partial payment, and escaping any other duties to perform under the contract. Of course, with the price of the stock declining, as it was in this case, the first option would be of no use.

■══■

Quicknotes

MATERIAL BREACH Breach of a contract's terms by one party that is so substantial as to relieve the other party from its obligations pursuant thereto.

REPUDIATION The actions or statements of a party to a contract that evidence his intent not to perform, or to continue performance, of his duties or obligations thereunder.

■══■

Truman L. Flatt & Sons Co. v. Schupf

Vendee (P) v. Vendor (D)

Ill. App. Ct., 271 Ill. App. 3d 983, 649 N.E.2d 990, *cert. denied*, 163 Ill. 2d 590, 657 N.E.2d 640 (1995).

NATURE OF CASE: Appeal from summary judgment for defendants in suit for specific performance of a real estate contract.

FACT SUMMARY: Flatt (P) backed out of a contract to purchase land from Schupf (D) when a condition that a rezoning request be granted was not satisfied, but later changed his mind and sued for specific performance of the contract.

🏛 RULE OF LAW
An anticipatory repudiation may be retracted by the repudiating party unless the other party has, before the withdrawal, manifested an election to rescind the contract, or changed his position in reliance on the repudiation.

FACTS: Flatt (P) had contracted with Schupf (D) to purchase some land for $160,000, contingent upon rezoning of the property. When his request for rezoning was denied, Flatt (P) wrote Schupf (D) offering a lower price for the land. When Schupf (D) did not accept the lower offer, Flatt (P) decided to go ahead with the purchase as provided by the contract and wrote a letter on June 14 informing Schupf (D). Schupf (D) replied on July 8 that the failure to waive the rezoning requirements, as well as the new offer to buy the property at less than contract price, had effectively voided the contract. Flatt (P) then sued for specific performance and the court granted Schupf's (D) motion for summary judgment because Flatt (P) had allegedly repudiated the contract. Flatt (P) appealed, claiming that he had not repudiated the contract and, even if he had, he timely retracted that repudiation.

ISSUE: May an anticipatory repudiation be retracted by the repudiating party unless the other party has, before the withdrawal, manifested an election to rescind the contract, or changed his position in reliance on the repudiation?

HOLDING AND DECISION: (Knecht, J.) Yes. An anticipatory repudiation may be retracted by the repudiating party unless the other party has, before the withdrawal, manifested an election to rescind the contract, or changed his position in reliance on the repudiation. Here, assuming Flatt's (P) request for a lower price constituted an anticipatory repudiation of the contract, he successfully retracted that repudiation in his letter of June 14, because Schupf (D) had not yet materially changed her position or indicated to Flatt (P) any intent to treat the contract as rescinded. Reversed and remanded.

▶ ANALYSIS

The doctrine of anticipatory repudiation requires a clear manifestation of an intent not to perform. Doubtful and indefinite statements that performance may or may not take place are not enough. The letter in this case created, at most, an ambiguous implication whether performance would occur.

━━■

Quicknotes

ANTICIPATORY REPUDIATION Breach of a contract subsequent to formation but prior to the time performance is due.

RELIANCE Dependence on a fact that causes a party to act or refrain from acting.

RESCISSION The canceling of an agreement and the return of the parties to their positions prior to the formation of the contract.

━━■

Hornell Brewing Co. v. Spry

Supplier (P) v. Distributor (D)

N.Y. Sup. Ct., 174 Misc. 2d 451, 664 N.Y.S.2d 698 (1997).

NATURE OF CASE: Action for declaratory judgment that defendant's rights have been terminated.

FACT SUMMARY: Hornell Brewing Co. (Hornell) (P) sought declaratory relief after Spry (D), who had an exclusive right to distribute Hornell's (P) beverages in Canada, failed to provide adequate assurance of due performance.

🏛 RULE OF LAW
One party's failure to respond to a request for adequate assurance of due performance constitutes a breach of the agreement, entitling the other party to suspend performance and terminate the agreement.

FACTS: Spry (D) was granted the exclusive right to purchase Hornell Brewing Co.'s (Hornell's) (P) beverages, including the popular "Arizona" drink, for distribution in Canada. When Spry (D) failed to remit timely payment for shipments of beverages received from Hornell (P), Hornell (P) de facto terminated its relationship with Spry (D). When Hornell (P) requested a declaratory judgment that Spry (D) had no continuing rights with respect to distribution of Hornell's (P) beverages, Spry (D) alleged that adequate assurance had been provided and that Hornell (P) had no right to demand any further assurances.

ISSUE: Does one party's failure to respond to a request for adequate assurance of due performance constitute a breach of the agreement, entitling the other party to suspend performance and terminate the agreement?

HOLDING AND DECISION: (Gans, J.) Yes. One party's failure to respond to a request for adequate assurance of due performance constitutes a breach of the agreement, entitling the other party to suspend performance and terminate the agreement. An enforceable contract existed between the parties based on the uncontroverted facts of their conduct. Hornell (P) had reasonable grounds for insecurity after several missed payments and bad checks, and properly requested assurances from the buyer, Spry (D), that he would be able to make the payments on time. When Spry (D) failed to adequately reply, Hornell (P) was entitled to suspend his performance and terminate the agreement. Hornell's (P) request for a declaratory judgment is granted.

▶ ANALYSIS

Under the Uniform Commercial Code § 2-609, a party that has reasonable grounds for insecurity may demand adequate assurance of due performance. Although this section applies only to the sale of goods, the Restatement (Second) of Contracts has a similar provision. Adequate assurance may take the form of a letter of credit or a bond.

■━■

Quicknotes

DECLARATORY JUDGMENT A judgment of the rights between opposing parties that is binding, but does not coercive relief (i.e., damages).

■━■

CHAPTER 1

Principles of Limitations

Quick Reference Rules of Law

11. *Roth v. Speck.*   An employee who wrongfully terminates his employment will be liable for any
lost profits which can be established (where appropriate) and the difference in salary that
the employer would be forced to pay someone of comparable skills.

156

Crabby's, Inc. v. Hamilton

Seller of real estate (P) v. Buyer of real estate (D)

Mo. Ct. App., 244 S.W.3d 209 (2008).

NATURE OF CASE: Appeal from judgment awarding damages to seller of land in action for breach of contract.

FACT SUMMARY: After Paragon Ventures, L.L.C. and Hamilton (collectively, "Buyers") (D) refused to close on an agreement to purchase real estate from Crabby's, Inc. (Seller) (P), and after Seller (P) brought suit for breach of contract on which Seller (P) prevailed, Buyers (D) contended that they had not waived a financing contingency provision in the agreement, and that the trial court had erroneously calculated Seller's (P) damages.

🏛 RULE OF LAW
(1) **A buyer under a real estate contract waives a condition in that contract through clear, unequivocal, and decisive acts showing the buyer's intentional relinquishment of the benefit of the condition.**
(2) **The sale price obtained in a sale of real property made by highly motivated sellers after a breach of contract for sale of the property constitutes substantial evidence of the property's fair market value where the subsequent sale is made just under a year after the breach.**

FACTS: Crabby's, Inc. (Seller) (P) put up for sale a restaurant and the land it was on. Hamilton, along with Paragon Ventures, L.L.C. (collectively, "Buyers") (D), agreed to purchase the property for $290,000. The contract contained a financing contingency provision that made it contingent on "Buyer's [sic] ability to obtain a conventional loan or loans in the amount of $232,000, payable over a period of not less than 15 years and bearing interest at a rate of not more than 5.5% per annum." The contract also provided that Buyers (D) would use reasonable diligence in seeking to obtain such a loan or loans, and that if Buyers (D) did not furnish Seller (P) with a copy of an effective written loan commitment within 30 days from the contract's effective date, the contract would automatically terminate. Buyers (D) applied for and were approved by a bank for a loan in the amount of $340,000.00. The bank agreed to loan them $225,000.00 amortized over 15 years on the real estate, $65,000.00 amortized over seven years on the equipment, and a $50,000.00 revolving line of credit all at the rate of interest of prime plus 1.5%. Buyers (D) did not apply for a loan with any other financial institution, and they never furnished Seller (P) with a copy of an effective written loan commitment within 30 days of the effective date of the contract. The parties extended the contract's closing date by around two weeks to permit certain repairs. This extension did not otherwise modify

the contract's terms. Following this extension, the parties discussed other additional repairs and this led to an agreement whereby Buyers (D) would receive a credit of $1,373.54 against the purchase price in lieu of additional repairs being made. This agreement also did not otherwise modify the contract's terms. By a second extension agreement, the closing date was again extended, by a little over two weeks, and the parties also entered into an agreement that allowed Buyers (D) to take possession of the property prior to closing so that they could start cleaning it. Buyers (D) obtained a key and took possession. Around this same time period, Buyers (D) made application for appropriate licenses to operate a restaurant on the property and had the utilities for the property transferred into Buyers' (D) name. Nothing in any of the subsequent agreements entered into between the parties altered any of the terms of the financing contingency contained in the original contract. Then, two days before the extended closing date, Buyers (D) informed Seller (P) of their intention not to close, notwithstanding that all matters required for closing had been addressed and all necessary paperwork was ready. Around a week later, Buyers (D) entered into an agreement to purchase a different restaurant and accompanying property for $170,000, and that sale closed. After Buyers (D) refused to close on Seller's (P) property, Seller's (P) realtor continuously tried to sell the property. Around 11½ months after Buyers (D) refused to close, the property sold for $235,000. Thereafter, Seller (P) brought a breach of contract action against Buyers (D), seeking damages equal to the difference between Buyers' (D) $290,000 contract price and the $235,000 price actually obtained when the property subsequently sold. Seller (P) also claimed real estate and personal property taxes, utilities, and mortgage interest accruing during that period as damages. The trial court determined that Buyers (D) had breached the contract, and awarded $95,547.30 to Seller (P). Buyers (D) appealed, arguing that the trial court had erred in finding they had breached the contract, arguing that by its terms the contract automatically terminated when they failed to provide Seller (P) with a copy of an effective written loan commitment as required by the financing contingency. They also argued that they had used reasonable diligence in finding a loan under the financing contingency, and, finally, they contended that the trial court's judgment was not supported by substantial evidence of the fair market value of the property as of the date the contract was breached by Buyers (D). In response, Seller (P) argued that Buyers (D) had waived the financing contingency provisions, and that the trial court's damages

Continued on next page.

calculation was not erroneous. The state's intermediate appellate court granted review.

ISSUE:

(1) Does a buyer under a real estate contract waive a condition in that contract through clear, unequivocal, and decisive acts showing the buyer's intentional relinquishment of the benefit of the condition?

(2) Does the sale price obtained in a sale of real property made by highly motivated sellers after a breach of contract for sale of the property constitute substantial evidence of the property's fair market value where the subsequent sale is made just under a year after the breach?

HOLDING AND DECISION: (Lynch, C.J.)

(1) Yes. A buyer under a real estate contract waives a condition in that contract through clear, unequivocal, and decisive acts showing the buyer's intentional relinquishment of the benefit of the condition. A provision in a real estate contract that makes the contract contingent upon the buyer's obtaining financing is a condition. Upon the nonoccurrence of the condition, the buyer is excused from performance. However, the buyer can elect to waive the contingency and proceed with the contract under the rule that a party may waive any condition of a contract in that party's favor. Parties to agreements may waive provisions of the contracts between them, and may do so either by an express agreement or through their conduct. Here, Buyers (D) waived the condition through their conduct, which manifested a clear, unequivocal, and decisive intentional relinquishment of the condition's benefits to them. Buyers (D) did not furnish Seller (P) with a copy of an effective written loan commitment within the time specified in the condition, so that the contract automatically terminated within 30 days of its being entered into. However, after that date, Buyers (D) entered into several contract amendments extending the closing date, providing Buyers (D) with a credit on the purchase price for repairs, and granting them the right to take possession of the property—which they did. Buyers (D) also put the property's utilities in their names, and, as late as just a few days before the extended closing date, were working on obtaining the licenses necessary for operating a restaurant on the property. Nothing in the contract amendments or subsequent agreements modified the financing contingency, which the parties expressly agreed remained unchanged. Thus, the only reasonable explanation possible for and consistent with Buyers' (D) signatures on these documents is their waiver of this contract requirement and the resulting automatic termination of the contract. Moreover, Buyers' (D) failure to apply for financing on the exact terms set out in the financing contingency, and their failure to seek a loan on such terms with more than one lender, evidences Buyers' (D) failure to use reasonable diligence to obtain such

financing as required by the contingency. Combined with their other conduct, these failures also evidence Buyers' (D) waiver of the entire financing contingency. All of these actions by Buyers (D) are clear, unequivocal, and decisive acts showing Buyers' (D) intentional relinquishment of the benefit of the entire financing contingency, and are so consistent with the intention to waive that contingency that no other reasonable explanation is possible. Affirmed as to this issue.

(2) Yes. The sale price obtained in a sale of real property made by highly motivated sellers after a breach of contract for sale of the property constitutes substantial evidence of the property's fair market value where the subsequent sale is made just under a year after the breach. Contrary to Buyers' (D) arguments, the subsequent sale was not too remote in time to constitute substantial evidence of fair market value, and, the sale was not a compelled sale. Therefore, the sale price obtained in the subsequent sale ($235,000) constituted substantial evidence of the property's fair market value. A seller's measure of damages for a buyer's breach of a contract for the sale of land with a structure on it is the difference between the purchase price and the fair market value of the property on the date of breach. If a seller sells the property within a reasonable time after breach, the sale price so obtained constitutes some evidence of market value. Here, Buyers (D) contend that 11½ months after breach is not a "reasonable time." State precedent provides that this timeframe does constitute a reasonable time. Accordingly, as a matter of law, the subsequent sale by Seller (P) occurred within a reasonable time after the date of Buyers' (D) breach of the contract, such that it provided substantial evidence to support the trial court's determination of the fair market value of the property on the date of Buyer's (D) breach of the contract. Buyers (D) also contend that the subsequent sale was a compelled sale, and, therefore, may not be used as evidence of fair market value, which is defined as a price obtained by a seller who is not under a compulsion to sell from a buyer who is not under a compulsion to buy. Here, although the evidence shows that Seller (P) was highly motivated to sell the property, there is no evidence that Seller (P) was under a compulsion to sell, or that the sale was in any way a forced or distress sale. Therefore, the sale price they obtained in the subsequent sale is substantial evidence of the fair market value of the property on the date of the breach. Affirmed as to this issue.

▶ ANALYSIS

Real estate conditions are intended to protect the buyer. Therefore, they are a condition of the buyer's duty, but not a condition of the seller's duty under the contract. Thus,

Continued on next page.

here, Seller (P) had no affirmative duties under the financing contingency.

■■■

Quicknotes

BREACH OF CONTRACT Unlawful failure by a party to perform its obligations pursuant to contract.

DAMAGES Monetary compensation that may be awarded by the court to a party who has sustained injury or loss to his person, property or rights due to another party's unlawful act, omission or negligence.

FAIR MARKET VALUE The price of particular property or goods that a buyer would offer and a seller would accept in the open market following full disclosure.

■■■

Handicapped Children's Education Board v. Lukaszewski

Employer (P) v. Speech therapist (D)

Wis. Sup. Ct., 112 Wis. 2d 197, 332 N.W.2d 774 (1983).

NATURE OF CASE: Appeal of award of damages for breach of contract.

FACT SUMMARY: Lukaszewski (D) reneged on a contract to provide speech therapy services on behalf of the Handicapped Children's Education Board (P).

🏛 RULE OF LAW
An employer who has to obtain an employee at a higher price upon breach of an employment contract may recover the difference.

FACTS: Lukaszewski (D) contracted with the Handicapped Children's Education Board (Board) (P) to provide speech therapy services. Subsequently, she was offered a better position. She resigned, but the resignation was rejected by the Board (P). Lukaszewski (D) then obtained medical documentation that the stress of the job was resulting in hypertension, whereupon she ceased appearing for work. The Board (P) searched for a replacement. The only applicant was more qualified, so the Board (P) had to hire at a higher salary. The Board (P) sued for the difference. The trial court entered judgment for the Board (P). The appellate court reversed, holding that a breach had occurred, but since the Board (P) had obtained a more qualified employee, it had not been damaged. The Board appealed.

ISSUE: May an employer who has to obtain an employee at a higher price upon breach of an employment contract recover the difference?

HOLDING AND DECISION: (Callow, J.) Yes. An employer who has to obtain an employee at a higher price upon breach of an employment contract may recover the difference. The non-breaching party is entitled to full compensation for the loss of his bargain. The court of appeals felt that the Board (P) had lost nothing, because the Board (P), although paying more, obtained a better "product." This is an incorrect analysis. The Board (P) did not contract for a better teacher at a higher price; it contracted for Lukaszewski (D) at a lower price. Since Lukaszewski's (D) breach forced the Board (P) to lose its bargained-for price, it is entitled to recover from Lukaszewski (D). Affirmed in part and reversed in part.

DISSENT: (Day, J.) Lukaszewski's (D) reason for leaving was legitimate, and therefore no breach occurred.

▶ ANALYSIS

The dissent did not address the coverability of damages issue. It suggested that the contract had been legitimately terminated. The dissent did not state the precise legal basis therefor, but it would seem that impossibility or impracticability of performance would be the grounds.

Quicknotes

BREACH OF CONTRACT Unlawful failure by a party to perform its obligations pursuant to contract.

IMPRACTICABILITY A doctrine relieving the parties to a contract from liability for nonperformance of their duties thereunder, if the subject matter of the contract ceases to exist.

American Standard, Inc. v. Schectman

Landowner (P) v. Construction grader (D)

N.Y. App. Div., 80 A.D.2d 318, *appeal denied*, 427 N.E.2d 512 (1981).

NATURE OF CASE: Appeal from award of damages for breach of contract.

FACT SUMMARY: Schectman (D) contended that the correct measure of damages for his failure to complete grading American Standard, Inc's (P) land was the diminution in value of the land, rather than the cost of completion.

🏛 RULE OF LAW
Only where the cost of completing the contract would entail unreasonable economic waste will the measure of damages for breach of a construction contract be diminution in value of the property in relation to what its value would have been if performance had been properly completed.

FACTS: Schectman (D) contracted to grade and to take down certain foundations to one foot below grade on American Standard, Inc.'s (American's) (P) land. Schectman's (D) performance substantially deviated from the grading specifications in the contract. American (P) sued for breach and was awarded damages equal to the cost of completing the grading properly. Schectman (D) appealed, contending the trial court erred by refusing to admit evidence that American (P) sold the property for only $3,000 less than its full market value and therefore it suffered no appreciable loss due to the breach. As a result, Schectman (D) argued, the correct measure of damages was this $3,000 diminution in value of the property due to the breach, rather than the cost of completion.

ISSUE: Will the measure of damages for breach of a construction contract be diminution in property value only where the cost of completion would entail unreasonable economic waste?

HOLDING AND DECISION: (Hancock, J.) Yes. The generally accepted measure of damages for breach of a construction contract is the cost of completing performance properly. Only where such cost of completion would entail unreasonable economic waste will the measure of damages be the diminution in the value of the property caused by the breach. Completing the job properly in this case would not require destruction of past work, only that performance be completed. The fact that the sale price of the property was not markedly affected by the breach is irrelevant to the measure of damages determination. No unreasonable economic waste would result from awarding cost of completion damages, therefore that measure was properly used. Affirmed.

▶ ANALYSIS

Some commentators criticize the result in this case as bestowing upon American Standard, Inc. a windfall recovery. Not only was it able to sell the property for virtually its fair market value, $183,000, it also received a judgment against Schectman (D) for $90,000. Other commentators justify cost of completion awards as protecting the plaintiff's subjective value ascribed to the property.

Quicknotes

WASTE The mistreatment of another's property by someone in lawful possession.

WINDFALL Sudden gain.

Hadley v. Baxendale

Mill operator (P) v. Shipping company (D)

Ex. Ch., 156 Eng. Rep. 145 (1854).

NATURE OF CASE: Action for damages for breach of a carrier contract.

FACT SUMMARY: Hadley (P), a mill operator in Gloucester, arranged to have Baxendale's (D) company, a carrier, ship his broken mill shaft to the engineer in Greenwich for a copy to be made. Hadley (P) suffered a £300 loss when Baxendale (D) unreasonably delayed shipping the mill shaft, causing the mill to be shut down longer than anticipated.

🏛 RULE OF LAW
A party injured by the breach of a contract may recover as damages those damages that are the direct, natural and immediate consequence of the breach and that can reasonably be said to have been in the contemplation of the parties when the contract was made.

FACTS: Hadley (P), a mill operator in Gloucester, arranged to have Baxendale's (D) shipping company return his broken mill shaft to the engineer in Greenwich who was to make a duplicate. Hadley (P) delivered the broken shaft to Baxendale (D) who in consideration for Hadley's (P) fee promised to deliver the shaft to Greenwich in a reasonable time. Baxendale (D) did not know that the mill was shut down while awaiting the new shaft. Baxendale (D) was negligent in delivering the shaft within a reasonable time. Reopening of the mill was delayed five days, costing Hadley (P) lost profits and paid-out wages of £300. Hadley (P) had paid Baxendale (D) £24 to ship the mill shaft. Baxendale (D) paid into court £25 in satisfaction of Hadley's (P) claim. The jury awarded an additional £25 for a total £50 award.

ISSUE: May a party injured by the breach of a contract recover as damages those damages that are the direct, natural and immediate consequence of the breach and that can reasonably be said to have been in the contemplation of the parties when the contract was made?

HOLDING AND DECISION: (Alderson, B.) Yes. A party injured by the breach of a contract may recover as damages those damages that are the direct, natural and immediate consequence of the breach and that can reasonably be said to have been in the contemplation of the parties when the contract was made. The jury requires a rule for its guidance in awarding damages justly. When a party breaches his contract the damages he pays ought to be those arising naturally from the breach itself, and, in addition, those as may reasonably be supposed to have been in contemplation of the parties, at the time they

made the contract, as the probable result of the breach of it. Therefore, if the special circumstances under which the contract was made were known to both parties, the resulting damages upon breach would be those reasonably contemplated as arising under those communicated and known circumstances. But if the special circumstances were unknown then damages can only be those expected to arise generally from the breach. Hadley's (P) telling Baxendale (D) that he ran a mill and his mill shaft which he wanted shipped was broken did not notify Baxendale (D) that the mill was shut down. Baxendale (D) could have believed reasonably that Hadley (P) had a spare shaft or that the shaft to be shipped was not the only defective machinery at the mill. Here, it does not follow that a loss of profits could fairly or reasonably have been contemplated by both parties in case of breach. Such a loss would not have flowed naturally from the breach without the special circumstances having been communicated to Baxendale (D). Reversed and remanded.

▶ ANALYSIS

This case lays down two rules guiding damages. First, only those damages as may fairly and reasonably be considered arising from the breach itself may be awarded. Second, those damages which may reasonably be supposed to have been in contemplation of the parties at the time they made the contract as the probable result of a breach of it may be awarded. The second is distinguished from the first because with the latter, both parties are aware of the special circumstances under which the contract is made. Usually those special circumstances are communicated by the plaintiff to the defendant before the making of the contract. But that is not an absolute condition. If the consequences of the breach are foreseeable, the party which breaches will be liable for the lost profits or expectation damages. Foreseeability and assumption of the risk are ways of describing the bargain. If there is an assumption of the risk, the seller or carrier must necessarily be aware of the consequences. A later English case held that there would be a lesser foreseeability for a common carrier than a seller, as a seller would tend to know the purpose and use of the item sold while the common carrier probably would not know the use of all items it carried. If all loss went on to the seller, this would obviously be an incentive not to enter into contracts. Courts balance what has become a "seller beware" attitude by placing limitations on full recovery. The loss must be foreseeable when the

Continued on next page.

contract is entered into. It cannot be overly speculative. The seller's breach must be judged by willingness, negligence, bad faith, and availability of replacement items. Restatement (First), § 331(2), would allow recovery in the situation in this case under an alternative theory. If the breach were one preventing the use and operation of property from which profits would have been made, damages can be measured by the rental value of the property or by interest on the value of the property. Uniform Commercial Code (U.C.C.) § 2-715(2) allows the buyer consequential damages for any loss which results from general or particular needs of which the seller had reason to know.

■═■

Quicknotes

CONSEQUENTIAL DAMAGES Monetary compensation that may be recovered in order to compensate for injuries or losses sustained as a result of damages that are not the direct or foreseeable result of the act of a party, but that nevertheless are the consequence of such act and which must be specifically pled and demonstrated.

U.C.C. § 2-715(2) Provides that any damages which seller is aware of and cannot cover against are includable as consequential damages.

■═■

Florafax International, Inc. v. GTE Market Resources, Inc.

Customer (P) v. Telecommunications company (D)

Okla. Sup. Ct., 933 P.2d 282 (1997).

NATURE OF CASE: Appeal from an order for plaintiff for lost profits.

FACT SUMMARY: Florafax International, Inc. (Florafax) (P) sued GTE Market Resources, Inc. (GTE) (D) for breach of contract and claimed damages for lost profits it stood to make from a collateral contract Florafax (P) had with a third party, but allegedly lost because of GTE's (D) breach.

🏛 RULE OF LAW
For recovery of lost profits, sufficient certainty must be shown that reasonable minds might believe from a preponderance of the evidence that such damages were actually suffered.

FACTS: Florafax International, Inc. (Florafax) (P), a flowers-by-wire company, had an agreement with a leading marketer of floral products to handle direct consumer telephone and Internet orders. Florafax (P) then entered into an agreement with GTE Market Resources, Inc. (GTE) (D) for telecommunication and telemarketing services. GTE (D) failed to provide sufficient telemarketing sales representatives to handle the Mother's Day calls for orders and, as a result, Florafax (P) lost customers. GTE's (D) failure to perform also led to termination of an agreement Florafax (P) had with a third-party client, and to additional costs Florafax (P) incurred when taking steps necessary to set up its own call answering center to perform the duties GTE (D) failed to provide. Florafax (P) sued GTE (D) for breach of contract and sought damages for its lost profits. The jury determined that GTE (D) breached its contract with Florafax (P) and awarded damages for all lost profits. GTE (D) appealed, claiming that lost profit damages cannot include profits from third party collateral contracts, or, if they are recoverable, they must be limited to a sixty-day period, since profits beyond that time would be too remote, speculative or uncertain.

ISSUE: For recovery of lost profits, must it be shown that there is sufficient certainty that reasonable minds might believe from a preponderance of the evidence that such damages were actually suffered?

HOLDING AND DECISION: (Lavender, J.) Yes. For recovery of lost profits, sufficient certainty must be shown that reasonable minds might believe from a preponderance of the evidence that such damages were actually suffered. Once it is clear that loss of business profits has been suffered by virtue of the breach, it is proper to let the jury decide what the loss is from the admissible evidence. In this case, not only was the fact and causation of lost profit damages adequately shown to a reasonable certainty, but the amount of lost profit damages awarded was sufficiently shown through competent evidence contained in the record to take the matter out of the realm of mere speculation, conjecture and surmise. Affirmed.

▶ ANALYSIS

The court explained the holding of *Hadley v. Baxendale*, 156 Eng. Rep. 145 (1854). Loss of future or anticipated profits is recoverable in a breach of contract action if the loss is within the contemplation of the parties at the time the contract was made, or if the loss flows directly or proximately from the breach, and the loss is capable of reasonably accurate measurement or estimate. This case fell under the second branch of the formulation.

Quicknotes

COLLATERAL CONTRACT A contract made prior to or contemporaneous with another contract.

SPECIAL DAMAGES Damages caused by a specific act that are not the usual consequence of that act and which must be specifically pled and proven.

Rockingham County v. Luten Bridge Co.

Customer (P) v. Telecommunications company (D)

35 F.2d 301 (4th Cir. 1929).

NATURE OF CASE: Appeal from directed verdict for plaintiff in action in damages for breach of contract.

FACT SUMMARY: Luten Bridge Co. (P) continued a construction contract after Rockingham County (D) had wrongfully notified it that the contract was being repudiated.

🏛 RULE OF LAW
After an absolute repudiation or a refusal to perform, the other party may not continue his performance in order to recover damages based on full performance.

FACTS: Rockingham County (D) contracted with Luten Bridge Co. (P) to construct a bridge. The contract was approved by a 3 to 2 majority of the County Commission, but after the contract was approved, one of the majority members resigned, and the other two failed to attend any more meetings. The minority, along with another commissioner, then acted as the Commission. After Luten (P) had begun minimal work, the newly constituted Commission (D), due to adverse public opinion, wrongfully repudiated the contract and informed Luten (P) that it would not perform. Luten (P), which had expended only a small amount of money on labor and materials at that point—perhaps gambling that the original majority on the Commission would reinstate the contract—proceeded to complete the bridge and brought suit in damages for breach of the entire contract. The trial court entered a directed verdict for Luten (P) on the full amount of its claim. The court of appeals granted review.

ISSUE: After an absolute repudiation or a refusal to perform, may the other party continue his performance in order to recover damages based on full performance?

HOLDING AND DECISION: (Parker, J.) No. After an absolute repudiation or a refusal to perform, the other party may not continue his performance in order to recover damages based on full performance. While Rockingham County (D) had no right to repudiate the contract, Luten (P) had a duty to cease its performance upon notification of an absolute, unqualified repudiation or a refusal to perform. Damages are then fixed at the moment of breach. The bridge could not be sold to anyone other than the County (D) and its completion therefore in no way mitigated damages. Luten's (P) only real interest was in lost profits which it could have recovered after the breach. Luten (P) may not recover for construction

and material costs after the repudiation. Reversed and remanded.

▶ ANALYSIS

The rule of mitigation of damages basically states that one cannot sue for a loss he could have avoided. Uniform Commercial Code § 2-610(a) states that a new party must be employed to mitigate damages, e.g., breach of employment contracts. Only reasonable mitigation efforts are required. No penalty is assessed for failing to successfully mitigate so long as a reasonable attempt was made. Failure to make a reasonable attempt will cause damages to be correspondingly reduced.

■━■

Quicknotes

COLLATERAL CONTRACT A contract made prior to or contemporaneous with another contract.

REPUDIATION The actions or statements of a party to a contract that evidence his intent not to perform, or to continue performance, of his duties or obligations thereunder.

SPECIAL DAMAGES Damages caused by a specific act that are not the usual consequence of that act and which must be specifically pled and proven.

■━■

Maness v. Collins

Former employee (P) v. Former employer (D)

Tenn. Ct. App., 2010 WL 4629614 (2010).

NATURE OF CASE: Appeal from judgment for plaintiff in action for breach of employment agreement, and cross-appeal from judgment for defendants on damages.

FACT SUMMARY: Maness (P) sold his business to SKM, LLC (D) and its owners (D). He contended that SKM (D) and the owners (D) breached the agreement for employment he had with them when they terminated him before the three-year employment term was up. SKM (D) and the owners (D) contended that they did not breach the agreement because they had just cause to terminate Maness (P), and that he was not entitled to damages because he had failed to mitigate his damages by looking for comparable work after his termination, notwithstanding that a non-competition agreement prohibited him from doing so.

🏛 RULE OF LAW

(1) The termination of an employee, who is employed under an employment agreement for a specific term, is not effected for just cause where the employer actively hinders the employee from performing his duties.

(2) An employer who has breached an employment agreement by terminating an employee covered under the agreement may not rely on the defense of mitigation of damages absent evidence that suitable alternative employment was available to the terminated employee.

FACTS: Maness (P), via an asset purchase agreement, sold his business to SKM, LLC (D), owned by three co-equal partners, Collins (D), Mike Smith (D), and Mike's son, Josh Smith (D). Josh Smith (D) was responsible for day-to-day management of the company. The agreement provided that Maness (P) would be an employee of SKM (D) for three years as a production manager and would be paid an annual salary. Maness (P) also entered a noncompetition agreement that prohibited him from competing directly or indirectly with SKM (D) throughout the United States for five years. As part of the noncompetition agreement, he averred that his skills were such that he could easily find alternative, commensurate employment or work that would not violate the provisions of the agreement. The relationship between Maness (P) and the company's owners deteriorated, as they clashed over his management style and restricted his authority to discipline and fire employees. In fact, they rehired an employee he had fired. Josh Smith (D) held a meeting with the SKM (D) employees in which he told them that Maness (P) no longer had any authority to correct employees or tell them what to do, but

Maness (P) was not informed of this meeting, nor were the other owners. When he complained, Maness (P) claimed, Mike Smith (D) told him to just stay in his office at his desk and draw his money. Maness (P), perceiving his authority to have been undercut, and finding employees increasingly disrespectful and belligerent toward him, became dissatisfied and idle. At some point, he reported to ownership that he had observed Josh Smith (D) in a drug transaction. Shortly thereafter, around five months after Maness (P) started working for SKM (D) as an employee, his employment was terminated on the grounds that he failed to fulfill his job duties, and that his actions and attitude were detrimental to the company's success. Maness (P) did not actively seek other work after his employment with SKM (D) was terminated. Maness (P) filed suit against SKM (D) and its owners, alleging breach of Maness's (P) employment agreement, and asserting that the non-competition agreement was unenforceable. At trial, Maness's (P) testimony about Josh Smith (D) was corroborated by SKM (D) employees, who attested to Josh Smith's (D) workplace drug use and dealing, and who attested to the meeting at which Josh Smith (D) informed employees that Maness (P) had no authority to discipline or terminate employees. The owners testified that Maness (P) was not interested in acquiring new customers, which they wanted him to do, and that he became idle and unproductive after they removed his authority to discipline and terminate employees. They believed there was just cause to fire him. Josh Smith (D) also testified that although he had a drug problem, and used drugs in the workplace, such use did not affect his performance, and he also testified that he never engaged in drug transactions at work. The trial court found that Josh Smith (D) had a severe drug addiction problem, and that Maness's (P) performance had been satisfactory until his authority had been undercut and removed. The court also found that although Maness (P) acted unprofessionally by becoming idle, he was dealing daily with "a drug-addicted business owner," namely, Josh Smith (D). Accordingly, the trial court found that the company and owners did not meet their burden of proof to show just cause for terminating Maness's (P) employment under the employment agreement. As to damages, the court found that Maness (P) had a duty to mitigate his damages, but took no action to do so by looking for other work. Maness (P) argued that looking for comparable work would have been pointless, as he was prohibited from doing so by the noncompetition agreement. The trial court determined that, in light of Maness's

Continued on next page.

(P) failure to make any effort to find work, he failed to mitigate his damages, and that such failure to mitigate precluded any award for damages. The parties cross-appealed, and the state's intermediate appellate court granted review.

ISSUE:

(1) Is the termination of an employee, who is employed under an employment agreement for a specific term, effected for just cause where the employer actively hinders the employee from performing his duties?

(2) May an employer who has breached an employment agreement by terminating an employee covered under the agreement rely on the defense of mitigation of damages absent evidence that suitable alternative employment was available to the terminated employee?

HOLDING AND DECISION: (Kirby, J.)

(1) No. The termination of an employee, who is employed under an employment agreement for a specific term, is not effected for just cause where the employer actively hinders the employee from performing his duties. The asset purchase agreement did not expressly specify that Maness (P) could be terminated for cause, just or otherwise. Therefore, under the plain language of the employment agreement, SKM (D) had an essentially unqualified obligation to employ Maness (P) for a period of three years, at the annual salary specified. However, state precedent provides that even where an employment agreement is for a definite term, the employer may nevertheless discharge the employee for just cause. Thus, SKM (D) and the owners (D) could terminate Maness's (P) employment for just cause without breaching the agreement. Whether Maness's (P) termination was for just cause is a question of fact, determined in light of all the circumstances. Here, viewed in isolation, Maness's (P) conduct would have provided just cause for his termination. However, the trial court, correctly viewing his conduct in the context of all the circumstances, determined, as a matter of fact, that Maness (P) was actively prevented from fulfilling his job responsibilities by Josh Smith (D) and SKM (D). Each party to a contract is under an implied obligation to restrain from doing any act that would delay or prevent the other party's performance of the contract, and each party has the right to proceed free of hindrance by the other party. Therefore, SKM (D) and the owners (D) did not have just cause to terminate Maness (P), and, therefore, they breached the asset purchase agreement, under which Maness (P) is entitled to recover. Affirmed as to this issue.

(2) No. An employer who has breached an employment agreement by terminating an employee covered under the agreement may not rely on the defense of mitigation of damages absent evidence that suitable alternative employment was available to the terminated employee. A party who has been wronged by a breach of contract [here, Maness (P)] may not unreasonably sit idly by

and allow damages to accumulate. This is known as the doctrine of avoidable consequences, often referred to as the plaintiff's obligation to mitigate his damages. Here, SKM (D) and the owners (D) failed to present evidence that comparable, suitable employment was available to Maness (P). Under state case law, the failure to mitigate damages is an affirmative defense, and where there has been a breach of an employment agreement by an employer, "the employer must prove both availability of suitable and comparable substitute employment and a lack of reasonable diligence on the part of the employee." Such evidence is necessary to quantify an employee's damages, since the measure of those damages is the compensation that the employee who has been wrongfully discharged would have received if the contract had been carried out according to its terms, provided that the employee has been unable to find comparable employment. Without such evidence, the computation of the employee's damages becomes problematic, since the employee may be entitled to some recovery despite a failure to mitigate, given that only the amount that the plaintiff would have earned in the exercise of reasonable diligence is applied to reduce his contractual damages. It is only where an employee through such diligence finds work that pays as much as, or more, than what the employee earned under the original employment agreement that the employee will be entitled to no recovery. If no proof of comparable, suitable substitute employment is presented to the trial court, then the trial court has no basis on which to determine the amount by which the plaintiff's damages should be reduced. Even where, as here, an employee avers that he could find alternative, commensurate employment or work, such a contractual acknowledgment does not relieve the breaching employer from presenting evidence of suitable, comparable employment to prove the plaintiff's failure to mitigate damages. Such an acknowledgement is not equivalent to a stipulation that the employee would have earned compensation that equaled or exceeded the compensation he would have received pursuant to the employment agreement. Thus, a trial court could not determine how much the employee would have been able to earn from alternative, commensurate work, and, therefore, the court would not be able to determine the amount by which the employee's damages should be reduced. Therefore, in the absence of evidence that suitable alternative employment was available to Maness (P), SKM (D) and the owners (D) cannot rely on the affirmative defense of mitigation of damages. Reversed as to this issue. Affirmed in part, reversed in part, and remanded.

Continued on next page.

▶ ANALYSIS

This decision illustrates the general rule that a breaching employer has the burden of proving the availability of substantially equivalent employment as part of its mitigation of damages defense. Some courts have carved out an exception to this general rule, holding that an employer is released from its burden of proving the availability of such equivalent employment if the employer proves that an employee has not made any reasonable efforts to obtain such work. Here, the court expressly rejected SKM's (D) and the owners' (D) invitation to adopt such an exception, reasoning that adopting the exception would create problems in calculating damages. In light of SKM's (D) and the owners' (D) failure to provide evidence of the availability of substantially equivalent employment, the trial court clearly erred in holding that Maness's (P) alleged failure to mitigate precluded him from any award of damages at all, as it had no evidence of how much to reduce his recovery by.

■═■

Quicknotes

BURDEN OF PROOF The duty of a party to introduce evidence to support a fact that is in dispute in an action.

DAMAGES Monetary compensation that may be awarded by the court to a party who has sustained injury or loss to his person, property or rights due to another party's unlawful act, omission or negligence.

■═■

Jetz Service Co. v. Salina Properties

Lessee (P) v. Lessor (D)

Kan. Ct. App., 19 Kan. App. 2d 144, 865 P.2d 1051 (1993).

NATURE OF CASE: Appeal from damages award for plaintiff in action for breach of a lease agreement.

FACT SUMMARY: Jetz Service Co. (P), which installs and maintains coin-operated laundry equipment, was awarded damages to cover its lost profits when Salina Properties (D) breached its lease.

🏛 RULE OF LAW
If the injured party could and would have entered into the subsequent contract, even if the contract had not been broken, and could have had the benefit of both, he can be said to have "lost volume" and the subsequent transaction is not a substitute for the broken contract.

FACTS: Salina Properties' (D) predecessor in title leased 175 square feet of an apartment complex to Jetz Service Co. (P), for use as a coin-operated laundry facility. Jetz Service (P) was entitled to the first $300 per month or 50%, whichever was greater, of the gross receipts from the machines it installed there. Salina Properties (D) disconnected all of Jetz Service's (P) machines sixteen months before the end of its lease agreement, and replaced them with its own equipment. Jetz Service (P) retrieved its property and stored it in one of its warehouses. Four sets of the laundry equipment were subsequently leased in the Kansas City area, although other suitable laundry equipment was available to complete this transaction. When Jetz Service (P) sued for damages, the trial court determined Jetz Service (P) was a "lost volume" lessee and awarded judgment for loss of profits and damages in the amount requested. Salina Properties (D) appealed, claiming that Jetz Service (P) failed to mitigate its damages, and failed to prove the requisite elements to recover lost profits.

ISSUE: If the injured party could and would have entered into the subsequent contract, even if the contract had not been broken, and could have had the benefit of both, can he be said to have "lost volume" and is the subsequent transaction not a substitute for the broken contract?

HOLDING AND DECISION: (Larson, J.) Yes. If the injured party could and would have entered into the subsequent contract, even if the contract had not been broken, and could have had the benefit of both, he can be said to have "lost volume" and the subsequent transaction is not a substitute for the broken contract. Adequate authority exists to apply the lost volume rule to volume providers of services. The evidence here showed that Jetz Service (P) had several warehouses in which it had available for lease about 1,500 washers and dryers, it would have

been able to fulfill the Kansas City lease without using the machines from Salina Properties (D), and it would have been able to enter into both transactions irrespective of the breach by Salina Properties (D). The trial court properly applied the status of lost volume lessee to Jetz Service (P) under the facts of this case. There was substantial competent evidence to justify the trial court's findings and judgment. Affirmed.

▶ ANALYSIS

The calculation of lost future profits was based upon historical past profits generated during the seven-month period preceding the breach by Salina Properties (D). Lost profits are presumed to have been contemplated by the parties. Fixed expenses or overhead are not deducted when computing lost profits.

■━■

Quicknotes

LOST-VOLUME SELLER A seller who can accommodate more than one buyer and for whom a buyer's breach does not release the goods for sale to another customer; in such a case, the appropriate measure of damages is the net profit the seller would have earned pursuant to the sale.

■━■

Zapata Hermanos Sucesores, S.A. v. Hearthside Baking Company, Inc.

Supplier (P) v. Debtor (D)

313 F.3d 385 (7th Cir. 2002), *cert. denied*, 540 U.S. 1068 (2003).

NATURE OF CASE: Appeal from award of attorneys' fees in action for breach of contract brought under international treaty.

FACT SUMMARY: Lenell (D), a U.S. corporation, which had been found to have breached its supply contract with Zapata Hermanos Sucesores, S.A. (Zapata), a Mexican corporation, contended that neither the Convention on Contracts for the International Sale of Goods, nor the inherent authority of the trial court, entitled Zapata to an award of all the attorneys' fees Zapata incurred in prosecuting its breach of contract action.

RULE OF LAW
(1) The term "loss" in Article 74 of the Convention on Contracts for the International Sale of Goods does not include attorneys' fees incurred in the litigation of a suit for breach of contract.
(2) A trial court does not have inherent authority to punish a litigant's bad faith, but non-tortious breach of contract through an award of attorneys' fees.

FACTS: Zapata Hermanos Sucesores, S.A. (Zapata) (P), a Mexican corporation that supplied Lenell (D), a U.S. corporation, sued Lenell (D) in U.S. District Court for breach of contract and won. Based both on a provision of the Convention on Contracts for the International Sale of Goods, and on the inherent authority of the courts to punish the conduct of litigation in bad faith, the district judge ordered Lenell (D) to pay Zapata (P) $550,000 in attorneys' fees. The Convention, of which both the United States and Mexico are signatories, provides remedies for breach of international contracts for the sale of goods. Zapata (P) brought suit under the Convention for money due under 110 invoices, amounting to around $900,000 and also sought prejudgment interest plus attorneys' fees, which it contended are "losses" within the meaning of the Convention and are therefore an automatic entitlement of a plaintiff who prevails in a suit under the Convention. Article 74 of the Convention provides that "damages for breach of contract by one party consist of a sum equal to the loss, including loss of profit, suffered by the other party as a consequence of the breach," provided the consequence was foreseeable at the time the contract was made. Article 7(2) provides that "questions concerning matters governed by this Convention which are not expressly settled in it are to be settled in conformity with the general principles on which it is based or, in the absence of such principles, in

conformity with the law applicable by virtue of the rules of private international law [i.e., conflicts of law rules]." The court of appeals granted review.

ISSUE:
(1) Does the term "loss" in Article 74 of the Convention on Contracts for the International Sale of Goods include attorneys' fees incurred in the litigation of a suit for breach of contract?
(2) Does a trial court have inherent authority to punish a litigant's bad faith, but non-tortious breach of contract through an award of attorneys' fees?

HOLDING AND DECISION: (Posner, J.)
(1) No. The term "loss" in Article 74 of the Convention on Contracts for the International Sale of Goods does not include attorneys' fees incurred in the litigation of a suit for breach of contract. Neither the Convention's background nor the cases under it indicate that "loss" is intended to include attorneys' fees. Although there is no suggestion to the contrary, it is clear that "loss" does not include attorneys' fees incurred in the litigation of a suit for breach of contract, though certain pre-litigation legal expenditures, for example expenditures designed to mitigate the plaintiff's damages, would probably be covered as "incidental" damages. The Convention is about contracts, not about procedure. The principles for determining when a losing party must reimburse the winner for the latter's expense of litigation are usually not a part of substantive contract law but are a part of procedural law. Although the Convention could have addressed the question of attorneys' fees, it did not, and there are no "principles" that can be drawn out of the provisions of the Convention for determining whether "loss" includes attorneys' fees. Therefore, the issue must be resolved by choice of law principles and under the substantive contract law of the nation the laws of which must be applied. Under Zapata's (P) reading, the Convention would get his attorneys' fees reimbursed more or less automatically. But this raises numerous problems. For example, if the defendant won, he could, under Zapata's interpretation, invoke the domestic law, if, as is likely other than in the United States, that domestic law entitled either side that wins to reimbursement of his fees by the loser. Also, a winning plaintiff might be able to waive his right to attorneys' fees under the Convention in favor of domestic law, which might be more or less generous than Article 74, since Article 74 requires that any loss must, to be

Continued on next page.

recoverable, be foreseeable, which beyond some level attorneys' fees, though reasonable ex post, might not be. Finally, it is unlikely that the United States would have signed the Convention had it thought that in doing so it was abandoning the hallowed American rule. The vast majority of the signatories of the Convention are nations in which the loser pays attorneys' fees and costs, so the question whether "loss" includes attorneys' fees would have held little interest for these nations. For all these reasons, "loss" in Article 74 does not include attorneys' fees. Reversed as to this issue.

(2) No. A trial court does not have inherent authority to punish a litigant's bad faith, but non-tortious, breach of contract through an award of attorneys' fees. The trial judge based his award of attorneys' fees in part on his desire to punish Lenell (D) for having failed to pay money it conceded it owed to Zapata (P). However, under U.S. common law (the law deciding any issues not expressly governed by the Convention), a breach of contract is not wrongful because it is neither tortious nor criminal on its own. Ordinarily, a breaching party will have to pay damages, and sometimes a breach can increase economic efficiency, which explains why the law does not view breaches, without more, as wrongful conduct. While common law courts will sometimes award punitive damages for breach of contract in bad faith, to prevail, a plaintiff must show that the breach of contract involved tortious misconduct, such as duress or fraud or abuse of fiduciary duty. Zapata (P) did not assert such misconduct here. In fact, Zapata (P) did not even request punitive damages, and the trial judge had no authority to award attorneys' fees in lieu of such damages. The issue of punitive damages as a sanction for breach of contract is a matter of substantive law, and, under the Erie doctrine, the federal court must follow state law on this issue, and the trial judge cannot circumvent this doctrine by renaming punitive damages "attorneys' fees." "The inherent authority of federal courts to punish misconduct before them is not a grant of authority to do good, rectify shortcomings of the common law (as by using an award of attorneys' fees to make up for an absence that the judge may deem regrettable of punitive damages for certain breaches of contract), or undermine the American rule on the award of attorneys' fees to the prevailing party in the absence of statute." Instead, the trial court's authority to punish is a residual one, limited to punishing misconduct occurring in the litigation itself, not in the events giving rise to the litigation or not adequately dealt with by other rules, such as Rules 11 and 37 of the Federal Rules of Civil Procedure, which Lenell (D) has not been accused of violating. Thus, the judge could have punished Lenell (D) only for misconduct in the litigation itself, and if the judge was punishing Lenell (D) for failing to pay Zapata (P) what it conceded it owed Zapata (D), this fault is largely attributable to the judge himself for failing to grant partial summary

judgment early in the proceedings based on his erroneous belief that he could not do so unless would give rise to an appealable judgment. Reversed as to this issue.

▶ *ANALYSIS*

As noted by the court, the so-called "American Rule" governing the award of attorneys' fees in litigation in the federal courts is that attorneys' fees are not ordinarily recoverable in the absence of a statute or enforceable contract providing therefor. The United States is in the minority of commercial jurisdictions that do not make prevailing parties truly whole by saddling their adversaries with the winners' legal expenses, an omission that does not (as does the vast majority of other jurisdictions' fee-shifting approach) put the winners in contract disputes into the same economic position as if the breaching parties had performed their required obligations under the contracts. There are exceptions to the American rule, however, that justify the awarding of attorneys' fees to the prevailing party, including the possibilities that the parties may have a valid contract term allowing for attorneys' fees, there may be an applicable statute granting such fees, or there may be an established court rule that allows for recovery.

Quicknotes

BREACH OF CONTRACT   Unlawful failure by a party to perform its obligations pursuant to contract.

Erlich v. Menezes

Homeowners (P) v. Contractor (D)

Cal. Sup. Ct., 21 Cal. 4th 543, 981 P.2d 978 (1999).

NATURE OF CASE: Appeal by contractor from adverse ruling in suit by homeowners.

FACT SUMMARY: Barry and Sandra Erlich (P) contracted with John Menezes (D) to build their "dream house." They moved in in December 1990. In February 1991, heavy rains came, and the house leaked from every conceivable location. The Erlichs (P) sued Menezes (D) not only for negligent breach of contract in the construction of their home, but sought damages for emotional distress as well.

🏛 RULE OF LAW
Damages for mental suffering and emotional distress are generally not recoverable in an action for the breach of an ordinary commercial contract.

FACTS: Barry and Sandra Erlich (P) contracted with John Menezes (D), a licensed general contractor, to build a "dream house" on their ocean-view lot. The house was built and the Erlichs (P) moved in in December 1990. In February 1991, the rains came, and the house leaked from every conceivable location. Despite extensive repair efforts, which included using sledgehammers and jackhammers to cut holes in the exterior walls and ceilings, application of new waterproofing materials on portions of the roof and exterior walls, and more caulk, the house leaked from the windows, from the roofs, and water seeped between the floors. Independent inspections revealed serious errors in the construction of the home's structural components. The Erlichs (P) sued Menezes (D) for breach of contract, fraud, negligent misrepresentation, and negligent construction. At trial, the Erlichs (P) testified that they suffered emotional distress as a result of the defective condition of the house and by Menezes's (D) invasive and unsuccessful repair attempts. The jury found that Menezes (D) had breached his construction contract by negligently constructing the house, but was not guilty of fraud or negligent misrepresentation. The jury awarded $406,700 as the cost of repairs, as well as $100,000 damages for emotional distress caused by the negligent construction, and Barry Erlich (P) received an additional $50,000 for physical pain and $15,000 for lost earnings. The court of appeals affirmed, and Menezes (D) appealed.

ISSUE: Are damages for mental suffering and emotional distress generally recoverable in an action for the breach of an ordinary commercial contract?

HOLDING AND DECISION: (Brown, J.) No. Damages for mental suffering and emotional distress are generally not recoverable in an action for the breach of an ordinary commercial contract since a preexisting contractual relationship, without more, will not support a recovery for mental suffering where the defendant's tortious conduct has resulted only in economic injury to the plaintiff. Unless the defendant has assumed a duty to plaintiff in which the emotional condition of the plaintiff is an object, recovery is available only if the emotional distress arises out of the defendant's breach of some other legal duty and the emotional distress is proximately caused by breach of the independent duty; even then, with rare exceptions, a breach of the duty must threaten physical injury, not simply damage to property or financial interests. Here, although the jury found that the contractor Menezes (D) had breached his construction contract by negligently constructing the house, the Erlichs (P) were not entitled to recover damages for mental distress since the claim for negligent breach of a contract is not sufficient to support tort damages for violation of an independent tort duty. Even assuming that Menezes's (D) negligence constituted a breach of a sufficient independent duty to the Erlichs (P), such a finding would not entitle them to emotional distress damages on the facts alleged. The breach (the negligent construction of the house) did not cause physical injury. The only physical injury alleged was for Barry Erlich's (P) heart disease which flowed from the emotional distress and not directly from the negligent construction. No California case has ever allowed recovery for emotional distress arising solely out of property damage. Cases permitting recovery for emotional distress typically involve mental anguish stemming from more personal undertakings the traumatic results of which were unavoidable, such as, for example, an infant injured during childbirth, misdiagnosed venereal disease and subsequent failure of a marriage, a fatal waterskiing accident, or the failure to adequately preserve a corpse. Reversed and remanded.

▶ ANALYSIS

In *Erlich*, the court explained that recovery for emotional disturbance will be excluded unless the breach also caused bodily harm or the contract or the breach is of such a kind that serious emotional disturbance was a particularly likely result since to permit emotional distress damages in cases of negligent construction of a personal residence when the negligent construction causes gross interference with the normal use and habitability of the residence would make the financial risks of construction agreements difficult to predict. Contract damages must be

Continued on next page.

clearly ascertainable in both nature and origin, and a rule focusing not on the risks which the contracting parties voluntarily assume, but on one party's possible future re-action to inadequate performance, cannot provide any reasonable limit on liability. As noted in *Erlich*, however, tort damages have been permitted in contract cases where a breach of duty directly causes physical injury; for breach of the covenant of good faith and fair dealing in insurance contracts; for wrongful discharge in violation of fundamen-tal public policy; or where the contract was fraudulently induced. In each of these cases, the duty that gives rise to tort liability is either completely independent of the con-tract or arises from conduct which is both intentional and intended to harm.

Quicknotes

BREACH OF CONTRACT Unlawful failure by a party to per-form its obligations pursuant to contract.

EMOTIONAL DISTRESS Extreme personal suffering which results in another's conduct and in which damages may be sought.

Roth v. Speck

Beauty shop owner (P) v. Employee (D)

D.C. Mun. Ct. App., 126 A.2d 153 (1956).

NATURE OF CASE: Action for breach of employment contract.

FACT SUMMARY: Roth (P) hired Speck (D) to work in his beauty shop for one year, but Speck (D) quit after six-and-one-half months.

🏛 RULE OF LAW
An employee who wrongfully terminates his employment will be liable for any lost profits which can be established (where appropriate) and the difference in salary that the employer would be forced to pay someone of comparable skills.

FACTS: Roth (P) hired Speck (D) for one year to be a beautician in his beauty shop. Speck (D) wrongfully quit after six-and-one-half months. Roth (P) brought suit for damages. At trial, the court found that lost profits could not be estimated because of the seasonal nature of the business and a number of other factors. It found that Speck (D) had another job with a $25 per week salary increase and that no satisfactory replacement could be found for the salary which Roth (P) had paid Speck (D). The court awarded Roth (P) $1.00 in damages since he had been unable to satisfactorily establish the amount of his injury.

ISSUE: Is an employee who wrongfully terminates his employment, liable for any lost profits which can be established (where appropriate) and the difference in salary that the employer would be forced to pay someone of comparable skills?

HOLDING AND DECISION: (Quinn, J.) Yes. An employee who wrongfully terminates his employment will be liable for any lost profits which can be established (where appropriate) and the difference in salary that the employer would be forced to pay someone of comparable skills. One of the measures of damages when an employee wrongfully terminates his employment is, in effect, "replacement" cost, i.e., the cost of hiring another employee of comparable ability if one could not be found at the same salary. The evidence adduced herein was that no satisfactory replacement could be found. Speck's (D) new employer offered him $25 per week more to work for him. This is a proper measure of damages since it would appear that Roth (P) would have to offer $25 per week more to find comparable help. Since lost profits could not be estimated due to too many intangible factors, Roth (P) cannot recover these damages. Reversed as to damages. Speck (D) is liable in damages for $25 for each week remaining on the contract.

⬧ ANALYSIS

Damages for lost profits will only be awarded where, at the time the contract was entered into, the employee knew or should have known that if he wrongfully terminated the employment, the employer would lose profits. The burden is on the employee to establish that his commissions would have been greater than his guaranteed salary so as to mitigate his damages. Mere difficulty in proof will not excuse the defendant of this burden.

■══■

Quicknotes

MITIGATION OF DAMAGES A plaintiff's implied obligation to reduce the damages incurred by taking reasonable steps to prevent additional injury.

■══■

CHAPTER 12

Reliance and Restitutionary Damages, Specific Performance, and Agreed Remedies

Quick Reference Rules of Law

Wartzman v. Hightower Productions, Ltd.

Law firm (D) v. Corporation (P)

Md. Ct. Spec. App., 53 Md. App. 656, 456 A.2d 82 (1983).

NATURE OF CASE: Appeal from award of damages for breach of contract.

FACT SUMMARY: Hightower Productions, Inc. (Hightower) (P) hired Wartzman (D), a law firm, to incorporate it, and when Wartzman (D) forgot a vital part of the process, Hightower (P), forced to cancel its project, sued Wartzman (D) for damages.

🏛 RULE OF LAW
Where a breach has prevented an anticipated gain and proof of loss is difficult to ascertain, a party can recover damages based upon his reliance interest on the contract, less any loss that can be proven that the injured party would have suffered if the contract were performed.

FACTS: Three men conceived of Hightower Productions, Inc. (Hightower) (P) as a corporate promotional venture in which an entertainer would live in a mobile perch to establish the world record for flagpole sitting. They hired Wartzman (D), a law firm, to incorporate it so they could sell stock to raise money for the venture. Wartzman (D) filed the articles of incorporation, and Hightower (P) hired an entertainer, a company to build the perch, and public relations specialists, and it sold stock. Hightower (P) still needed to sell more stock when Wartzman (D) announced that Hightower (P) had been structured incorrectly and that a securities attorney would need to be hired for approximately $15,000. Hightower (P) asked Wartzman (D) to pay the costs of restructuring, but they refused. The stockholders decided to discontinue the project because of the added costs that accrued because of this mistake. Hightower (P) sued Wartzman (D) for failure to create a corporation authorized to issue stock. The jury returned a verdict in favor of Hightower (P), and Wartzman (D) appealed.

ISSUE: Where a breach has prevented an anticipated gain and proof of loss is difficult to ascertain, can a party recover damages based on his reliance interest on the contract, less any loss that can be proven that the injured party would have suffered if the contract were performed?

HOLDING AND DECISION: (Getty, J.) Yes. Where a breach has prevented an anticipated gain and proof of loss is difficult to ascertain, a party can recover damages based upon his reliance interest on the contract, less any loss that can be proven that the injured party would have suffered if the contract were performed. If anticipated profits are too speculative to be determined, moneys spent in part performance or in preparation for performing the contract are recoverable. These damages are limited if it can be shown that full performance would have resulted in a loss. It is the responsibility of the breaching party to show that performance of the contract would have resulted in a net loss. Ordinarily, profits lost due to a breach of contract are recoverable. Wartzman (D) contended that its failure to incorporate Hightower (P) correctly was only a collateral issue as to why the project failed. However, the project could only have worked if stock had been sold to raise money. Without this, there were no funds to continue. Additionally, it would be impossible to prove that the project would have ultimately failed. Therefore, reliance damages were an appropriate remedy. The jury instructions were correct in that the ultimate success of the venture need not be proven, nor could Wartzman (D) have claimed that Hightower (P) did not mitigate its damages by hiring a securities attorney for $15,000. It was not required to spend huge amounts of money to mitigate. Affirmed.

▶ ANALYSIS

One of the main factors affecting determination of how much a party receives in reliance damages is whether that party tried to mitigate its damages. Here, the court held that Hightower (P) had no duty to mitigate; rather Wartzman (D) bore the responsibility of mitigating damages by paying for the securities expert itself. Some courts use this "equal opportunity" exception, but it is not accepted by all courts.

■=■

Quicknotes

BREACH OF CONTRACT Unlawful failure by a party to perform its obligations pursuant to contract.

MITIGATION Reduction in penalty.

■=■

Walser v. Toyota Motor Sales, U.S.A., Inc.

Dealer (P) v. Auto manufacturer (D)

43 F.3d 396 (8th Cir. 1994).

NATURE OF CASE: Appeal from damages award for plaintiffs in a promissory estoppel claim.

FACT SUMMARY: Walser (P) alleged that the district court erred in instructing the jury that damages were limited to the out-of-pocket expenditures made in reliance on Toyota's (D) promise of a dealership.

🏛 RULE OF LAW
In determining damages on a promissory estoppel claim for breach, whether to charge full contract damages, or something less, is a matter of discretion delegated to district courts.

FACTS: Walser (P) was negotiating with Toyota (D) for a Lexus dealership and was told that a letter of intent had been formally approved by Lexus management. In reliance on that statement, Walser's (P) father had agreed to purchase property for the proposed Lexus dealership. When informed that Lexus would not be issuing the letter of intent to him, Walser (P) sued for breach of contract, promissory estoppel, fraud, joint venture, statutory breach, intentional interference with contractual relations and interference with a prospective business advantage. The district court dismissed all charges except for the promissory estoppel, breach of contract, and fraud claims. The jury returned a verdict in favor of Walser (P) only on the promissory estoppel claim, and awarded damages in accordance with the district court's instructions to limit damages to out-of-pocket expenses. Walser (P) appealed, claiming the district court had erred in its instructions.

ISSUE: In determining damages on a promissory estoppel claim for breach, is it a matter of discretion delegated to district courts whether to charge full contract damages, or something less?

HOLDING AND DECISION: (Hansen, J.) Yes. In determining damages on a promissory estoppel claim for breach, whether to charge full contract damages, or something less, is a matter of discretion delegated to district courts. A district court's discretionary decision will not be disturbed on review if that decision remains within the range of choice available to the district court, accounts for all relevant factors, and does not constitute a clear error of judgment. The district court did not abuse its discretion in limiting the award of damages on the promissory estoppel claim to out-of-pocket expenses. Affirmed.

▶ ANALYSIS

Some courts have held that recovery for promissory estoppel cases should be limited only to the amount of actual reliance. Other courts have granted expectation damages and lost profits. Certainty and foreseeability are other factors considered by courts in making damages awards.

Quicknotes

PROMISSORY ESTOPPEL A promise that is enforceable if the promisor should reasonably expect that it will induce action or forbearance on the part of the promisee, and does in fact cause such action or forbearance, and it is the only means of avoiding injustice.

RELIANCE Dependence on a fact that causes a party to act or refrain from acting.

United States ex rel. Coastal Steel Erectors, Inc. v. Algernon Blair, Inc.

Federal government (P) v. General contractor (D)

479 F.2d 638 (4th Cir. 1973).

NATURE OF CASE: Appeal by subcontractor in action to recover in quantum meruit for labor and equipment furnished.

FACT SUMMARY: Blair (D), as general contractor, was sued by its subcontractor in the name of the United States (P) to recover for the labor and equipment that had been supplied before the subcontractor ceased work on the project due to a breach of contract by Blair (D).

🏛 RULE OF LAW
A subcontractor who justifiably ceases work under a contract because of the prime contractor's breach may recover in quantum meruit the value of labor and equipment already furnished pursuant to the contract irrespective of whether he would have been entitled to recover in a suit on the contract.

FACTS: Blair (D) was acting as general contractor in constructing a naval base and had subcontracted certain work to Coastal Steel Erectors, Inc. (Coastal). Coastal stopped performance when 28% of its work was done because of a material breach of the subcontract by Blair (D). Another subcontractor was hired to complete the job. Coastal then brought an action, in the name of the United States (P), to recover for labor and equipment furnished. The district court found $37,000 was still due Coastal under the contract, but held that it would have lost more than that if it had to complete the contract. Therefore, there could be no recovery on the contract.

ISSUE: May a subcontractor who justifiably ceases work under a contract because of the prime contractor's breach recover in quantum meruit the value of labor and equipment already furnished pursuant to the contract irrespective of whether he would have been entitled to recover in a suit on the contract?

HOLDING AND DECISION: (Craven, J.) Yes. A subcontractor who justifiably ceases work under a contract because of the prime contractor's breach may recover in quantum meruit the value of labor and equipment already furnished pursuant to the contract irrespective of whether he would have been entitled to recover in a suit on the contract. Whether or not he would be entitled to recover in a suit on the contract, a subcontractor who justifiably ceases work under a contract because of the prime contractor's breach, as in this case, may recover in quantum meruit the value of the labor and equipment already supplied. The impact of quantum meruit is to allow a promisee, such as Coastal, to recover the value of services

he gave to the defendant irrespective of whether he would have lost money on the contract and been unable to recover in a suit on the contract. The standard for measuring the reasonable value of services rendered is the amount for which such services could have been purchased from one in the plaintiff's position at the time and place the services were rendered. The case must be remanded for a finding as to the reasonable value of the labor and equipment Coastal furnished. Reversed and remanded.

▶ ANALYSIS

According to Palmer, the courts regularly deny restitution of the value of the plaintiff's performance where he has fully performed and the defendant's obligation is to pay money. He notes this is incongruous, since restitution of an amount in excess of the contract price for full performance has been permitted in many decisions where the plaintiff has only partially performed. 1 G. Palmer, The Law of Restitution 378–379 (1978).

∎≡∎

Quicknotes

QUANTUM MERUIT Equitable doctrine allowing recovery for labor and materials provided by one party, even though no contract was entered into, in order to avoid unjust enrichment by the benefited party.

RESTITUTION The return or restoration of what the defendant has gained in a transaction to prevent the unjust enrichment of the defendant.

∎≡∎

Lancellotti v. Thomas

Purchaser of business (P) v. Business owner (D)

Pa. Super. Ct., 341 Pa. Super. 1, 491 A.2d 117 (1985).

NATURE OF CASE: Appeal of award of damages for breach of contract.

FACT SUMMARY: Lancellotti (P) backed out of an agreement to purchase a business from Thomas (D) who had been paid $25,000.

> 🏛 **RULE OF LAW**
> A party breaching a contract may be entitled to restitution to prevent forfeiture.

FACTS: Lancellotti (P) contracted to buy Thomas's (D) business. Pursuant to this, Lancellotti (P) paid $25,000. A dispute subsequently arose regarding certain improvements called for in the contract, and Lancellotti (P) eventually abandoned the business. Lancellotti (P) sued for a return of the $25,000. Thomas (D) counterclaimed for $6,665 in rent, which had been deferred under the contract. The trial court instructed the jury that a breaching party was not entitled to restitution. The jury awarded Thomas (D) $6,665. Lancellotti (P) appealed.

ISSUE: May a party breaching a contract be entitled to restitution to prevent forfeiture?

HOLDING AND DECISION: (Spaeth, J.) Yes. A party breaching a contract may be entitled to restitution to prevent forfeiture. The common law rule held that a breaching party was not so entitled, on the premise that a wrongdoer should not profit from his wrongdoing. However, the common law rule has been slowly eroded. Recognizing that the purpose of contract law is not to punish, courts have increasingly permitted breaching parties to recover if a forfeiture would otherwise occur and prejudice to the nonbreaching party will not occur. This is the position of the Uniform Commercial Code (U.C.C.) and Restatement. Here, the trial court instructed the jury that a breaching party could not recover, so once the jury found that Lancellotti (P) had breached, his recourse was foreclosed. The matter must be remanded for a determination of whether restitution would prejudice Thomas (D).

DISSENT: (Tamilia, J.) The U.C.C., cited by the majority, is inapplicable here, as the contract did not involve goods. This being so, any departure from the common law rule must come from the Pennsylvania Supreme Court, which as yet has not seen fit to change the common law rule in this jurisdiction and has not adopted the Restatement position Most importantly, however, for determining the outcome of the case—and ignored by the majority—is the trial court's determination that the agreement clearly captures the parties' agreement. The record shows that Lancellotti (P) engaged in bad faith "sharp practice;" to

provide him with restitution is to reward him for his bad faith conduct—a result inconsistent with equity.

> ▶ **ANALYSIS**
>
> The acceptance of the rule stated here has been slow in coming. While the law of contracts is not criminal law, a breaching party does appear to have "done wrong." For this reason, the law has been reluctant to help the breacher. The rule has evolved as contract law has come to focus more on economics and less on morality.

■━■

Quicknotes

EQUITY Fairness; justice; the determination of a matter consistent with principles of fairness and not in strict compliance with rules of law.

FORFEITURE The loss of a right or interest as a penalty for failing to fulfill an obligation.

RESTITUTION The return or restoration of what the defendant has gained in a transaction to prevent the unjust enrichment of the defendant.

■━■

Ventura v. Titan Sports, Inc.

Employee (P) v. Former employer (D)

65 F.3d 725 (8th Cir. 1995), *cert. denied*, 516 U.S. 1174 (1996).

NATURE OF CASE: Appeal from judgment for plaintiff in suit for recovery in quantum meruit.

FACT SUMMARY: Jesse Ventura (P) was awarded quantum meruit recovery of royalties for videotape exploitation of his television performances while employed by Titan Sports, Inc. (D).

 RULE OF LAW
Intellectual property rights are benefits upon which an action for unjust enrichment may be based.

FACTS: Ventura (P) was paid to wrestle for Titan Sports, Inc. (Titan) (D) for several years before branching out into an acting career. He returned to Titan (D) as a commentator under an oral agreement that made no mention of videotape royalties or licenses. After hiring a talent agent, Ventura (P) continued working for Titan (D) under a new contract that waived royalties, until he left and began working for WCW, Titan's (D) main competitor. When Ventura (P) sued Titan (D) for lost royalties for the use of his likeness on videotapes produced by Titan (D), a jury found that Titan (D) had defrauded Ventura (P), and awarded quantum meruit damages. The district court concluded that a jury trial was not appropriate, vacated the jury verdict, and entered findings of fact and conclusions of law consistent with the verdict. Titan (D) appealed, alleging that Ventura (P) was not entitled to quantum meruit damages because he had provided his services under an express contract.

ISSUE: Are intellectual property rights benefits upon which an action for unjust enrichment may be based?

HOLDING AND DECISION: (Magill, J.) Yes. Intellectual property rights are benefits upon which an action for unjust enrichment may be based. Titan's (D) rights are limited by Ventura's (P) right to publicity. We believe the Minnesota Supreme Court would recognize the tort of violation of publicity rights, which protects pecuniary interests. Titan's (D) violation of this right makes Titan's (D) use of Ventura's (P) commentary without his consent unjust. The district court correctly found that the agreement between Ventura (P) and Titan (D) precluding royalties for videotape exploitation included only his performance as a wrestler. There was no agreement concerning the payment of royalties for his performance as a commentator. The court further found that Ventura (P) later justifiably relied on Titan's (D) fraudulent misrepresentations of its royalty policy, and as a result suffered damages. Thus the court rescinded the agreements, and permitted Ventura (P) to recover in quantum meruit. There is no

basis for concluding that the district court's findings were clearly erroneous or lacked sufficient evidentiary support. Affirmed.

DISSENT: (Arnold, J.) The court found a right of publicity under Minnesota law in the absence of any evidence that Minnesota's courts would welcome this cause of action. It is hardly unjust, from an economic viewpoint, that Titan (D) should receive the full benefit from selling copies of videotapes that it created. Titan (D), as entrepreneur, staged the wrestling matches, hired the various wrestlers, hired the announcers, and, above all, took the risks that the venture would fail to turn a profit. If there is any unjust enrichment in this case, it is in allowing Mr. Ventura (P) a recovery under these circumstances.

▶ *ANALYSIS*

The court in this case allowed recovery in restitution. Titan (D) was found to have been unjustly enriched, and Ventura (P) was entitled to the value of his services. In addition to finding a violation of Ventura's (P) right to publicity, the court also found that his contract had been rendered unenforceable due to fraud, thus entitling Ventura (P) to restitution on those grounds as well.

■═■

Quicknotes

QUANTUM MERUIT Equitable doctrine allowing recovery for labor and materials provided by one party, even though no contract was entered into, in order to avoid unjust enrichment by the benefited party.

RESTITUTION The return or restoration of what the defendant has gained in a transaction to prevent the unjust enrichment of the defendant.

RIGHT TO PRIVACY Those personal liberties or relationships that are protected against unwarranted governmental interference.

UNJUST ENRICHMENT The unlawful acquisition of money or property of another for which both law and equity require restitution to be made.

■═■

City Stores Co. v. Ammerman

Department stores (P) v. Promoters (D)

266 F. Supp. 766 (D.D.C. 1967), *aff'd*, 394 F.2d 950 (D.C. Cir. 1968).

NATURE OF CASE: Action for specific performance of a contract.

FACT SUMMARY: Promoters (D) of a proposed shopping center, in return for Lansburgh's Department Store's (P) expression of preference for their site over that of a competitor's, agreed, in the event they were issued a permit, to offer Lansburgh (P) a tenancy on rental and terms equal to that of the other stores in the center and then reneged on the offer.

RULE OF LAW

(1) A binding option contract is formed, despite the existence of express and implied conditions precedent and material terms remaining to be decided, where the substance of the agreement is clear.

(2) An option contract involving further negotiations on details and construction of a building may be specifically enforced where damages would be inadequate or impracticable, and the importance of specific performance to the plaintiff outweighs the difficulties of supervision by the court.

FACTS: Ammerman (D), the promoter of a proposed suburban shopping center, was having considerable difficulty in persuading the Board of County Supervisors to rezone the land for that use. In order to impress the Board, Ammerman (D) secured from Lansburgh's Department Store (P), which was owned by City Stores Co. (P), a letter expressing its preference for the project over that of Ammerman's (D) major competitor. In return, Ammerman (D) agreed, in the event he was successful in receiving a building permit, to accept Lansburgh's (P) as a tenant on the rental and terms at least equal to that of the other stores in the center. Ammerman (D), who had promised another tenant to keep the stores in the center down to three, refused to accept Lansburgh's (P) when Sears offered it better terms. Lansburgh's (P) sued for specific performance, and Ammerman (D) defended on the grounds that the option with Lansburgh (P) was lacking in material terms, and therefore void, that specific performance was not an appropriate remedy, and that it would result in hardship to them.

ISSUE:

(1) Is a binding option contract formed, despite the existence of express and implied conditions precedent and material terms remaining to be decided, where the substance of the agreement is clear?

(2) May an option contract involving further negotiations on details and construction of a building be specifically enforced where damages would be inadequate or impracticable, and the importance of specific performance to the plaintiff outweighs the difficulties of supervision by the court?

HOLDING AND DECISION: (Gasch, J.)

(1) Yes. A binding option contract is formed, despite the existence of express and implied conditions precedent and material terms remaining to be decided, where the substance of the agreement is clear. The rule that where material terms remain to be decided, there is no contract at all, applies only where the parties fail to reach an enforceable agreement. An option contract, though in the form of an offer, is a true contract which is binding on the offeror, and subject to the offeree's acceptance or rejection. The option here, although lacking in material terms, is nonetheless a binding contract.

(2) Yes. An option contract involving further negotiations on details and construction of a building may be specifically enforced where damages would be inadequate or impracticable, and the importance of specific performance to the plaintiff outweighs the difficulties of supervision by the court. Here, while the crucial elements of rate of rental and the amount of space can readily be determined from other leases entered into by Ammerman (D), some details of design, construction, and price of the building to be occupied were left open for further negotiations. However, it would be unfair to allow Ammerman (D), who has already reaped the benefits of his bargain with Lansburgh's (P), to object merely on the ground of the incompleteness or uncertainty of the agreement. Even were it possible to arrive at a precise measure of damages for breach of this contract—which it is not—money damages would not compensate Lansburgh's (P) for its loss of the right to participate in the shopping center. Finally, the difficulties of supervision are here diminished since the court can look to the other leases the promoters have made for guidance. As for any hardship the promoters may suffer as a result of not being able to accept Sears, they have not suggested that this would ruin them financially, but only that they would make less money. This is not a sufficient basis to deny specific performance. The option will be specifically enforced.

Continued on next page.

▶ *ANALYSIS*

More courts are today willing to depart from the estab-lished rule that equity will not order specific performance of a building or repair contract by emphasizing the inade-quacy of the damages factor. These courts have variously held that damages are inadequate where the contract calls for construction on the contractor's own land, where the plaintiff is financially unable to complete the work and not await an award of damages before he can live in the house, or where a business tenant seeks repairs on a short-term lease. Even where damages are arguably inad-equate, many courts, reluctant to oversee the enforcement of their decrees, and the attendant supervision required, will still refuse to order specific performance.

■══■

Quicknotes

OPTION CONTRACT A contract pursuant to which a seller agrees that property will be available for the buyer to purchase at a specified price and within a certain time period.

SPECIFIC PERFORMANCE An equitable remedy whereby the court requires the parties to perform their obligations pursuant to a contract.

■══■

Reier Broadcasting Company, Inc. v. Kramer

Broadcasting company/employer (P) v. Athletic coach/employee (D)

Mont. Sup. Ct., 316 Mont. 301, 72 P.3d 944 (2003).

NATURE OF CASE: Appeal from order denying motion for relief from judgment in suit seeking an injunction to prevent a breach of an employment agreement.

FACT SUMMARY: Reier Broadcasting Company, Inc. (Reier) (P) contended that a personal services employment agreement it had with Kramer (D) was not subject to a state statute that prohibited the use of an injunction to prevent of a breach of a contract that could not be specifically enforced.

> 🏛 **RULE OF LAW**
> A statute that provides that an injunction may not be granted to prevent the breach of a contract, the performance of which would not be specifically enforced, applies to a negative covenant in a personal services employment agreement so that an injunction may not prevent the personal services from being performed elsewhere during the life of the contract.

FACTS: Reier Broadcasting Company, Inc. (Reier) (P), a broadcasting company that had exclusive rights to broadcast certain university athletic events until 2002, entered into an employment contract with Kramer (D), the university's head football coach, for exclusive rights with him. The contract remained in force until 2004 and specified that Kramer (D) could not provide similar services to any other broadcaster. When Reier's (P) contract with the university expired in 2002, the university sought bids from other broadcasters. Reier (P) noticed that the university's Request for Proposal required the successful offeror to broadcast interviews and conduct a commentary program with Kramer (D) in violation of the Reier-Kramer employment agreement. The university declined to change its Request for Proposal, and awarded broadcast rights to another broadcaster, Clear Channel Communication (Clear Channel). The university also notified Kramer (D) that he was expected to provide interviews to Clear Channel despite the exclusivity clause in his contract with Reier (P). Reier (P) brought suit for a temporary restraining order (TRO) and injunction to prevent Kramer (D) from providing services to Clear Channel. The TRO was granted, but the court declined to convert it into an injunction based on a state statute that prohibited the issuance of an injunction to prevent the breach of a contract the performance of which would not be specifically enforced. Reier (P) moved to alter or amend the court's judgment, and this motion was denied. The state's highest court granted review.

ISSUE: Does a statute that provides that an injunction may not be granted to prevent the breach of a contract, the performance of which would not be specifically enforced, apply to a negative covenant in a personal services employment agreement so that an injunction may not prevent the personal services from being performed elsewhere during the life of the contract?

HOLDING AND DECISION: (Leaphart, J.) Yes. A statute that provides that an injunction may not be granted to prevent the breach of a contract, the performance of which would not be specifically enforced, applies to a negative covenant in a personal services employment agreement so that an injunction may not prevent the personal services from being performed elsewhere during the life of the contract. The trial court correctly relied on a state statute that provides that "an obligation to render personal service" cannot be specifically enforced. The court also correctly reasoned that since the Reier-Kramer contract was one for personal services, that contract could not be specifically enforced, so that it could not be enforced by injunction. Reier (P) argues that the statute prohibiting an injunction applies only to affirmative covenants, not to negative covenants that prohibit the performance of services that are special or unique. According to Reier (P), contracts based on special or unique personal services, or in which a person holds a unique position, may be indirectly enforced by restraining the person from providing services to another. This is an issue of first impression in this state. Other states that have ruled on this issue have interpreted statutes similar to the one here to prevent the enforcement of negative covenants in personal services contracts. Those courts have reasoned that an injunction of a negative covenant would amount to the enforcement of the affirmative part of the contract, and thus be in violation of the statute. Thus, here, if an injunction were granted, Kramer (D) could perform only for Reier (P), if at all—it's not just that he could not perform for Clear Channel—and this would result in the indirect specific enforcement of the contract. The reasoning of those courts is sound. Affirmed.

DISSENT: (Cotter, J.) Enforcement of the negative covenant in the contract between Reier (P) and Kramer (D) would not run afoul of the statute involved here, and it would not serve as an indirect enforcement of the affirmative part of the contract. Reier (P) is simply seeking to prevent Kramer (D) from violating the non-competition

Continued on next page.

provisions of the contract—provisions that were specifically bargained for by Kramer (D), at the encouragement and behest of the university. The university, which helped negotiate the contract, is acting in bad faith, and its position is offensive. Additionally, a party that has accepted and used the benefits that it has contractually secured for itself is estopped from denying the validity of binding force of the contract. Therefore, not only should the negative covenant here be enforced by injunction, but, in addition, the university and Kramer (D) should be estopped from challenging the contract's enforceability.

▌ *ANALYSIS*

The Restatement (Second) position on this issue, in § 367(2), is that an injunction will not be issued if the probable result would be to compel an "undesirable" continuance of personal relations or "to leave the employee without other reasonable means of making a living." Also, the court in this case relied on California precedent [*Anderson v. Neal Institutes Co.*, 37 Cal. App. 174, 173 P. 779 (Cal. Ct. App. 1918)] in reaching its conclusion. However, as the court points out, the California legislature responded immediately to that decision by amending the statute at issue to allow for the use of injunctive relief to enforce a negative covenant where the promised service is of a unique character the loss of which cannot be adequately compensated in damages. In its current form, the statute states, "[a]n injunction may not be granted . . . to prevent the breach of a contract the performance of which would not be specifically enforced . . . other than a contract in writing for the rendition of personal services . . . where the promised service is of a special, unique, [or] unusual . . . character, which gives it peculiar value. . . ." The court in this case could have suggested that if the state's legislature wanted to similarly amend the statute, it could have done so, and that its failure to so amend the statute is an indication that it did not intend to follow the California legislature's policy decision.

■═■

Quicknotes

BREACH The violation of an obligation imposed pursuant to contract or law, by acting or failing to act.

INJUNCTION A court order requiring a person to do, or prohibiting that person from doing, a specific act.

■═■

Barrie School v. Patch

Private school (P) v. Parent of student (D)

Md. Ct. App. [highest court], 401 Md. 497, 933 A.2d 382 (2007).

NATURE OF CASE: Appeal from affirmance of judgment for defendants in action for breach of contract to enforce a liquidated damages provision.

FACT SUMMARY: The Barrie School (P) contended that it was not required to mitigate damages where the liquidated damages provisions of its enrollment contract were valid and did not constitute a penalty, so that the Patches (D), who had breached the enrollment contract, were required to pay the liquidated damages.

🏛 RULE OF LAW
A non-breaching party has no duty to mitigate damages where the parties agree to a valid liquidated sum in the event of a breach.

FACTS: The Patches (D) enrolled their daughter in The Barrie School (P), a private school. They entered a re-enrollment agreement (Agreement) with the school for the following academic year. The Agreement provided for a $1,000.00 non-refundable deposit and payment of the remaining tuition balance of $13,490.00 in two installments. The Agreement contained an escape clause that allowed for unilateral cancellation, provided that the head of the school received written notice by certified letter before May 31, 2004. Under § 3 of the Agreement, the Patches (D) were obligated to pay the full tuition if they failed to meet the withdrawal deadline. The Patches (D) did not cancel the Agreement on or before May 31, 2004. Instead, 44 days later, they attempted to cancel by faxing a notice to the school, in which they demanded return of their deposit. The school demanded payment of the balance of the full amount of tuition, as required by the contract, but the Patches (D) refused to do so. The school filed suit against the Patches (D) for breach of contract plus 12% interest, and attorney's fees. The Patches (D) countered by asserting that the Agreement had been procured by fraud, that it was a contract of adhesion, that the damages constituted a penalty, that The Barrie School (P) had a duty to mitigate any damages, and that the Agreement was unenforceable because it violated public policy and the state's anti-competition laws. The Patches (D) also counterclaimed for a return of their deposit, interest, and attorney's fees. Although no evidence of mitigation was presented at trial, it turned out the number of students enrolled for the academic year at issue exceeded the school's original budget projections. The trial court ruled that the contract was valid and had been breached by the Patches (D). It also ruled that there was no fraud in the inducement to enter into the Agreement, and that the Agreement was not a contract of adhesion. As to the liquidated damages provision, the court held that it was valid, but also held that The Barrie School's (P) failure to mitigate its damages was fatal to its claim. Accordingly, the court entered judgment for the Patches (D). The state's intermediate appellate court affirmed, and the state's highest court granted review.

ISSUE: Does a non-breaching party have a duty to mitigate damages where the parties agree to a valid liquidated sum in the event of a breach?

HOLDING AND DECISION: (Raker, J.) No. A non-breaching party has no duty to mitigate damages where the parties agree to a valid liquidated sum in the event of a breach. The party seeking to set aside a liquidated damages provision has the burden of proving that the provision should not be enforced. This gives the non-breaching party the advantage inherent in stipulated damages clauses, that of eliminating the need to prove damages. It also upholds the general principle that assumes that bargains are enforceable and that the party asking the court to invalidate a bargain should demonstrate the justice of his or her view. Valid liquidated damages clauses are enforceable, and the validity of such clauses is determined by looking to the stipulated loss at the time of the contract's formation, not actual losses resulting from breach. Here, the lower courts correctly determined that the liquidated damages clause at issue was not a penalty, because the specified damages amount was a reasonable forecast of just compensation for potential harm caused by a breach of the Agreement, and because that amount was neither grossly excessive nor out of all proportion to an amount that might have been expected at the time of contracting. In addition, the actual damages resulting from breach would have been very difficult to estimate at the time of contracting, as it would be almost impossible to assign an exact amount as to the impact of losing one child for the school year. Despite the validity of the liquidated damages provision, the Patches (D) argue that, in keeping with general contract law principles, there exists a duty to mitigate damages even in the face of a valid liquidated damages clause. The mitigation of damages doctrine helps to determine the proper amount of damages for a breach of contract. Liquidated damages differ fundamentally from mitigation of damages. While mitigation is part of a court's assessment of actual damages that have resulted from a breach of contract, liquidated damages clauses are the remedy the parties to a contract have determined to be proper in the event of breach. Where the parties to a contract have

Continued on next page.

included a reasonable liquidated damages sum that stipulates damages in the event of breach, that sum replaces any determination of actual loss. From this, it logically follows that once a court has determined that a liquidate damages provision is valid, it need not inquire as to the amount of actual damages, and the need for mitigation of damages is precluded. To hold otherwise, would blunt the Agreement's purpose. Here, the Agreement's liquidated damages clause specified a comprehensive sum that eliminated the need to calculate actual losses, including any mitigation of damages that might have occurred. Accordingly, The Barrie School (P) had no duty to mitigate damages. The same rationale applies to the Patches' (D) argument that the school suffered no actual harm, because it filled the spot that was to be taken their daughter. The no-actual-harm defense negates the benefit of an agreed-upon or stipulated damages clause and deviates from the accepted principle that the time of contract formation is the appropriate point from which to judge the reasonableness of a stipulated amount of damages. Moreover, such a defense, if given effect, would potentially generate uncertainty in the calculation of damages, because courts could then give greater damages than contemplated when the damages actually exceeded the stipulated amount. Finally, as to the Patches' (D) arguments that the contract was one of adhesion and unconscionable, the lower courts did not err in concluding that the Agreement was neither. First, the Patches (D) were under no compulsion to send their daughter to The Barrie School (P) in the first place, and, second, the Agreement was not extremely unfair. To the contrary, it gave the Patches (D) a meaningful opportunity to cancel the entire Agreement upon timely notification and receive a full refund. In sum, the Agreement was an arm's-length business transaction. Reversed and remanded.

DISSENT: (Bell, C.J.) The majority is wrong in concluding that where a liquidated damages clause is valid there is no need for the non-breaching party to mitigate its damages. It is a long-held, and well-settled, general principle of contract law that contract remedies are to be compensatory, not punitive. The majority maintains that the time of the contract formation is the appropriate point from which to judge the reasonableness of a liquidated damages provision. However, this prospective viewpoint is not the best vantage point for determining the reasonableness of the liquidated damages clause. Instead, because the validity of a liquidated damages does not become an issue until one of the parties breaches the contract, the review of a liquidated damages clause to determine whether it is a penalty should include the effect of the breach, at the least, whether actual damage have been incurred. Ordinarily, unless actual damages are extremely difficult to determine, the validity of a liquidated damages clause should be determined from all the circumstances—those existing at the making of the contract as well as those existing at the time of the breach, including consideration of the actual damages sustained. Here, it is clear that the

Patches (D) breached the Agreement. However, the evidence shows that the school did not suffer harm commensurate to the sum fixed as liquidated damages. Awarding the school a full year's tuition is grossly disproportionate to, and in excess of, the harm it actually suffered—which was none, since its enrollment projections were exceeded. Contrary to the majority's view, a no-actual-harm defense is consistent with liquidated damages provisions. If the actual loss is less than the stipulated amount, the liquidated damages will not be deemed a penalty unless they are excessive. However, if the actual loss is greater, then the stipulated amount will be the limit of recovery. Where, as here, if the stipulated amount will lead to an excessive recovery, the liquidated damages clause will be deemed a penalty, and the non-breaching party will have to prove its actual damages—just as in any other breach of contract action.

▶ *ANALYSIS*

It would seem that under a "freedom of contract" approach, the penalty limitation on liquidated damage clauses should be abolished and such clauses should be enforced unless they are the product of some defect in the bargaining process, such as fraud or coercion. Some commentators advocate such a position. Others would create a presumption that a liquidated damages clause is valid absent a showing that the clause is unconscionable. Still, others would apply the penalty limitation to situations where there may be an opportunity and incentive to induce a breach, but otherwise would not impose the penalty limitation.

■═■

Quicknotes

BREACH OF CONTRACT Unlawful failure by a party to perform its obligations pursuant to contract.

COUNTERCLAIM An independent cause of action brought by a defendant to a lawsuit in order to oppose or deduct from the plaintiff's claim.

FRAUD A false representation of facts with the intent that another will rely on the misrepresentation to his detriment.

JUST COMPENSATION The right guaranteed by the Fifth Amendment to the United States Constitution; when property is taken for public use by the state, a person is to receive adequate compensation in order to restore him to the position he enjoyed prior to the appropriation.

LIQUIDATED DAMAGES An amount of money specified in a contract representing the damages owed in the event of breach.

MITIGATION OF DAMAGES A plaintiff's implied obligation to take reasonable steps to attempt to minimize damages after injury has occurred.

■═■

Glossary

Common Latin Words and Phrases Encountered in the Law

A FORTIORI: Because one fact exists or has been proven, therefore a second fact that is related to the first fact must also exist.

A PRIORI: From the cause to the effect. A term of logic used to denote that when one generally accepted truth is shown to be a cause, another particular effect must necessarily follow.

AB INITIO: From the beginning; a condition which has existed throughout, as in a marriage which was void ab initio.

ACTUS REUS: The wrongful act; in criminal law, such action sufficient to trigger criminal liability.

AD VALOREM: According to value; an ad valorem tax is imposed upon an item located within the taxing jurisdiction calculated by the value of such item.

AMICUS CURIAE: Friend of the court. Its most common usage takes the form of an amicus curiae brief, filed by a person who is not a party to an action but is nonetheless allowed to offer an argument supporting his legal interests.

ARGUENDO: In arguing. A statement, possibly hypothetical, made for the purpose of argument, is one made arguendo.

BILL QUIA TIMET: A bill to quiet title (establish ownership) to real property.

BONA FIDE: True, honest, or genuine. May refer to a person's legal position based on good faith or lacking notice of fraud (such as a bona fide purchaser for value) or to the authenticity of a particular document (such as a bona fide last will and testament).

CAUSA MORTIS: With approaching death in mind. A gift causa mortis is a gift given by a party who feels certain that death is imminent.

CAVEAT EMPTOR: Let the buyer beware. This maxim is reflected in the rule of law that a buyer purchases at his own risk because it is his responsibility to examine, judge, test, and otherwise inspect what he is buying.

CERTIORARI: A writ of review. Petitions for review of a case by the United States Supreme Court are most often done by means of a writ of certiorari.

CONTRA: On the other hand. Opposite. Contrary to.

CORAM NOBIS: Before us; writs of error directed to the court that originally rendered the judgment.

CORAM VOBIS: Before you; writs of error directed by an appellate court to a lower court to correct a factual error.

CORPUS DELICTI: The body of the crime; the requisite elements of a crime amounting to objective proof that a crime has been committed.

CUM TESTAMENTO ANNEXO, ADMINISTRATOR (ADMINISTRATOR C.T.A.): With will annexed; an administrator c.t.a. settles an estate pursuant to a will in which he is not appointed.

DE BONIS NON, ADMINISTRATOR (ADMINISTRATOR D.B.N.): Of goods not administered; an administrator d.b.n. settles a partially settled estate.

DE FACTO: In fact; in reality; actually. Existing in fact but not officially approved or engendered.

DE JURE: By right; lawful. Describes a condition that is legitimate "as a matter of law," in contrast to the term "de facto," which connotes something existing in fact but not legally sanctioned or authorized. For example, de facto segregation refers to segregation brought about by housing patterns, etc., whereas de jure segregation refers to segregation created by law.

DE MINIMIS: Of minimal importance; insignificant; a trifle; not worth bothering about.

DE NOVO: Anew; a second time; afresh. A trial de novo is a new trial held at the appellate level as if the case originated there and the trial at a lower level had not taken place.

DICTA: Generally used as an abbreviated form of obiter dicta, a term describing those portions of a judicial opinion incidental or not necessary to resolution of the specific question before the court. Such nonessential statements and remarks are not considered to be binding precedent.

DUCES TECUM: Refers to a particular type of writ or subpoena requesting a party or organization to produce certain documents in their possession.

EN BANC: Full bench. Where a court sits with all justices present rather than the usual quorum.

EX PARTE: For one side or one party only. An ex parte proceeding is one undertaken for the benefit of only one party, without notice to, or an appearance by, an adverse party.

EX POST FACTO: After the fact. An ex post facto law is a law that retroactively changes the consequences of a prior act.

EX REL.: Abbreviated form of the term "ex relatione," meaning upon relation or information. When the state brings an action in which it has no interest against an individual at the instigation of one who has a private interest in the matter.

FORUM NON CONVENIENS: Inconvenient forum. Although a court may have jurisdiction over the case, the action should be tried in a more conveniently located court, one to which parties and witnesses may more easily travel, for example.

GUARDIAN AD LITEM: A guardian of an infant as to litigation, appointed to represent the infant and pursue his/her rights.

HABEAS CORPUS: You have the body. The modern writ of habeas corpus is a writ directing that a person (body) being detained (such as a prisoner) be brought before the court so that the legality of his detention can be judicially ascertained.

IN CAMERA: In private, in chambers. When a hearing is held before a judge in his chambers or when all spectators are excluded from the courtroom.

IN FORMA PAUPERIS: In the manner of a pauper. A party who proceeds in forma pauperis because of his poverty is one who is allowed to bring suit without liability for costs.

INFRA: Below, under. A word referring the reader to a later part of a book. (The opposite of supra.)

IN LOCO PARENTIS: In the place of a parent.

IN PARI DELICTO: Equally wrong; a court of equity will not grant requested relief to an applicant who is in pari delicto, or as much at fault in the transactions giving rise to the controversy as is the opponent of the applicant.

IN PARI MATERIA: On like subject matter or upon the same matter. Statutes relating to the same person or things are said to be in pari materia. It is a general rule of statutory construction that such statutes should be construed together, i.e., looked at as if they together constituted one law.

IN PERSONAM: Against the person. Jurisdiction over the person of an individual.

IN RE: In the matter of. Used to designate a proceeding involving an estate or other property.

IN REM: A term that signifies an action against the res, or thing. An action in rem is basically one that is taken directly against property, as distinguished from an action in personam, i.e., against the person.

INTER ALIA: Among other things. Used to show that the whole of a statement, pleading, list, statute, etc., has not been set forth in its entirety.

INTER PARTES: Between the parties. May refer to contracts, conveyances or other transactions having legal significance.

INTER VIVOS: Between the living. An inter vivos gift is a gift made by a living grantor, as distinguished from bequests contained in a will, which pass upon the death of the testator.

IPSO FACTO: By the mere fact itself.

JUS: Law or the entire body of law.

LEX LOCI: The law of the place; the notion that the rights of parties to a legal proceeding are governed by the law of the place where those rights arose.

MALUM IN SE: Evil or wrong in and of itself; inherently wrong. This term describes an act that is wrong by its very nature, as opposed to one which would not be wrong but for the fact that there is a specific legal prohibition against it (malum prohibitum).

MALUM PROHIBITUM: Wrong because prohibited, but not inherently evil. Used to describe something that is wrong because it is expressly forbidden by law but that is not in and of itself evil, e.g., speeding.

MANDAMUS: We command. A writ directing an official to take a certain action.

MENS REA: A guilty mind; a criminal intent. A term used to signify the mental state that accompanies a crime or other prohibited act. Some crimes require only a general mens rea (general intent to do the prohibited act), but others, like assault with intent to murder, require the existence of a specific mens rea.

MODUS OPERANDI: Method of operating; generally refers to the manner or style of a criminal in committing crimes, admissible in appropriate cases as evidence of the identity of a defendant.

NEXUS: A connection to.

NISI PRIUS: A court of first impression. A nisi prius court is one where issues of fact are tried before a judge or jury.

N.O.V. (NON OBSTANTE VEREDICTO): Notwithstanding the verdict. A judgment n.o.v. is a judgment given in favor of one party despite the fact that a verdict was returned in favor of the other party, the justification being that the verdict either had no reasonable support in fact or was contrary to law.

NUNC PRO TUNC: Now for then. This phrase refers to actions that may be taken and will then have full retroactive effect.

PENDENTE LITE: Pending the suit; pending litigation under way.

PER CAPITA: By head; beneficiaries of an estate, if they take in equal shares, take per capita.

PER CURIAM: By the court; signifies an opinion ostensibly written "by the whole court" and with no identified author.

PER SE: By itself, in itself; inherently.

PER STIRPES: By representation. Used primarily in the law of wills to describe the method of distribution where a person, generally because of death, is unable to take that which is left to him by the will of another, and therefore his heirs divide such property between them rather than take under the will individually.

PRIMA FACIE: On its face, at first sight. A prima facie case is one that is sufficient on its face, meaning that the evidence supporting it is adequate to establish the case until contradicted or overcome by other evidence.

PRO TANTO: For so much; as far as it goes. Often used in eminent domain cases when a property owner receives partial payment for his land without prejudice to his right to bring suit for the full amount he claims his land to be worth.

QUANTUM MERUIT: As much as he deserves. Refers to recovery based on the doctrine of unjust enrichment in those cases in which a party has rendered valuable services or furnished materials that were accepted and enjoyed by another under circumstances that would reasonably notify the recipient that the rendering party expected to be paid. In essence, the law implies a contract to pay the reasonable value of the services or materials furnished.

QUASI: Almost like; as if; nearly. This term is essentially used to signify that one subject or thing is almost analogous to another but that material differences between them do exist. For example, a quasi-criminal proceeding is one that is not strictly criminal but shares enough of the same characteristics to require some of the same safeguards (e.g., procedural due process must be followed in a parole hearing).

QUID PRO QUO: Something for something. In contract law, the consideration, something of value, passed between the parties to render the contract binding.

RES GESTAE: Things done; in evidence law, this principle justifies the admission of a statement that would otherwise be hearsay when it is made so closely to the event in question as to be said to be a part of it, or with such spontaneity as not to have the possibility of falsehood.

RES IPSA LOQUITUR: The thing speaks for itself. This doctrine gives rise to a rebuttable presumption of negligence when the instrumentality causing the injury was within the exclusive control of the defendant, and the injury was one that does not normally occur unless a person has been negligent.

RES JUDICATA: A matter adjudged. Doctrine which provides that once a court of competent jurisdiction has rendered a final judgment or decree on the merits, that judgment or decree is conclusive upon the parties to the case and prevents them from engaging in any other litigation on the points and issues determined therein.

RESPONDEAT SUPERIOR: Let the master reply. This doctrine holds the master liable for the wrongful acts of his servant (or the principal for his agent) in those cases in which the servant (or agent) was acting within the scope of his authority at the time of the injury.

STARE DECISIS: To stand by or adhere to that which has been decided. The common law doctrine of stare decisis attempts to give security and certainty to the law by following the policy that once a principle of law as applicable to a certain set of facts has been set forth in a decision, it forms a precedent which will subsequently be followed, even though a different decision might be made were it the first time the question had arisen. Of course, stare decisis is not an inviolable principle and is departed from in instances where there is good cause (e.g., considerations of public policy led the Supreme Court to disregard prior decisions sanctioning segregation).

SUPRA: Above. A word referring a reader to an earlier part of a book.

ULTRA VIRES: Beyond the power. This phrase is most commonly used to refer to actions taken by a corporation that are beyond the power or legal authority of the corporation.

Addendum of French Derivatives

IN PAIS: Not pursuant to legal proceedings.

CHATTEL: Tangible personal property.

CY PRES: Doctrine permitting courts to apply trust funds to purposes not expressed in the trust but necessary to carry out the settlor's intent.

PER AUTRE VIE: For another's life; during another's life. In property law, an estate may be granted that will terminate upon the death of someone other than the grantee.

PROFIT A PRENDRE: A license to remove minerals or other produce from land.

VOIR DIRE: Process of questioning jurors as to their predispositions about the case or parties to a proceeding in order to identify those jurors displaying bias or prejudice.

Casenote® Legal Briefs